A SAILOR, A CHICKEN,
AN INCREDIBLE VOYAGE

A SAILOR, A CHICKEN, AN INCREDIBLE VOYAGE

The Seafaring Adventures of Guirec and Monique

GUIREC SOUDÉE

with **Véronique de Bure**

Translated by **David Warriner**

GREYSTONE BOOKS
Vancouver / Berkeley

First published in English by Greystone Books in 2021
Originally published in French as *Le Monde selon Guirec
et Monique: Un marin, une poule, un incroyable voyage*,
copyright © 2019 by Flammarion, Paris
English translation copyright © 2021 by David Warriner

21 22 23 24 25   5 4 3 2 1

Greystone Books Ltd.
greystonebooks.com

Cataloguing data available from Library and Archives Canada
ISBN 978-1-77164-704-5 (cloth)
ISBN 978-1-77164-705-2 (epub)

Copy editing by James Penco
Proofreading by Alison Strobel
Jacket and text design by Fiona Siu
Jacket and interior photographs by Guirec Soudée,
except where credited otherwise
Map by Fiona Siu

Printed and bound in Canada on FSC® certified paper at Friesens.
The FSC® label means that materials used for the product have
been responsibly sourced.

Greystone Books gratefully acknowledges the Musqueam, Squamish, and
Tsleil-Waututh peoples on whose land our office is located.

Greystone Books thanks the Canada Council for the Arts, the British
Columbia Arts Council, the Province of British Columbia through the
Book Publishing Tax Credit, and the Government of Canada for
supporting our publishing activities.

Canadä

Contents

For my father, Stany, and Yvinec, his island paradise.
See, Dad, I took your advice: he who dares, wins!

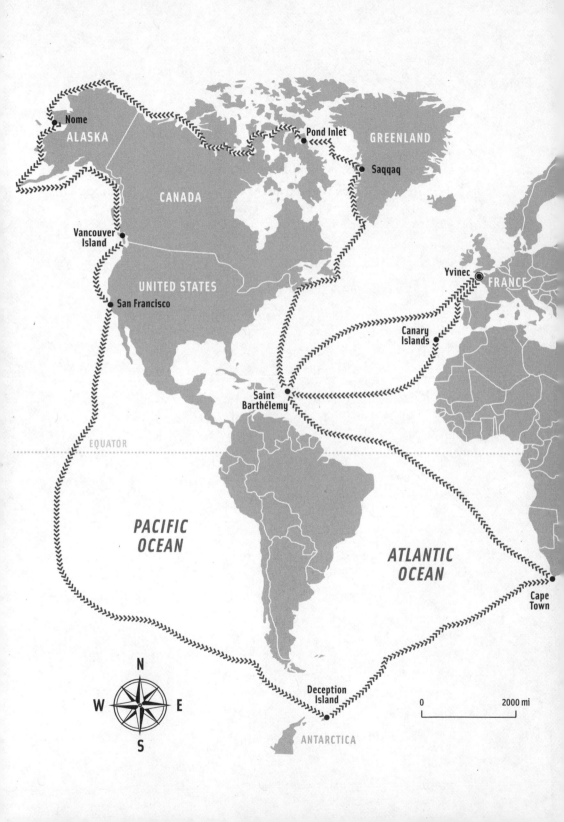

Nome

ALASKA

Pond Inlet

GREENLAND

Saqqaq

CANADA

Vancouver
Island

Yvinec

FRANCE

UNITED STATES

San Francisco

Canary
Islands

Saint
Barthélemy

EQUATOR

PACIFIC
OCEAN

ATLANTIC
OCEAN

Cape
Town

Deception
Island

ANTARCTICA

N
W   E
S

0   2000 mi

LOOK, MONIQUE, THAT'S where we are. Vancouver Island, it's called. Pretty, isn't it?

And all the way up there? That's Greenland! Remember Disko Bay? What a blast we had up there, just the two of us. For sure, we froze our feathers off, but plenty of things up there made us work up a sweat, didn't they? Now, Momo, look at my finger. See where I'm pointing? There. See all that blue? That's the Pacific Ocean. And all those little dots in the middle of the blue? Those are islands.

Stop clucking, Momo. Listen to me. So this place here, that's Polynesia. There they make garlands out of flowers, and everything smells of vanilla and coconut. Ah, it's so, so sweet. That's where we're going. It's going to be a long journey, Monique. A very long journey. But at the end, when we get there, there will be soft, white-sandy beaches and clear, turquoise-blue water, just like on Yvinec. That's my little island in France. I'll take you there one day. Polynesia's going to feel so nice after all that ice. You'll see; it's a bit like the Canary Islands, where you come from. In this paradise, you'll be able to catch all the fish you like. And we'll go windsurfing, stand-up paddleboarding, and even kitesurfing! No, we won't jump too high, I promise. So what do you say?

~~~~~~~~

WE DIDN'T END up going to paradise, Momo. Not that one, anyway. They wouldn't have us there. Well, they said they didn't want you there. And I won't go anywhere without you.

But it's okay; we'll find our own paradise.

Monique eats from her new *bol breton*

Where It All Began

~~~~~~

DECEMBER 2012

At last, I had my boat.

I couldn't find one locally in Brittany, so I had to go all the way down to the south of France—to Martigues, a picturesque little port town just outside of Marseille. Who'd have thought that a young guy like me, Guirec, from the little village of Plougrescant, on the northern coast of Brittany, would end up scoring a sailboat from a glitzy marina on the Mediterranean?

The owners made it clear on the phone: "You're coming a long way, so don't come for nothing. It's forty thousand euros. We're not letting it go for any less."

"Okay," I said, and off I went.

I didn't have the forty thousand. Scrimping together all my savings, plus what I'd earned on my working holiday in Australia, I had thirty-one thousand. But I wanted that boat.

I had spent ages combing all the classified ads of Brittany and scouring all the local marinas for boats for sale, to no avail. I

1

had seen dozens of sailboats, but nothing was quite what I was looking for—or within my budget. I needed a boat that could skim across the ocean waves. Down south, *Lungta* was waiting for me. Her name was a good omen. She was named after the Tibetan wind horse, a symbol of good fortune found on traditional prayer flags.

The first time I saw her, *Lungta* was out of the water on her cradle, shining bright under the brilliant blue skies of Provence. I knew this was the boat for me as soon as I laid eyes on her. She was perfect. Just over thirty feet long, she was a decent size and seemed to be in pretty good shape. Solid enough too, and just as tidy on the inside as she was on the outside—though I have to admit I wasn't a huge fan of the orange-colored hull. But that was nothing a coat or two of fresh paint couldn't fix.

I said "seemed to be" in good shape because the truth was that I knew nothing at all about cruiser yachts. I'd never set foot on an oceangoing vessel before, and as soon as we began discussing the technical details, I was completely out of my depth. I just smiled and nodded and pretended I knew what I was talking about. One of the two young owners, Damien, soon put me at ease. As I explained what I was planning to do—sail solo across the Atlantic and get close to the ice around the North Pole—I could see him getting all starry-eyed.

I mean, how could he not take me seriously? I had traveled the length of France to come and see this boat. Like a true seafarer, I inspected the hull, pointed out a fault or two, pretended I'd found a weak spot here and there. I listened to the sound of the engine, made sure it was clean, checked for play in the rudder, gave the mast a shake, unfurled the sails, and tested the fittings.

To do what I set out to achieve, I explained, I would have to fix up a lot of things, replace some parts, have the hull inspected for durability, you name it. The longer the conversation went on, the more I bartered. In the end, I negotiated well: they let her go for twenty-nine thousand. At last, I was the owner of a great boat!

A few weeks later, I came back down to Martigues to put the boat in the water. I enlisted three friends to come and help: my buddy Romain and two seasoned sailors, Kiki and Étienne. I was no stranger to being on the water, but I'd always been more of a windsurfer than a sailor. At the helm of a sailboat, I was clueless. There was no way I could have sailed this boat back to Brittany without their help.

We set sail in December, of all months, and the forecast was terrible. But we weren't too bothered. At least we'd get to see how the boat fared when the going got rough!

Suffice it to say that Brittany, in northern France, isn't exactly right next door to Provence, on the southeast coast—especially when you're traveling by sailboat. You have to sail all the way down the Spanish coast to the end of the Mediterranean, round Gibraltar to the south, then make your way back up the coast of Portugal before crossing the Bay of Biscay back to the north-west tip of France. Fortunately, the weather improved, and in the magical Mediterranean we rang in the new year at sea. It was after we passed Gibraltar that things started to get hairy. Kiki and Étienne had to get home, so they bid us farewell in Cádiz, in southwestern Spain. Romain and I put on a brave face, but we knew we were in over our heads.

It was such a hard slog; it took us ten days to make our way up the coast of Portugal, and we were exhausted when we made land again in Galicia—in the north of Spain—in mid-January.

The sketchy weather conditions, coupled with our lack of experience, put us in a risky situation, to say the least. At one point, we even thought we were going to lose the boat. It was taking on water, and there was no way to see where it was coming from. I remember Romain, who was just as much of a rookie as I was, yelling in a panic, "We're going down, Guirec! We're sinking!"

We figured there was no way we'd make it across the Bay of Biscay, a body of water notorious for its strong winds and high swells. Both of us were exhausted, and I was flat broke. So we made the decision to leave the boat in Spain and head home. Romain went back to the alpine town of Annecy, while I headed to Paris, where my eldest sister, Valentine, would give me a room to stay for a while.

I needed money, so I scoured all the ads I could in Paris and found a job selling windows. The ad promised high sales potential and attractive earnings, so I jumped at the opportunity. We were paid on commission, and I was so motivated that I soon became the top-selling salesman in the store. I'm sure I could have sold replacement windows for the whole Palace of Versailles if I'd tried!

Five months later, my bank balance was a lot healthier and the weather was much nicer. I went back to Spain with a childhood friend to get the boat. It was a good thing my friend had solid sea legs, because we had a rough time out there. It was summertime, so neither of us suspected we'd encounter twenty-foot swells. It didn't take long before we started having issues with our battery. By the time we got to Brittany, the engine was out of commission, and we couldn't even turn on the GPS.

One moonless night, just offshore from the Sept-Îles archipelago in southern Brittany, we were nearly scared to death. The current was so strong that it was carrying us backward faster than we could sail ourselves forward. By daybreak, we were dangerously close to washing up on the rocks. Fortunately, the wind and currents shifted as the tide came in, and we were carried away, farther north and then east, toward Yvinec, my family's little island. We made it just before nightfall, and it wasn't soon enough! We anchored in the bay right in front of my family's place. It was the fifth of July, and I was happy and proud to have sailed my boat home.

Yvinec is the most magical place in the world. There's only one house on that little island, and it's ours. The mainland isn't far away—only about half a mile—and when the tide is out, you can walk ashore. But when the tide is in, we're cut off from the world. I'll never grow tired of the moonlike landscapes surrounding this little island. The scenery is always changing as the tides and seasons come and go. The light is never exactly the same from one day to the next, and neither is the sound of the waves that lull us to sleep every night.

The sea has always been my backyard and my playground. Growing up, I was always outside, whatever the weather. We had a few canoes, and I used to paddle one offshore to go fishing and set my lobster traps. I'd get out of bed at five in the morning to head outside, and stay out until sunset. I could easily spend ten hours a day on the water. By the time I was four or five years old, I was already building rafts out of wooden pallets. I was lucky to have a father who trusted me completely. He gave me a lot of freedom to make my own choices when I was growing up, but others disagreed with his laissez-faire approach. Especially on stormy days, when not a single other boat was on the water, my sisters used to worry. "You're out of your mind," they used to tell my father. "He's going to die out there, and you'll forever regret that you never stopped him." He simply trusted that I knew what I was doing, and let me get on with it.

As far as I was concerned, it didn't matter if a gale was blowing; if it was time for me to pull up my traps, I just had to go out there and get it done. I was never very far from shore, so if worst came to worst, I could always swim my way back to dry land. When I wasn't out fishing, I was always windsurfing, surfing, kitesurfing, or snorkeling. I was crazy about the ocean! It didn't matter if it was summer or winter, I only ever wore a T-shirt and shorts and always walked around barefoot.

People in the village used to call me the barefoot little island boy. Whenever I'd go over to the doctor's office or to the grocery store, I used to say that someone had stolen my shoes. I remember one winter that was harsher than usual. Some ice had formed in the bottom of my little boat, and I used my bare heels to smash it. The water temperature would drop to about forty-five degrees Fahrenheit in winter, but I still went diving as if it were summertime. Nothing could stop me from being in the water—not wind, not cold, and certainly not fear.

Yvinec made me who I am. My little island is the reason I'm so happy in my own company and passionate about what I do. I live for the ocean, just like my father. It was his childhood dream to live on an island, and after he and my mother divorced, he wanted to make Yvinec his home. He was a keen sailor, and sailed across the Atlantic twice with a crew. Unfortunately, he and I rarely sailed together. But when I was young, he'd tell me all about his adventures, and I'd say, "One day, you and me, we're going to sail away together and go all around the world!" I often used to flip through the photo albums my father kept in the living room, which were yellowed by time and warped by moisture. I loved letting my mind wander across those distant seas he would speak of so fondly. And I thought that one day, I too would follow in his footsteps.

I spent the summer fixing up my boat. Sometimes friends would come over to lend a hand. I was determined to set sail by the end of August. To be ready on time, I had a lot of work to get done. But I wasn't afraid of hard work.

I never found it easy to knuckle down at school, though—let's just say I never really found my place in the education system. It wasn't for lack of trying. I gave plenty of schools a shot—thirteen, to be exact! I made my way through all the nearby schools, and went as far afield as Paris. When I was sixteen years old, I was so frustrated that I said, "That's it, Dad. I'm done with school."

Not knowing what else to do, my father arranged for me to stay home and brought in tutors to give me private lessons. I was a teenager who couldn't wait to learn all about life, and I knew there was nothing for me in any school textbooks. The tutors soon realized I was a lost cause, academically speaking. They were all very nice, and we ended up talking about the great wide open sea and the adventures of life much more than school work. And whenever my father wasn't around, I would take my tutors out fishing instead, and they loved it! The next year, my parents enrolled me in another high school about an hour's drive away in Saint-Brieuc, the nearest big town. Needless to say, I was bored to tears! I spent my days gazing out the window, calculating the tide times, and thinking about my lobster traps.

I turned eighteen in January that year. That was when I started to ask myself existential questions. I figured I had another whole year of high school left to go before I graduated, and that would only just be the beginning. I'd have to go on to university and get a degree if I wanted to get a decent job. But what would I study, and what kind of job would I want to do? I just couldn't see myself chained to a desk for the next forty years, and I came to realize that if I went down the road the system wanted me to go, it would really clip my wings. I felt a calling to travel and was desperate to maintain a sense of freedom. What I really wanted to do was to sail the world, but I knew that I'd need to make some money first.

So I called it all quits. I said goodbye to my little island, my family, my latest high school, and the comfort of a life path that was all mapped out for me. I sold my motorcycle, bought a plane ticket to Australia, a French-English dictionary, and a Lonely Planet guide, and headed out into the great unknown with all of two hundred euros in my pocket. My whole family tried to talk me out of it. I ignored their advice and insisted on going overseas to learn English and see something new.

Of course, I could have gone to England or Ireland instead, but that would have been too close to home. I dreamed of being completely out of my comfort zone, of seeing kangaroos, platypuses, and koalas, and I longed to surf the waves of the Pacific and Indian oceans. And heading off to Australia with nothing but two hundred euros and five words of English in my pocket would certainly be a challenge. Even my father, who had always stood by my choices in life, had a hard time understanding my decision. "I don't get it," he said. "You're barely eighteen years old; you have your own apartment, a motorcycle, and everything else you need. You've got it easy, and now you're going to throw it all away." He couldn't grasp why I would ever give that all up to go to the ends of the world and live on the streets.

I'm not exaggerating when I say I lived on the streets. When I got to Sydney, I ended up sleeping on the sidewalk for the first few nights and woke up to find rats crawling over me. After dark, I was an outcast, and only at daybreak did I feel like a normal person again. Before I set off for Australia, everyone had wanted to put me in touch with people they knew over there, but I was determined to see how I could manage on my own. I soon left the big city and headed inland. I had read that it was fruit-picking season, and I thought I'd try my luck. It turned out to be the right decision, because I found work harvesting apples, watermelons, and grapes.

It wasn't long before I built up a little nest egg and could afford to buy myself a bicycle. I then pedaled my way across the whole southwest of the country, eating pretty much nothing but oat flakes and powdered milk. Every cent I earned counted. Every cent I kept in my pocket got me one step closer to buying my boat. Along the way, I worked as a gardener and pool cleaner, waited tables, and washed dishes—and then I arrived in Carnarvon. I ran into some young people who told me I might as well turn right back around, because there was no work to be had there. I figured they probably hadn't looked hard enough.

Walking around the port, I chatted with a few fishing-boat captains. One of them was furious; he was missing a crew member after someone failed to show up, and he was already late heading out to sea.

"Have you ever worked on a shrimp trawler?" he asked me.

"Of course! That's what I do for a living back in France," I bluffed.

"Great. Climb aboard. We're leaving in half an hour, and we won't be back for three weeks," he told me.

And just like that, off I went to sea. It ended up being more than a month before we made it back again. The skipper soon realized I had never worked on a shrimp trawler before, but he showed me the ropes. I worked like a madman for nearly twenty hours a day on a shark-infested sea, sorting shrimp through nets that were booby-trapped with deadly fish, and snakes too. One day, I came very close to losing my leg, and another time, I was knocked out cold by a giant sea star. But I didn't care. I would stop at nothing to buy myself a sailboat so I could set sail and see the world.

~~~~~~~~

I STILL WANTED to leave my little island by the end of August. But the list of things I had to fix on the boat just kept growing. Crossing the Bay of Biscay had really taken its toll on the vessel. The engine needed an overhaul. The sails weren't in as good a shape as I'd thought. When the tide went all the way out, I was using support crutches to keep the boat upright, but several times I went out to find the boat lying on her side, the crutches completely broken.

One morning at high tide, when the boat was at anchor, I noticed that she was sitting very low in the water. What the heck, I thought. There was water all over the cabin floor! It had seeped in through the propeller shaft seal, submerging the batteries, causing them to short-circuit and puff out gray smoke. Battery acid had then leaked into the boat, damaging some of the electronics. Obviously, I would have to repair the damage, and that would cost money. And at that point, it was already September.

I figured I would finally be able to set sail around the end of November. By then, the boat would just need a good cleaning and supplies for a full month at sea. I was quickly running out of time, though. I planned to repaint the hull white and green—the color of hope—before I left. I would also rename the boat *Yvinec*, so that I would never feel too far away from my little island. The Breton painter and seafarer Yvon Le Corre made the stencil for me.

As I turned my attention to the hull, I was a little concerned to see there were a few small patches of corrosion to repair, but Manu, a friend who knows boats inside and out, helped to set my mind at ease. "You just have to treat the surface," he said. "First you scrape away the rust, then sand the area, and apply antifouling before you put the paint on. It's hard work, but it's nothing serious."

Keen to fix the damage quickly, I grabbed a hammer and a stiff metal brush and set about doing the job, following Manu's instructions very carefully. I gently hammered away the rust, then scrubbed with the metal brush until I got down to the bare steel of the hull.

Suddenly, a jet of water squirted into my face. Oh no—I had made a hole in my boat! I was absolutely furious. After all the trouble I had gone to for this damn boat! I had poured blood, sweat, and tears into it, only to have a punctured hull ten days before I was supposed to set sail!

But there was no way I was going back to square one again. I plugged the hole with a screw and some Sikaflex sealant, made sure the water couldn't get through again, and went back to very carefully hammering and scraping, until—*whoosh!*—not one, not two, but three more jets of water spurted forth. I was definitely in over my head now. I called Manu, and he laughed at me over the phone, saying he would come right over.

But as soon as Manu saw the holes, he realized this was no laughing matter. As it turned out, the metal in places was barely thicker than a sheet of tissue paper, and the rust had spread farther than we'd suspected. "Guirec, you can't go to sea in a boat like this," he said. "The rust is eating her alive. You have to redo the whole hull."

That was too much for me to hear. It had been three years since I'd quit school and a year since I'd bought my boat—a boat I had spent four solid months repairing and preparing for my first solo Atlantic crossing. I had poured all my energy and my savings into this project. I had invested time and money in equipment, clothing, and food for my journey. And now I had to give up on the idea?

I thought I'd bought a boat that was seaworthy, but it had turned out to be a giant cheese grater. I didn't blame the former owners. They themselves had bought a freshly painted boat that was cosmetically sound, a boat they had barely sailed. They couldn't have known the boat was in this kind of condition.

I knew the sensible thing to do would be to wait until I had the means to get a big job like this done properly. It wouldn't be the end of the world to wait another six months. It was always an option to go back to Paris and sell more windows to fill my bank account. But did I really want to put this off—again? And how long would it take to redo the entire hull? I didn't have the money for that. It was a completely irrational idea to even consider embarking on a solo crossing with a punctured hull. But was crossing the Atlantic solo really a rational thing to do in the first place?

If you let the first hurdle get in your way, you'll never get anywhere. There's always a good excuse not to leave, and there's always something that's not quite perfect. And there are always a million little things that still need tweaking when you think you've done it all. Too bad; a few damn holes weren't going to sink me.

And so, I plugged the perforations, welded a few patches over the top, and hoisted my sails. I brought the welding machine along too, just in case.

~~~~~~~

I MANAGED TO LEAVE at the end of November, by the skin of my teeth, right after I had painted *Yvinec* in green letters on one side of the hull—because there wasn't enough time to do both sides. I brought the stencil and the can of paint with me. I figured I could always do the rest at my first port of call. Any sailor who clapped eyes on me and my old boat would have told me I was crazy and irresponsible and tried to talk me out of it, and they wouldn't have been wrong. But life is too short to have any regrets. There's no point in planning for every eventuality, because that only keeps you from getting anywhere. You can't cross a bridge until you get to it, can you?

Before I climbed aboard, there was only one thing left to do, which was to set my family's minds at ease. I had been deliberately vague with them about my plans. It was better that way, for all of us. I had never told any of them what I was really setting out to do—it wasn't to sail across the ocean. It was to sail to the ends of the earth. I wanted to sail all the way to the top of the globe, where few humans had ever ventured. I wanted to experience true solitude, the real thing, amid the most immense of white winter landscapes. Where did that urge come from?

Who had whispered the idea into my ear? Maybe it was some documentary I'd seen, or some story I'd heard. Perhaps it was something I'd read; I can't remember. But one thing was for sure: I dreamed of seeing polar bears, sailing through great fields of floating ice, and touching icebergs with my bare hands.

I told my parents I was going to cross the Atlantic, and that if I enjoyed the experience, I would keep going. As it was, they found that idea very disconcerting. I didn't have enough experience, and my boat was riddled with rust, they said. I figured I'd better not tell them about my dream to spend a winter in the sea ice. I have to admit I wasn't very sure of it myself. What if the boat did sink?

"What will you do if something happens out there in the middle of the ocean?" they asked me.

"Don't worry; I'm equipped for that," I replied.

That wasn't true. I had nothing. Well, only an old VHF radio—which would allow me to communicate with other boats, but only within a very short range—and an old GPS. I didn't have an emergency beacon. Those were way too expensive. And as for flares, they would be no use in the open ocean. Unless a container ship happened to be in the vicinity, there would be no one to see them.

"If you haven't heard from me in two months from now, then you can start to worry," I told my parents, trying to reassure them.

I had no solo sailing experience whatsoever. The traditional route from France to the Caribbean passes to the south of the Azores High area, via the Canary Islands and Cape Verde. Sailors can then pick up the warm trade winds that blow steadily from east to west. As I was far from being a seasoned sailor, I decided against blazing my own trail, for once, and opted to follow the route most traveled.

The day before I set sail, I had to call my friend Romain to ask him to explain to me again how to get a fix—or how to calculate my position in terms of longitude and latitude on a marine chart. Oh, if that had been the only thing I still needed to learn! Never mind, I thought. I had the willingness and the desire to learn what I had to, and I wasn't afraid. I would just pick up what I needed to know on the fly. I've always preferred to learn by doing, rather than by teaching myself theory. I've always trusted my instincts. I was definitely counting on my lucky star as I set sail on this adventure. I might have been crazy, but I've always trusted that life will work itself out the right way.

~~~~~~~

I CHECKED ALL my gear before I set out, of course. The engine was still temperamental and needed a lot of fussing with, to the point where I even considered doing without it entirely. The sails would be good enough. I had bought new batteries and replaced the wind generator, so I would be good for power. Navigation-wise, I had paper marine charts, and electronic charts on my iPad. As for tools, I packed enough to be able to repair anything that might feasibly happen to the boat. I had a compressor and generator if I needed them, plus my trusty welding machine. I was well equipped, and I found that reassuring. I had plenty of clothes and food supplies, of course, as well as all my water toys: windsurf boards, masts, booms, and sails; stand-up paddleboard and paddle; surfboard; and kitesurfing and diving gear. My sailboat was so well stocked, it was a full-on surf shop, as well as a mini grocery and hardware store!

It's amazing how much you can pack into a little sailboat. The only problem was, everything was so well packed that whenever I wanted to retrieve anything, I needed the patience to pull everything out and put it back in its place again.

Technically speaking, *Yvinec* is a swing-keel sailboat. It's important for monohull sailboats to have a keel, because a keel provides weight at the bottom of the hull to counteract the weight of the wind in the sails, which helps to prevent capsizing. Sailboats with a fixed keel are more stable and easier to right if they do capsize, because the keel is longer and provides a greater counterbalance—but the downside is generally a deeper draft, which means they sit deeper in the water.

Instead of a fixed keel, *Yvinec* has a swing keel, which can be raised—like a centerboard in a dinghy—to let her sail in shallower waters. But this also makes her a less stable boat, harder to sail upwind, and more likely to capsize when the keel is lifted. The real advantage is that you don't have to worry when the tide goes out; all you have to do is lift the keel, drop anchor, and put out the crutches for the boat to rest upright until the tide comes back in.

A few days before I headed off, my parents each came to pay me a visit, and to bring me some basic groceries: butter, cereal, UHT milk (the shelf-stable Tetra-Pak milk commonly found in France), mini yogurts, and canned cod liver. All the basics for a Frenchman! Then I went to the local farmers' market in Tréguier to pick up some of the other good stuff I knew I couldn't live without: a few sticks of *saucisson*, slabs of pâté, and wheels of cheese. And finally, right before I climbed aboard once and for all, I wolfed down a delicious traditional Breton crepe, to savor one last taste of home!

I wanted to set sail on my own. No one was there when I left, and that was the way I wanted it to be. A journalist from *Ouest-France*, the local newspaper, had wanted to write an article about me, some kind of little-guy-from-a-little-village adventure story, but I'd told him that I'd rather he didn't. In my mind, I didn't really know where I was going or what I was doing, so I certainly didn't want anyone to write about me! I wanted to keep a low profile. I started the engine, let it warm up a little, and listened as it went from a rumble to a purr. And then I gently eased *Yvinec* away from the dock and headed down the Jaudy river estuary toward the ocean.

I had to motor along the tidal estuary for a good forty minutes before reaching open water. The shores of the Jaudy are always a scenic sight. All the way along, tiny white-sand coves alternate with woodland areas, where great flocks of birds fly skyward as the boats sail by. I passed the majestic Château de Kestellic, with its pink granite walls, slate roof, and palm trees standing guard out front. Next, I sailed past the picturesque village of La Roche Jaune, then through the ominously named Baie de l'Enfer (which means Bay of Hell). As I neared the open water, a dolphin crested the surface, as if to show me the way. As I sailed past my home on the little island of Yvinec, I could see my father standing on top of the big rocky outcrop at the farthermost tip, waving his arms. My heart swelled with joy and pride as I waved enthusiastically in return. Finally, I was on my way!

Not long after that, the engine suddenly sputtered to a halt. Seriously? Was this some sort of joke? Unfortunately, it wasn't. It was a serious problem. The part that controls the engine throttle and cutoff had broken—that's not something to take lightly! Barely an hour had passed since I left the marina, and already I was in trouble.

There was only one thing for it: I pulled out my generator and welding machine, which I had never suspected I would need to use so soon. Time to get to work! I was no expert, but I managed to repair the part, and it looked like it would hold. I started the engine again and kept going.

But the same thing happened again. And again. Each time I welded the part back together, I tried to do a better job. I must have been trying too hard, because I ended up nicking the end of my finger and fingernail on the angle grinder. I winced in pain as I inspected the wound. It was a pretty deep cut, and I disinfected it with rubbing alcohol before bandaging it up.

By now, the sun was setting, and I was going into my first night as a solo seafarer. Shortly before midnight, the wind came in. I hoisted the sails and killed the engine, and *Yvinec* glided along in the silence of the ocean, by the light of the moon.

Little by little, the wind picked up, and a nice swell started to build. The gusts blew through, stronger and stronger, buffeting *Yvinec* as they passed. At daybreak, I noticed there was a serious problem with the self-steering system. The blade had blown off of the wind vane—which is connected to the rudder and keeps the boat sailing a safe course in relation to the apparent wind. This eliminates the need for a sailor to be constantly at the helm. It's a purely analog piece of equipment; there's nothing electronic about it, and that's a good thing. Back in the day, before automatic pilots existed, every seafaring sailboat had a self-steering wind vane. Even today, most oceangoing sailboats, except for the faster racing boats, still have a similar setup. It's a basic mechanical system that can often handle the sea better than a high-tech automatic pilot. Ideally, boats should have both, and that had been the case with *Yvinec*—until now.

Now I would have to stop in Spain to fix the wind vane before I set my sights on the Caribbean. I would make do with the automatic pilot until then. At least that's what I thought, until the automatic pilot also failed, while I was still sailing down the western coast of Brittany just off the Finistère peninsula. The automatic pilot makes it possible for solo sailors to move around the boat, and essentially have a life on board, without having to stay at the helm the whole time. It's an absolute must in terms of giving a skipper time to eat, rest, and sleep. All you have to do is program a route and hit the "Auto" button, and you won't deviate from your course. It's as simple as that. But now things had become complicated. No matter how positive a person I usually am, and how much I always saw potential solutions rather than problems, I knew this would be a major setback. I had to think quickly. What was I going to do?

I had no more navigation aids, so I would have to hold the tiller the whole time to keep us on course. One thing was for sure, I wouldn't get very far like that. At this point, I was nearly halfway between my home port in Brittany and my destination in Spain, with nothing but open water right ahead of me.

I had a dilemma. Should I throw caution to the wind and forge ahead into the Bay of Biscay to take on its peaks, troughs, and swells aboard a boat that was far from being in good shape? Or turn around and head back to the south coast of the Finistère peninsula in western Brittany? For once in my life, I decided to do the sensible thing and head back to Brittany. I would take the time to fix what had broken, and set off again with the right equipment.

And so, I turned the boat around and set a northeasterly course toward the southern shores of the Finistère peninsula. It was pitch dark when I finally drew near the coast. After thirty hours nonstop at the helm, I was exhausted.

After a good night's sleep at anchor, I made myself hot chocolate and a bowl of cereal for breakfast, then I made my way to shore. I sailed into Port-la-Forêt, which is a true mecca for sailors. The marina there is huge, with more a thousand slips. Port-la-Forêt is also home to a renowned training center for offshore sailing. Among sailors, this place is known as the *vallée des fous*— "the valley of the crazies"—I guess because we're either crazy about what we do, or we have to be crazy to do it! Many of the world's finest sailors have passed through here, including Michel Desjoyeaux—the two-time winner of the Vendée Globe single-handed yacht race—as well as professional sailors like Vincent Riou and Armel Le Cléac'h, the cream of the crop of ocean adventurers. I didn't have any trouble finding a marine electronics specialist in a place like this.

There was no arguing with the expert's verdict. I had to install a new automatic pilot system that would be tougher than the old one. And it was going to cost 4,800 euros for the equipment alone, plus 500 euros for labor. I didn't have a penny of that, but I had to find a way to pay for it. Since my return from Australia, I had managed to get by on my own, doing odd jobs here and there to cover my expenses. As a matter of pride, I had always politely declined any help. I'm fortunate to have a family that is relatively well off, but I'd never wanted to take advantage of that.

This time, though, I didn't have the choice. To earn six thousand euros, I would have to delay my trip by several months, and that would be an even bigger blow to my pride. And so, for the first—and what I hoped would be the last—time, I decided to accept my older sister Nolwenn's offer to help. She looked after me a lot when I was little, and has always been like a second mother to me.

The repairs put *Yvinec* out of action for a week. I made the most of the time by fixing up a few things around the boat. I installed a basic AIS (Automatic Identification System) receiver that would detect other boats equipped with the same system, helping to avoid collisions. The circuit board on the refrigerator was fried, so I replaced that. And, most importantly, I replaced the alternator, which I should have done earlier. If that were to fail, I wouldn't be able to recharge my batteries and would really be in trouble.

I also installed a float switch on the bilge pump so that it would kick in as soon as any water entered the boat. This kind of thing can really come in handy if, for some reason, the boat is left for an extended time with no one on board. It's every sailor's nightmare to return to their boat and find it underwater. I had somehow also neglected to plan for this contingency. It was sobering to think that at any time, I might have been at risk of running out of power or sinking!

I had been at the marina for a few days when a journalist by the name of Aziz came by to say hello. We struck up a good rapport, and I agreed that he could write an article about me. He asked me so many questions. A couple of days later, I couldn't believe my eyes when I opened the newspaper and found myself face-to-face with a half-page spread showing *Yvinec*, and me giving the thumbs-up. This is what the article said:

GUIREC SOUDÉE TAKES ON THE WORLD BY SAILBOAT

Aboard his sailboat Yvinec, *Guirec Soudée is going to travel around the world solo. He's already sailed his way around Brittany from the Côtes-d'Armor region, and has called in to Port-la-Forêt to make a pit stop and to repair some equipment. Now he's just waiting for the wind to blow his way before he sets off again. Nothing can stop Guirec Soudée. When this twenty-one-year-old young man from Brittany sets his mind to something, he won't let go of it . . .*

It was funny to see myself in the newspaper. As soon as I set foot in the little café in the marina that morning, where I had already become a regular, people were keen to show their support. "Respect, Guirec!" they said. "What you're doing is great!" Seeing them all standing at the bar with their espressos, then gathering around me to shoot the breeze, I was worried they would take me for someone I wasn't—a seasoned sailor. Feeling a little sheepish, I smiled and tried to just go with the flow. The worst thing was that I was the one who still had lots of questions to ask them, not the other way around. But it was clear from the article that I was a quirky kind of character, and that distracted them from the fact that I barely knew what I was doing.

After a week in the marina, *Yvinec* was ready to go again, and my wallet was emptier than ever before. The time had come to leave Port-la-Forêt and wave goodbye to my new friends. *Au revoir, les amis!* The great sailor is off on his way around the world, and setting sail for . . . the port next door, Concarneau. The truth was,

I needed to earn a bit of money, and the weather was going to stop me from getting much farther anyway.

~~~~~~~~~~

THE MARINAS HERE are full of people like me, people who are crazy about the sea. We're like one big family. It's easy to strike up a conversation with a complete stranger here and find that you have plenty in common. As soon as I docked in Concarneau, Michael and Erwan, two sailors whose boat was docked next to mine, took me under their wing and helped me earn a few euros. One day I helped them on a fishing expedition. Another day we went out to pull up lobster traps. And another time I had my hands full cleaning seaweed out of the fishing nets. They made sure I didn't go hungry either by filling my belly with the pollack, crab, and langoustine we caught.

It wasn't long before I got to know Olivier, who has a handsome ketch—a two-masted sailboat. During the season, he's a sailing instructor at Les Glénans, one of the top sailing schools in Europe. He's not the type to have the wool pulled over his eyes. He soon pegged me as the amateur I was, and wasn't afraid to give me a piece of his mind. "You can't be serious, Guirec! Don't tell me you're going to cross the Bay of Biscay all by yourself! Have you even thought about the weather? It's the middle of winter, man!" he said. To that, I mumbled a sheepish reply that it would all be fine, more to try to convince myself than to set his mind at ease. He must have thought I was out of my mind, a kid who had no idea what he was getting himself into.

Olivier introduced me to a guy named Xavier. He was getting ready to sail around the world too, aboard his Figaro—a sleek sailboat built for racing. The three of us soon realized we shared the same thirst for adventure on the high seas. And we all started getting ready to set sail across the Bay of Biscay before charting a course to the Caribbean. But the weather was still too bad to head out to sea. I ended up spending Christmas and New Year's with my friends in the marina before there was a decent break in the weather. My family tried to persuade me to come home for Christmas—I was still only an hour or two down the road, after all—but in my mind I had already left.

~~~~~~~~

I LEFT CONCARNEAU on January 16. I was sailing solo, but I wasn't really on my own. Two other sailboats left the dock at the same time as *Yvinec*—Olivier's ketch and Xavier's Figaro. It was nice to see my friends' boats so close by as we all headed the same way, though I could only enjoy their company while it lasted. They were too fast for me to follow, and just seventy-two hours later, they were already out of sight.

I should have listened to Olivier's advice, but my stubbornness prevailed. The Bay of Biscay had been bad enough when Romain and I had sailed it together—but alone, it was hellish. I was freezing the whole time and the spray kept blasting me in the face. I thought I could make it all the way to A Coruña, on the northern coast of Spain, but I was too optimistic. After three days of high seas and a solid Force 5 wind, gusting 6, I had to make land about eighty nautical miles sooner, in Ribadeo.

It was pitch dark when I moored *Yvinec* at the dock, and I was feeling a little the worse for wear. I hadn't slept much at all, and the crossing had shaken my confidence quite a bit. Needless to say, I was happy to make it to dry land. What's more, as I approached the coast, I had an unpleasant surprise when I ventured way too close to some shallows—I guess I needed to brush up on my chart reading! The waves there were huge and sounded like thunder as they crashed over the shoal in a horrendous sea of white water and smoky spray. *Yvinec* was rolling dangerously in the swell; this was a pretty close call.

It was a very pleasant surprise to run into Xavier at the marina, though. He'd had to give up on the idea of making it all the way to A Coruña too. We spent a few days in Ribadeo before we set sail again. This time, I was determined to make it down to the southern climes quickly. Soon after, though, I had to make land again, this time at A Coruña. The forecast was terrible, so it really wasn't wise to be at sea. I found this frustrating, to say the least.

One morning, after a few days in the marina, I got up and poked my head out of the cockpit to see a magnificent wooden sailboat moored right alongside *Yvinec*. There was a young woman puttering around on deck, who seemed to be having some trouble. I pulled on a T-shirt and jumped out onto the dock to introduce myself. "Hi, I'm Guirec!" I said, cheerfully.

Her name was Alexandra, and she had just inherited her father's sailboat, a magnificent old sloop that must have been nearly a hundred years old. A thing of beauty. I was happy to lend a hand. It must have looked like I knew what I was doing, because she was very keen to put me to work. Before I knew it, I had found myself a job. It was good to earn a bit of cash so I could tinker on *Yvinec* a little more, stock up at the local grocery store, and feast on some more tapas.

After a month in A Coruña, with favorable weather in the forecast and a tidy nest egg of about a thousand euros in my pocket, I was set to continue on my way.

I was just checking the last things over when a friendly guy wandered over to say hello. "Time to head out, is it?" he asked.

We introduced ourselves. His name was Kevin, and his girlfriend's name was Lucie. They were leaving today too, aboard their Gin Fizz cruiser with the equally bubbly name of *Mousse*, and we were headed the same way.

"It's time to get going!" they said. "We're not going to stay too close to the coast; there's no wind. Best to head offshore."

Oh, really? What are they talking about? I wondered. Why were they heading offshore? Why make the route any longer than it already was? Later, that would all be obvious. But right then, I figured they could do what they pleased. I was going to stick to my plan, and we agreed to meet up in Peniche, on the Portuguese coast.

As I approached the marina in Peniche, the sun wasn't up yet. I love sailing into a marina in the dark. You can see the lights sparkling in the distance, they seem so close, and you figure you're nearly there—but you still have hours at the helm before you reach the first navigation buoys. When you eventually enter the channel, the lights guide you in—green to starboard side, red to port—as you glide through the deep, dark silence of the night. There's no one watching. You can make all the rookie mistakes you like, because there's no one there to judge you. It's just you, your boat, the sea, and the stars.

AFTER CALLING IN at Peniche, I planned to sail down the coast toward Gibraltar, then chart a course farther offshore toward Madeira that would take me well away from the coast of Morocco. It wasn't the easiest route, and I would have to be especially vigilant because of heavy marine traffic—but according to the forecast, if I sailed a straight line from Peniche, there wouldn't be a breath of wind. It just goes to show, heading offshore to catch the wind doesn't always work in your favor.

I thought it would take me five or six days to get where I was going. The winds were light the first night, but the next morning there was barely a breath. I didn't want to have to start the engine, because it's noisy, it pollutes the environment, and it costs money. On the bright side, the sun was out and the temperature was a balmy sixty degrees Fahrenheit. I set the self-steering, and *Yvinec* glided along nicely all by herself.

I closed my eyes for a while to enjoy the moment. Then, deciding to make the most of the calm conditions, I climbed the mast. The view from up there is amazing! Like an overexcited boy, I laughed and shouted, made grand declarations to the ocean, and yelled at the top of my lungs. Other than the dolphins and gulls, there was no one around to hear. It did me a world of good to let off some steam. At the same time, I was mindful not to get too carried away. When you're more than forty feet up in the air, you tend to sway around a lot, and it would be easy to slip and fall. It's not usually a good idea to climb the mast without a safety line, and there was no one out here to come to my rescue if I got into trouble. With that sobering thought, I tightly grasped everything within my reach—rungs, lines, and all—as I made my way safely down onto the deck. It wasn't so bad down there, after all that excitement.

We still had a very light tailwind. In Peniche, Kevin and Lucie had shared plenty of sailing tips with me, specifically how to pole out the genoa jib to sail "wing on wing" downwind, with the genoa out to one side of the boat and the mainsail to the other, so both would stay filled and catch the most wind. When the winds were light, this would make for comfortable sailing. The good thing about cruising along at a leisurely three knots is that it's the perfect speed to cast a fishing line. And fish for supper was a very attractive prospect indeed, after all the canned food I'd been eating. I carefully prepared my lines, set my lures, and cast them out. Fingers crossed!

As I waited for the fish to bite, I went down into the galley to prepare some spaghetti carbonara. From the tiny cabin window down there, the view right above the water's surface was spectacular. Pasta in hand, I climbed back on deck and started talking to myself. "Oh, fantastic, there's space to dine alfresco on the patio! What a prime location! Does anyone mind if I take this table?" With a great big smile, I sat with my face to the sun and dug in to the pasta with my fork, eating it right from the pan. It wasn't the fanciest way to dine, but the food stayed warm.

I kept half an eye on my lines as I ate. Nothing was moving at all. Where were all the fish? I had done everything I was supposed to do, and it hadn't worked. Oh well, I sighed, as I resigned myself to yet another night of eating just pasta.

And how come the wind wasn't picking up either? It wasn't quite dead calm, but it was close enough. At this pace, it felt like it was going to take forever to get to Madeira. According to the GPS estimate, we would get there in four days and eighteen hours. Not much earlier, the estimate had been four days and five hours. This kind of thing changes all the time; that's just the way it is when you're sailing. You know when you're leaving, but you never know when you're going to arrive.

Suffice it to say that I was happy when we drew closer to Madeira and Funchal was finally in sight. It was the beginning of March, and the marina was full to bursting. There wasn't a single slip to be had. I had to drop anchor in the bay, outside the seawall. I could have done without that, because the sea was pretty rough. That made for a rolly anchorage, so we were literally tossing and turning in the choppy water. But from a financial perspective, it wasn't a bad thing. At least I was saving the cost of a slip in the marina. It wasn't exactly a priority for me to be forking out what little cash I had for water that was barely drinkable, showers that were lukewarm at best, and washrooms of questionable cleanliness.

Kevin and Lucie had been waiting for me for the last few days, and soon enough I spotted Xavier's Figaro too. We weren't sailing side by side, but at least we were following each other. The four of us met for dinner that night aboard Kevin and Lucie's Gin Fizz. I brought a tuna I had finally managed to catch the day before, and we prepared a carpaccio that was simply divine.

Funchal is a fantastic port of call, because there's plenty to do on shore. During the daytime, I would often go ashore and make my way up into the hills. The slopes were steep and sandy, but the flower-lined paths up there offered some incredible views of the city down below kissing the ocean. In the evening, I would head back to *Yvinec* in my dinghy and settle down for another night at anchor, then feast my eyes on the view the next morning as I tucked in to my bowl of chocolate-flavored cereal. Peace and quiet—that was another benefit of anchoring outside the marina that I came to appreciate.

The time had come for me to set sail again and chart my course to the Canary Islands, my final port of call before embarking on the great Atlantic crossing. On my way out of the Madeira archipelago, I decided to make a stop on the remote island of Selvagem Grande, around 150 nautical miles to the south. The island is a nature reserve, so I'd needed to obtain a visitor permit from the authorities in Funchal first. The only inhabitants were two rangers named Jake and Carlos, their dog, Selvagem, a colony of monk seals, and thousands of Cory's shearwaters. These birds are a protected species, and they make their nests to raise their chicks in the tiniest of crevices in the rocky cliffs. Jake and Carlos took me under their wing right away. They showed me every nook and cranny of their island, fed me local delicacies, and even taught me how to bake my own bread!

One morning, I took Carlos scuba diving; it was his first time. These waters are renowned as some of the cleanest and most unspoiled in the world, so the scenery underwater was extraordinary. Moray eels, anemones, sea stars, scorpion fish, and barred hogfish, and even a large tuna all swam toward us fearlessly. This was probably the most memorable dive of my life. Ever since I was a young boy, I've loved being under the water. It doesn't matter whether I'm free diving, snorkeling, or scuba diving, there's nothing quite like the feeling of floating weightlessly in another world. It's like being in outer space, or at least the way I imagine it.

My hosts extended such a warm welcome that I ended up staying four days longer than I had planned. They even sent me on my way with a good twenty pounds of sea salt they had harvested themselves, to help me preserve my future catches. I certainly hoped their gift would bring me luck on the fishing front. I felt sad to be leaving them behind. I figured you must have to really enjoy your own company to live in a lighthouse in the middle of nowhere. But they seemed happy. As always, after these brief and intense encounters that are so typical of the sailing way of life, I wondered whether I would see Jake and Carlos again someday.

I set sail to the south, heading for the island of Lanzarote in the Canary Islands. It wasn't far—less than a hundred nautical miles from Selvagem Grande. Once more, however, the wind was playing hard to get. I had to adjust my course toward the island of Tenerife instead, and after twelve hours of smooth, steady sailing, it came into my sights. Soon we were gliding our way into the marina at Santa Cruz, the island's capital.

I made the most of this pit stop by stocking up on food and supplies. I pretty much swept the supermarket shelves clean and crammed my pantry full to bursting to make sure I'd have enough provisions to keep me going all the way to the Caribbean. Depending on the wind, the Atlantic crossing could take anywhere from three weeks to more than a month. As I was unloading my groceries, I met Jonas, a young Frenchman who was traveling around the world and looking to hitch a ride to the Caribbean. We struck up a rapport right away, but I had to explain that it was important for me to sail solo and live this adventure alone. He understood, and didn't seem to be offended at all. He was curious to find out more about what I was doing, in fact. I invited him aboard and we spent the evening chatting about our respective plans.

The next day, I set off again for the south coast of the island, which has a reputation for being a paradise for water and wind sports. I figured I deserved to have some fun for a while. No sooner had I arrived in the beachfront town of El Medano than I found myself shooting the breeze with a guy named Iao. He worked at the Bahia Water Sports Center, the surf school in front of where I had moored *Yvinec*.

I love windsurfing, surfing, and kitesurfing, so I was really in my element here. The only problem was, if I wanted to keep my wallet flush and stock up on fresh produce before I embarked on the long crossing, I'd have to earn a bit more cash. Naturally, I found myself a sweet gig teaching a French couple kitesurfing!

After a couple of weeks doing this sort of thing, I knew I had to think about raising anchor if I wanted to take advantage of the favorable trade winds. For the first time in my life, I was going to be at sea for a whole month, completely alone. I couldn't wait to get out there.

The only thing still nagging at me was that I would have liked to bring a little animal companion on board with me. My father thought it was a great idea for me to have some company. He even suggested I take Igloo, our golden retriever who always came out on the water with me back home. But life on the sailboat would have been too hard for him. He's a big dog who needs space.

I wanted an animal for company, but not your typical pet, not the kind you usually see on a boat cruising the ocean. And if I was going to get an animal, it might as well be a useful one. That's when the idea of getting a chicken crossed my mind. A hen would barely take up any space, wouldn't make too much noise, and could even lay eggs! This was a fantastic idea, my father agreed. He started asking around back home and got in touch with some specialized breeders of hens. But according to them, life on a sailboat would be far too stressful for a hen, and a stressed hen would never lay eggs. This was obviously disappointing to hear, but I moved on.

Still, the chicken idea kept running through my mind as the day of my grand departure drew closer. Eating healthily is a constant challenge on a sailboat, so it would be a real luxury to have fresh eggs in the middle of the ocean! And there wasn't necessarily any reason why my hen would be stressed, I told myself. If I took good care of her, if I built her a comfortable coop and fed her properly, why wouldn't she lay eggs for me? And weren't chickens friendly, sociable creatures too? I had to admit, I had no idea. I asked Iao, and he talked to some friends, who talked to their friends, and a few days later, a big cardboard box was delivered to the surf school.

Inside was a cute little bundle of feathers—a pretty copper-colored hen with a scarlet comb on top of her head and matching wattle under her chin. As soon as I opened the box, she turned her neck to the right, then to the left, jerking her head back and forth as she looked around curiously to take in her new surroundings. I scooped her up in my hands, and she was so soft and warm. She was quite content to be held and didn't try to get away. She seemed bright-eyed and curious—and quite docile, dare I say.

That was how I ended up going to sea with a chicken! Before I brought her back to the boat, I went into town to buy a few things, so I could build her a little place to call her own aboard *Yvinec*. A few planks of wood to build a coop, a bag of wood shavings for bedding, and a big sack of special grain for egg-laying hens was all I needed. Even before I walked out of the surf school with my hen in a cardboard box, I had already taken her under my wing.

As we left the building, the hen poked her head curiously out of a hole in the side of the box, clearly wondering what was happening and where I was taking her. People pointed and laughed as I carried her out onto the jetty and into my dinghy. Once we were on board, I opened the box. Out she hopped, and started to wander around as comfortably as if she were in a farmyard. With tiny little steps, she explored all around the floor of the dinghy, and even climbed up onto the inflatable sides. It didn't take long for her to find her sea legs! I could tell the two of us were going to have fun together. Even as I started the engine for us to motor away from the shore, she remained completely unruffled. During the short journey across the bay to reach *Yvinec*, I kept one hand on her to make sure she didn't fall into the water.

When we arrived at the sailboat, I picked my hen up and placed her gently on the deck. Before she went off to explore her new digs, she gave her feathers a cautious little shake. She walked all over the boat, poking her beak into every little nook and cranny. So far, so good. Now, where was I going to put her? I couldn't just let her wander around completely freely; I had no idea how she would fare when the seas got rough. And I had to find somewhere comfortable for her to sleep, anyway. Because chickens go to bed early, don't they?

This hen of mine still needed a name. Where I come from, in Brittany, it's traditional to eat out of a *bol breton*, a ceramic bowl with your name on it. I had a few of these on board, including one with my name on it—Guirec—of course. There were two others as well, which must have been left behind by previous owners. One of the bowls bore the name Jeannette, and the other, Monique.

I weighed up these names for a moment and soon decided on Monique. That sounded to me like a good name for a hen! She quickly found her bearings, leaving lots of little presents behind as she went—I hadn't thought about that. I was going to have my work cut out for me, cleaning up after her. I wondered if it was possible to toilet-train a chicken and teach it some basic principles of hygiene. I didn't have a clue. Wait, where did she think she was going now? No, Monique! You're not going into the cabin! I scooped her up and put her down again at the opposite end of the boat. "Listen to me, Monique," I said. "This is my home, down here. Be patient, and you'll have your own little home too. Just give me a bit of time to build it for you."

I thought the ideal place to put my little feathered co-skipper would be in the cockpit, at the stern of the boat, below the tiller, where there would be the least movement and where she would be well sheltered from the wind and the spray. I set up my generator and jigsaw tool, and got to work. Under Monique's watchful eye, I built a basic coop between two cross braces in the cockpit. It didn't take long for me to see that she was the clingy type. More than a few times, I had to shoo her away from the jigsaw blade. I adopted her so that she would lay eggs for me, not so she would end up on my plate as slices of roast chicken! I spread some wood shavings over the floor of her coop, added a little sand and a few pebbles I had scooped up from the beach, and gave her a cup of fresh water with the Monique bowl, into which I had sprinkled a good handful of grain. Mission accomplished! "What do you think, Monique?" I asked. "Monique?"

Where had she gone now? I found her below deck, inside the cabin. I didn't know what she was so interested in down there, but I wasn't having any of it. I was fine with her pooping outside, where I figured it would be easy enough to live with in the wind, rain, and fresh sea air, but inside the cabin? That was out of the question. I carried her back up on deck. Again, I tried to explain that on a sailboat, a little discipline went a long way. She cocked her head and looked at me with her tiny, beady eyes. I showed her the way to her coop. "Here you go, Monique. You can go inside here. This is your home," I said to her.

Warily, she ventured first one foot inside, then the other, turned around and walked out, turned her neck left and right, went back inside, scrabbled around in the wood shavings, dipped her beak into the water, pecked at a few grains (scattering them everywhere), and came back out again. That went pretty well, I thought.

What wasn't going so well, however, was my plan to sail off into the sunset. The wind wasn't blowing in the right direction. I would just have to be patient for a while. I decided to make the best of the situation and introduce Monique to the joys of water sports. After all, partners who play together, stay together! The easiest thing to try first was stand-up paddleboarding. With my board and paddle under one arm and Monique under the other, out I went.

She wasn't too keen in the beginning. I put her on the board and she flapped her wings, as if she wanted to take off. I brought her right back to the center line, stepped onto the board, and started to paddle. Monique didn't seem to think this was a good idea, but she soon settled. She kept turning her head in all directions, and everyone on the beach was laughing.

A short while later, I decided to give Monique a windsurfing lesson. I put her on the board and set off as gently as I could, but it was quite windy and she started to flap her wings again. So, I lifted her up and put her on the boom instead, the part I was holding onto, and she stayed there quite calmly, her feet wrapped around the soft, rounded perch. She even seemed to enjoy the experience.

Monique would always go to bed as soon as the sun went down. Sometimes, when I was sure she wasn't going to wake up, I slipped away for a while. I wasn't going to be staying much longer in El Medano, so I wanted to make the most of what time I had left. I would jump in my dinghy and head ashore to hang out with Iao and his buddies. Before I went to bed, I would check on Monique to make sure she had enough water in her cup. It was almost always empty. I couldn't believe how much she drank. Were all chickens this thirsty? I would rummage around in the wood shavings to see whether she had hidden an egg in there, but no, there was still no egg. What if the experts back in Brittany were right, and a hen would not lay eggs at sea?

As soon as she came out of her coop in the morning, Monique would follow me around. She was always so interested in everything I did, and she certainly took an interest in my chocolate-flavored breakfast cereal. She was so insistent that she even pecked at my hand to get a little closer to the bowl. Wasn't she happy with the grain I was feeding her? I pointed to the name painted in black on my ceramic bowl. "See where it says Guirec, right here? Guirec, that's me. This is my bowl. You have your own bowl, and it says Monique on it. And I don't go pecking in your bowl, do I?"

My words fell on deaf ears. By now she was wriggling around all over the place, so I scooped her up and held her in my lap. She was heavier than I thought. Her coat was coppery red, with some lighter-colored feathers underneath—the same shade as the little spots of rust on my boat, and my suntan! Monique certainly wasn't shy. Could you tame a chicken? I wondered. Would she eventually know her name and listen to me?

The next morning, while I was having my breakfast, I took my eye off Monique for a moment—and she disappeared. Where had she gone? She must be walking around on deck, I thought. In the morning she liked to warm her feathers in the sun. I put my bowl of cereal down and went up on deck. I couldn't see her anywhere. Oh no, she hadn't fallen in the water, had she? Suddenly, I heard her singing. Phew! I followed the sound, and there she was, sitting very still, with her legs folded under her, nestled right up against the mast, of all things. Gently I tiptoed closer, trying not to frighten her. "Oh, Monique, I was worried about you," I said. No reaction. All of a sudden, she stood up, puffed out her feathers, showing her fluffy white underbelly, and—*plop!*—out popped an egg!

"Good job, Monique!" I cried. And she started to sing.

And they said Monique would never lay eggs at sea!

PART 1

Our Atlantic Crossing

W E'RE OFF! We finally set sail on April 17, 2014, at seven in the evening. All being well, we should be in the Caribbean around the first week of May. The wind is light, but that's not a bad thing for Monique. It'll give her time to ease gently into life on the open ocean.

I hoist the mainsail and unfurl the genoa. The bay of El Medano slips away in our wake as *Yvinec* glides through the crystal-blue water. It's a magical moment. I'm sitting on the deck with my legs dangling over the edge of the boat and my feet hanging in midair. Monique is perched on my shoulder. Life is pretty sweet.

I'm chatty by nature, so I give Monique a running commentary as we sail along, telling her all about the sea, the wind, the currents, and the swell. I point to the island of Tenerife, with its red mountain and black-sand beaches. I tell her where we're going as she gazes back one last time at the island where she hatched. I know it's doing me good to talk to her. She's soaking up some of the sadness that's tearing at my heart, the way it does every time I leave a place where I've made new friends. "Wow, look at that, Monique!" I suddenly exclaim, as four, five—no, six!—dolphins crest the surface at our bow. It's amazing! They're leaping all around us now. Talk about giving *Yvinec* a special send-off! There's a huge smile on my face as we sail off into the distance, escorted by this pod of dolphins performing a ballet we'll never forget.

As the sun slips into the water ahead of *Yvinec*'s bow, I can't believe this is actually happening. The big blue, the great wide ocean I've been dreaming of for so long, is finally opening up and welcoming us with outstretched arms.

It's time for Monique to hit the hay, and I watch her strut away to her sleeping quarters. "Sweet dreams, Monique! See you tomorrow!"

Now, I'm all alone. Let the solo crossing begin! I'm excited, and a little anxious too. Crossing an ocean is no small undertaking, especially on a sailboat that's far from perfect. *Yvinec* is in better shape than when we left Brittany, but she still has plenty of flaws.

I figure that if we do sink, I'll grab my paddleboard and jump into the dinghy. We'll drift on the currents and eventually end up somewhere. The sea is pretty calm and the currents are favorable, running with the trade winds. Like Alain Bombard, who set out to prove a point that it was perfectly possible to sail across the ocean without any provisions, I'll survive on plankton and fish if I have to. But I'll also have fresh eggs, thanks to Monique! If you stop to assess every single risk you encounter in life, you'll never get anywhere or do anything. Instead, I like to believe that if I think positively, positive things will happen!

Here in this moment, all around me, there is nothing except the deep, dark ocean and a few twinkling lights in the distance— my sole seafaring companions in the Atlantic night. I relax as the swell and the chop lull me into a sense of security. It's not that hard to raise anchor and set sail.

The trick to spending a night at sea is to split it into shifts. The wind is light right now, so I decide it's a good time to place my trust in the boat and get some sleep. I've killed the engine, because it's too noisy. I don't have that much diesel on board, so I'd rather save it if I don't absolutely need it. I'm not in a hurry, either; there's no one waiting for me when I get to the other side. I know the wind will pick up again. I just have to be patient.

DAY 1, APRIL 18

I wake up around seven in the morning. I've slept for at least a couple of hours without interruption; what a luxury! The sky is overcast and a light breeze is picking up, so I raise the sails. When I was growing up on the coast, I used to drag my father out of bed so he would come fishing with me. When we were out on the water, I would conjure up all kinds of daydreams in my mind. I imagined us discovering the hidden treasures of the ocean, or exploring desert islands inhabited by exotic animals. The ocean has always fueled my imagination.

Monique is still inside her little coop. She turns to look at me as I approach.

"Good morning, Monique! Sleep well?" I ask.

Of course, she doesn't reply, but I sense she understands what I'm saying; she knows that I'm taking an interest in her. As far as chickens go, Monique seems like she's pretty smart. I think she's starting to respond to her name when I call her.

I pour some water into her dish and pick up her bowl to fill it with grain. She follows me around the deck and I have a hard time trying to stop her from wandering down into the cabin. I can see the attraction; there are provisions stacked all over the place down there, even in the bathroom—now unusable. Monique seems to go crazy whenever there's food around. I fill her bowl with grain, and she's right on my heels as I place it back down in her coop. She dives right in, and grain flies everywhere—making her fresh water all cloudy.

As Monique devours her breakfast, I head down into the galley to make my own. Eating healthily is a must when you're at sea. You can't allow yourself to have any slumps in energy, because you always need to have your wits about you, even if the conditions look easy. The weather can change rapidly, and you might have to make a decision or execute a maneuver without warning. You need quick reflexes. And for that, your body needs fuel. Breakfast is the most important meal of the day for me, and it has to fill me up, because I usually won't eat anything else until around five in the afternoon. So in the morning, I warm up a bowl of milk with some powdered chocolate, and I add whatever cereal I feel like too. I like to make myself a couple of slices of toast with butter and jam as well. If it's not raining, I take my bowl up on deck and check my sails at the same time.

I scan the sky. These clouds don't look like they're going away soon, but they're nothing to worry about. The air is warm already, and I know it's going to be a hot day. I'm barefoot, wearing nothing but boardshorts. Yesterday there were still some boats around, but now we really are alone out here, Monique and me. She's wandering around the deck now, exploring.

"Monique! Monique? Come here!" I cry.

She looks at me hesitantly.

"Monique?"

Stiffly and somewhat awkwardly, she lifts first one leg, then the other, making her way over to me in no great hurry. Why does she seem so reluctant? Maybe she's feeling shy today? But no—as soon as she's by my side, she hops up onto the bench seat, then onto my thigh, with all the confidence in the world. The wind has tousled her plumage, and she looks pretty funny. I pet her gently and smooth her feathers back into place. Then I try to put her down on the deck, but she's not having any of it—she flaps her wings and grips my arm with her claws. Ah, I realize, she has her eye on my breakfast. I place a morsel of cereal in the palm of my hand and offer it to her. Aha! She's going to stick to me like glue from now on. At least it will be easy for me to keep an eye on her. And I can use food to tame her a little.

When I get up to wash my bowl, she follows me like a little dog. Dishes on *Yvinec* get washed with seawater, like on many boats. It tends to leave a residue on everything, and makes even stainless steel utensils go rusty over time. I try to avoid that by giving everything a quick rinse with fresh water—cold, of course, because there's no hot water on board. But it's never enough; they're always poorly washed, and poorly rinsed. I figure it's not a huge deal, because I'm not exactly the cleanest either while I'm at sea! I can't afford to waste fresh water—in lieu of a shower, I pour a bucket of seawater over my head, and if I'm lucky, I get to rinse myself off with rainwater. I do use fresh water to rinse my mouth out after brushing my teeth, though. I tried using seawater, and it was really gross. Fresh water is a rare and precious commodity when you're at sea. I have my stocks of bottled mineral water and a water tank that can collect and store about forty gallons of rainwater—but that's no good if it doesn't rain. What's more, there are two of us now, and Monique is always thirsty.

Because I'm setting out for an experience to remember, I've brought some notebooks on board with me and I'm going to write everything down. Every day, I make a note of the weather, wind speed, boat speed, what I eat, what I catch fishing, and whatever other random things I'd like to remember. The only problem is, I don't have anything exciting to report yet! Still, I make an effort to write the date—I underline it the way we always did at school—and time, our boat speed and position, the direction we're sailing, and how the sails are trimmed. Today I jot down a few brief notes: *2014-04-18, 11:45 AM. Position N27°02'44", W17°28'11". Speed: 4.5–5 knots. Wind: 8 knots. Heading 218°. Monique laid an egg yesterday, and she's laid another one today. Not much wind when we set off yesterday, but fantastic sunset and lots of dolphins jumping six feet in the air.*

We're struggling to go any faster than five knots. The wind's blowing from behind us, so to improve our boat speed, I decide to fly the spinnaker. That's not an easy thing to do. It's a gigantic sail with a surface area of about three hundred square feet. It's almost impossible to rig on your own. The first time I tried, I was with Kevin and Lucie in Portugal. Since then, I've honed my technique, but it's still a big and physically challenging job, especially to lower it. But the spinnaker doesn't help that much today, and by the time the sun goes down, the sea looks like it's standing still.

I'm always worried we might crash into another boat in the dark, so all my senses are on high alert. Even though the wind is light and steady, I don't want to let my guard down, because the weather could turn in a flash. I set my alarm and try to catch forty winks. Every half-hour at least, I get up to check the sails and self-steering, then I go back below deck to snooze for another half-hour. Sometimes, I'm only awake for a moment or two. Other times, if I have to trim the sails, I might be up on deck for longer.

People often ask me what it's like at night, whether I sleep. Well, no, I tell them. I don't sleep. Not like everyone else sleeps, never a full seven or eight hours, never a whole night. In the middle of the ocean, the seabed is over twelve thousand feet below your boat, so dropping anchor and settling down for a quiet night's sleep is out of the question. Even if you're not keeping watch the whole night long, you're essentially on-call around the clock.

My anchor chain is 250 feet long, but that doesn't mean I can cast anchor in water that deep; the deepest water I can moor in is about 75 feet. Anchors don't just sink vertically and instantly immobilize a boat; they have to catch on the seabed, and will only hold fast when the boat pulls the chain tight. For a boat to be securely anchored, the chain has to run at a diagonal. And you always have to let out more chain than you think you'll need, because it's not just the anchor that keeps the boat from moving, but also the weight of the chain on the seabed. If you don't let out enough chain, and go ashore to explore for a while, you might not find your boat where you left it. (This is not a rare occurrence!) So when I drop anchor, I always let out plenty of chain for extra peace of mind, and, because I'd rather be safe than sorry, I use a second anchor too.

Around midnight, I wake to the sound of the spinnaker flapping. The wind has shifted, and it's total chaos above deck. The spinnaker has twisted itself around the genoa like a dishrag. There's no way I can lower it without untangling them first—I know there are techniques for that, but I don't know any of them! When these things happen, you have to act fast, without hesitation—but without panicking either, because you don't want to damage your equipment. Logically, if there's a problem, that means there's a solution. You can't have one without the other! The solution I come up with probably isn't the best, but it's the only one that springs to mind. The spinnaker has wrapped itself around the genoa in one direction, so logically, to untangle it, I just have to turn it the same number of times in the opposite direction. So I start the engine, grab the helm, and motor *Yvinec* around in circles until the sail is completely free again. It works! Now I can go back to bed.

Sailing a boat really isn't rocket science. All it takes is common sense, quick reflexes, and a little creativity!

The rest of the day turns out to be calm. I spend time tinkering with the self-steering, which could use a little fine-tuning.

As we forge steadily ahead, I glance over at Monique. So far, I've been letting her roam free, but that might not be the best idea. For one thing, she's making lots of little messes all over the deck.

DAY 3, APRIL 20

This morning at sunrise, I get up to check the sails and the self-steering, and everything is fine. I'm still tired, so I figure I'll go back to bed for a while. I'm just falling back asleep when Monique decides to serenade me. Of course, she's right above my berth and she starts clucking at the top of her lungs! I bury my head in the duvet, to no avail. There's no way I'm going back to sleep now, so I might as well get out of bed. It's just my luck to end up with a hen who thinks she's a rooster!

And so I go back up on deck, give Monique her breakfast, and, with a grumble, put her back in her coop.

The weather is still cloudy, and it's going to be another hot day. *Yvinec* glides slowly through the water under the power of the spinnaker. I'm getting the hang of the self-steering now. In the light breeze, the boat is staying on a steady, comfortable course. To pass the time and stay in shape, I work out as best I can. I take one of the cushions from the benches in the cockpit and take it up to the bow to do some push-ups. Of course, Monique is curious and comes over to see what I'm doing. Just for fun, I pick her up and put her on my back. She won't stop flapping. Thanks for the claw massage, Momo! I turn onto my back, set Monique down on my stomach, and off we go for a few ab crunches. Talk about a change of scenery from the gym! It's breathtaking here. I turn on my GoPro, thinking this would be a funny thing to film.

It's too hot to keep Monique cooped up, so I let her wander around on deck. She's an explorer at heart, but she's leaving plenty of souvenirs behind! When it gets too dirty, I clean up after her. I throw a bucket of seawater over the deck and give it a good scrub with a brush, then rinse with another bucket of water so it all disappears into the ocean. Times like these, I tell myself that if Monique were to fall overboard, I'd get over it. It would be a shame about the eggs, though.

To keep busy, I fish. I prepare my bait and my lures, then I cast my lines. It works pretty well. Yesterday, I hauled in two fish. There's no shortage of them in this ocean, and they're all safe to eat. I have no idea what kinds of fish those were, but I ate them both and lived to tell the tale! When you're fishing so far offshore, you don't have to worry about toxins in the fish. If I catch one that's too small, I decide to let it live a longer life and put it back in the water. The same goes for any that are too big. I don't have the refrigerator plugged in because it drains the batteries, so I'd rather avoid the mess.

DAY 4, APRIL 21

Finally, after two days of gray skies, the weather is glorious! *Yvinec* sways gently in the swell to compensate and stay her course. Monique manages to keep her balance by bending first one leg, then the other. She has it all figured out! She's developed her own morning routine. After her breakfast, she goes for a run around the deck, feathers flapping in the wind. She still has the reflex to peck at the ground with her beak, but there's not much to scavenge there. Then, when she feels she's going to lay an egg, she retreats to her coop. When I hear her cluck, I know I can go and collect my egg. If, for whatever reason, she can't get into her coop, she makes sure I know it. She stands right in front of the door and squawks. So if I have to change the bedding and clean the inside of the coop, I prefer to wait until the afternoon.

Obviously, as soon as I'm up to my elbows in cleaning it out, she wants to come in!

It's a beautiful day. A good breeze is beginning to fill in, so I disengage the self-steering and take the helm. Monique sits beside me and soaks up the sun. We're both very happy here, I think.

That afternoon, I catch a fabulous mahi-mahi. These are commonly found between Cape Verde and the Caribbean.

Because it's nice out, I take the opportunity to wipe down the hatches and cabin windows. After yesterday's mist and all the spray, I couldn't see much of the scenery from inside the cabin. When I'm done, I'm happy to see out again through the Plexiglas! I bask in the hot sun as the hull glides gently through the picture-perfect ocean. Monique seems to be in a good mood, and I've caught a delicious fish for dinner. Life is good. I put on some music and dance like crazy on the deck. I must look like I'm out of my mind, dancing my heart out on a sailboat in the middle of the ocean with a chicken to keep me company. So what? No one can see me.

We're treated to a fantastic surprise this afternoon—by a school of flying fish! I had never seen one before. There are ten, maybe fifteen of them, leaping out of the water all around *Yvinec*, gliding through the air before diving below the surface, and then zigzagging their way to launch themselves skyward again. They look like synchronized swimmers. Suddenly, one of them flops onto the deck of the boat. The poor little thing isn't moving and must have knocked itself out. Right away, Monique dashes over for a closer look. It's crazy how inquisitive this hen can be! She starts eagerly pecking away at the fish and clearly likes what she's tasted, because a few minutes later there's nothing left of it. No sooner has she finished than she starts scanning the deck with her beady eyes, hoping there are more fish where that came from. I'm keen for a taste too, if she'd let me grab one! Fortunately, another one soon lands right at my feet. Monique hurries over, but too late. This time, it's my turn. Soon, more fish are landing on the deck and the two of us are dashing to and fro, seeing who will be the first to claim the latest catch. I can't believe how quickly Monique can run! She's so much more sure-footed on deck too. Most of the time, she runs right past me, grabs the fish before I can, and makes short work of it. She swallows the smaller ones whole, even if they are still alive and kicking. I can just imagine them wriggling around in her stomach!

In the end, I still manage to collect enough fish to fry up for dinner. Yum, they are delicious! Talk about a gift that fell from the sky!

By sundown, Monique is fast asleep in her coop. Alone on deck, I watch as the sun slips into its watery bed for the night. There's nothing quite like a sunset at sea. The colors are so wild they defy description. There are simply no words—in any language—to explain this fire in the sky and the twisting, turning flames of red, orange, yellow, and purple that paint so many parallel worlds on the horizon. Every night is different, and just as magical as the last. My soul melts into its flamboyant beauty, and I lose all sense of time, but not my sense of self. I gaze into the sky and just one ray of this fading light is enough to fill my heart forever.

It's not the same when the sun rises. It's a different feeling; there's something more solemn about it. It makes me realize how alone I am out here. As the day dawns, it feels as if I'm witnessing the birth of the world.

DAY 5, APRIL 22

The wind has picked up and there's a nice swell running. It's taken me by surprise—the spinnaker has torn loose and is dragging in the water! It's my fault; I should have hauled it in sooner.

When I take a closer look at the nylon, I'm relieved to see the damage isn't catastrophic. I cut a decent length of Insignia sail-repair tape, which is just like a roll of Scotch tape, only stronger. Unfortunately, the tear is on a yellow stripe in the sail, and my repair tape is black. Oh well, it's not the most aesthetically pleasing of repairs, but the black-on-yellow does make *Yvinec* look a bit like a pirate ship!

The swell is making it difficult for me just to keep my balance, so you can imagine how challenging a task it is to wash the dishes. I have to hold on to the edge of the sink with one hand while I rinse the dishes under the faucet with the other. Monique, true to her habits, pokes her head through the cabin window to see what I'm up to. Of course she wants to come in, but I shoo her away; that's the game we play. She's stubborn though, and clearly isn't happy to be kept outside today. I push her away again, and she suddenly nips my finger with her beak! It seems crossing the Atlantic can turn even the most mild-mannered hen into a ferocious beast.

We keep sailing toward Cape Verde. Overnight, a big wave must have broken over the back of the boat, because the next morning I find the roof of Monique's coop has torn right off. She's soaked to the skin and whimpering like a little dog, the poor thing. I pick her up and rinse her off gently with fresh water before drying her as best I can and wrapping her up in a towel. But guess what I find when I glance around the wreckage of her coop? She's laid an egg! Way to go, Momo!

A short while later, I sweep the wet wood shavings into a bucket and throw them overboard. After all, it's biodegradable! Then I set about cleaning and fixing up the coop. Monique's not happy because I've taken her bowl and dish out of there. She stands guard by the door, clucking like crazy, not wanting to let me put my hand in there. I get it; she's defending her territory, but she's trying my patience.

"Hey, Monique!" I say. "Don't you want me to make your space clean again? I'm doing this for you, you know!"

But she doesn't reply, and just keeps kicking up a fuss.

I go fetch my saw and a few planks of wood to repair the roof. I know I'll have to reinforce it if I don't want this to happen again. Once the structure is solid, I apply some silicone sealant to make it waterproof. Finally, I spread some fresh wood shavings inside and fill Monique's dish with water.

"There you go, Monique. Are you happy now?" I ask.

She dunks her beak into the dish for a drink and, one by one it seems, rearranges all the wood shavings to her liking. When she's done, the rearrangement looks just the same to me, but it must make sense to her. By the end of the day, the sun is out again, the clouds have almost all dissipated, and I decide to fly the spinnaker to increase our boat speed. The sail billows yellow, red, and orange as it fills with wind; black repair-tape aside, it's a perfect color-match with the sun. Ah, a sailboat always looks so elegant with the spinnaker flying!

We're sailing full speed with the self-steering engaged. We've covered 140 nautical miles in twenty-four hours at a top speed of nearly nine knots. *Yvinec* is surfing the waves, and Monique, ever the daredevil, is figure skating all over the deck.

We're not far from Cape Verde now. I'd love to stop; I've always dreamed of going there. After a week at sea, it would be nice to set foot on dry land and discover a new country. But I've run out of money. I'm completely broke. What would I do there with all of sixty cents in my pocket?

DAY 6, APRIL 23

We're barely two hundred nautical miles from Cape Verde now. The sky is clear, but the wind has really picked up and there's a rolling swell. I have to reef the sails to reduce the surface area; otherwise the self-steering can't cope. The closer we get to the archipelago, the more time I have to spend trimming the sails and checking the self-steering, day and night. If a big gust blows through, the spinnaker won't be able to handle the sudden and intense increase in wind strength. I have to be constantly on the lookout for danger signs. If the spinnaker fails, the boat will lurch sharply one way or the other. The mainsail or the genoa might fill with wind from the wrong side and cause us to jibe or tack without warning, and such a sudden change of direction would be incredibly dangerous.

The swell is getting big now, and the troughs between the waves must be at least twenty feet deep. *Yvinec* is well and truly surfing down the faces of the waves. I've had to take the spinnaker down. This is the biggest swell I've ever encountered. Things got pretty hairy when I crossed the Bay of Biscay, but these conditions are something else entirely. The swell is higher, and longer. A few months ago, I would never have been able to handle anything like this.

Based on what I'd heard, I thought that it was going to be smooth sailing once we got into the Atlantic. With the steady trade winds blowing from behind us and the seas not too rough, this was supposed to be easy—so smooth you could put a bottle on the table and it wouldn't slide off, people had said.

This time, even though Monique has become an expert at sliding from one end of the deck to the other, things are getting dangerous. Sometimes, she perches perilously close to the edge to feel the wind blowing through her feathers. It wouldn't take much of a gust for her to be swept overboard. If she keeps messing around, she'll never make it across to the other side with me.

When she scurries and flaps her way to the front of the boat, where it pitches and rolls the most, I yell, "No, Monique! Come back here!" But she won't listen. Then she gets blasted by the spray and wobbles her way back, soaking wet and bedraggled, looking like she's been through the washing machine. If I don't see her wander back toward the cockpit, I scan the rigging, squinting at the mast, sails, and lines to see where she is. If she does fall in the water, by the time I can turn around and go back for her, it will be too late.

I have to figure out a way to keep her inside her coop when the boat starts to heel too sharply to one side. I dig around in my tools and materials and find a piece of old fishing net, which I attach to the front of her coop. It's a simple system that will keep her safe without—pardon the pun—cooping her up. That way she can still enjoy the fresh air and keep me company. And the more the journey goes on, the more I realize I need the company.

DAY 7, APRIL 24

This morning, I find another egg in Monique's coop! Seven eggs in seven days; that's amazing! It's still warm when I pick it up. Very gently, I write the number 7 on the shell with a black marker, and put it into an egg carton. I've been numbering every one of Monique's eggs. That way, I know what order to eat them in, starting with the ones she laid first and working my way through to the freshest. It's the next best thing to an expiry date. Because I still have a few eggs left from the grocery store in El Medano, I'd rather finish those before I start to eat Monique's. There's always a risk she might stop laying eggs.

When I'm at sea, I try to ration my supplies. I'm frugal with everything on board, not just Monique's eggs. You never know how long a crossing like this is going to take. For instance, I love good chocolate. So to make sure my supplies last until I make it to shore again, I limit myself to two squares a day, and not a single piece more. Yesterday though, I could have easily eaten a whole bar.

With a tinge of regret, I watch Cape Verde slowly disappear into the distance on my GPS screen. It's too bad; it would have been great to dance under the hot sun to Cesária Évora's beautiful song "Sodade." But sadly, it is not to be. This is the first time I've decided not to make a stopover in a place I've never been before. It's frustrating. And to be honest, it's getting me down. Before embarking on a transatlantic voyage, most sailors call in at Cape Verde. It's the last place you can stop before committing to the long Atlantic crossing. This is where everyone stops to gather their strength and stock up on fresh water and food, not to mention enjoy the vibrant colors and festive atmosphere of the islands before the solitude of the open ocean really sinks in. But I can't stop there, because I don't have any money.

DAY 9, APRIL 26

Today is another exhilarating day surfing the swell and the waves. The self-steering is holding fast and keeping us on course, and my morale is back. We've been gone for eight nights now, and Monique has laid eight eggs. Isn't that fantastic?

Now I'm reading in the sun at the front of the boat, and Monique is sitting in my lap. *The Long Way* by Bernard Moitessier is a fascinating read. It's the story of his first nonstop solo race aboard his sailboat *Joshua*. That was nearly fifty years ago. Where I come from, every sailor has read it. I'm not usually much of a reader on dry land, but out here, I can really take the time to appreciate a book. I raided my father's bookshelf before I set off, so I have lots of accounts of other sailors' experiences on board. I still have so much to learn about sailing, and the books are helping with that. But reading about the authors' adventures at sea is what really floats my boat, if you'll pardon the expression. In my little reading library, there's another book by Moitessier about sailing around Cape Horn; I'd love to go there myself one day. Ernest Shackleton's *South: The Endurance Expedition* is essential reading for any sailor serious about heading into the ice, and Jimmy Cornell's *World Cruising Routes* is an endless source of important information about navigating the world.

The more the days go by, the more it feels like Monique and I are partners in this adventure together. There's no way I could ever entertain the idea of eating roast chicken now! It's surprising, actually, how easy it is to tame a hen—and for her to tame a solo sailor like me! It's starting to feel like we're in sync with one another. She knows her name and comes when I call her. Well, when she wants to; she's still very strong-willed. Sometimes, she stubbornly turns her back on me and saunters off to the other end of the boat instead.

No matter how independent Monique seems, though, there's one thing that always brings her running right back to me, and that's food! It's unbelievable what a glutton she is. As soon as I start cooking anything in the galley, she tries to sneak in through the window if it's open. "No, Monique!" I shout, and she backs off. But right away she tries her luck again, so I have to raise my voice a little louder. She knows I'm shooing her away. She's sneaky. If I turn my back for a second when I'm rinsing my pasta, she hops into the colander and starts pecking away. She's not afraid of anything—especially not of me. When I'm peeling carrots or potatoes, she's quick to steal the peelings that fall into the sink. I don't mind her doing that; I can't be at odds with her all the time. I'm actually getting used to her being constantly under my feet. She makes me laugh, and I don't have the heart to keep shooing her away. So more and more often, I've been letting her keep me company inside the cabin. The only place that's completely off-limits to her now is my berth, because that's where I sleep. To everywhere else on board, I have admitted defeat.

Perched on the table or the bench beside me, she has taken to eating right out of my bowl or my spoon. She'll even try to snatch the food right out of my mouth if I'm not careful! Food drives her absolutely crazy. When I've had enough of her begging, or if I just want to be left alone for a while, I'll put her back in her coop. It's partly my fault, of course. I encouraged her to eat off my spoon and plate before, so I can't really blame her.

Often, when I take the helm, she comes and perches on the tiller and looks out to the horizon. I can't help but wonder what's going through her mind. Do chickens think? Chickens, I have no idea, but Monique certainly has a mind of her own! Am I really bonding with her, or is she just helping me to feel less lonely? One thing's for sure, she's all I have, and I like to take good care of her.

She finally seems to have gotten the message about not being wanted inside the cabin and has found the perfect spot to keep an eye on me when I'm cooking: right at the top of the deck stairs, with her head just inside the cabin and her behind in the open air. When she's not there, I'll find her peering in from the tiny cabin window over the galley. There's just enough of an opening for her to stick her head in, and just enough space for me to reach my hand out.

DAY 11, APRIL 28

The sailing is smooth. No fish today.

It's the perfect time to make scrambled eggs for dinner. Monique's are the best eggs I've ever tasted. These ones taste kind of salty, maybe because she's been eating fish recently.

Sometimes instead of just keeping watch at night, I take the helm for fun. I like to pick a star, point the nose of the boat that way, and follow. When there's a clear sky, it's magical out here. My senses have never been sharper. I notice everything. I'm always listening to what my sailboat is telling me. I hear every little creak and squeak. Sometimes the sails sound like they're making music. I listen to the rigging as it sings in the wind; it's becoming a familiar song. If I keep an ear out, I'll be ready for whatever might come our way.

DAY 12, APRIL 29

After twelve days at sea, I'm starting to get bored. I open up my notebook and reread all the entries I've made so far.

It's hard to believe what a big deal I thought this crossing would be. It was a childhood dream that grew larger in my mind with every story my father told me. I've come to realize that it's not that hard after all. I find that I'm getting impatient already. I just want to get to the other side of this ocean so I can start planning my next adventure. I'm keen to head north to Greenland. I want to see polar bears, seals, and Arctic foxes. Wouldn't it be amazing to hunker down for the winter there and let the ice and snow set in around us?

I'm getting cabin fever, and it's making me reflect on my life. I've always set my sights firmly on what lies ahead of me, so I'm surprised to find myself looking back. I haven't seen my family for nearly a year. My sisters have had babies I've never seen. But my father is the person I think about the most. I'm the youngest of his eight children; he had me late in life. He and I have always been very close. He was the last person I called before I left. He's the only one who understands me. He's the only one who never told me I was crazy when I told people what I was planning to do, the only one to give me any words of encouragement. The harder my mother and sisters tried to discourage me, the more I wanted to show them what I was capable of. I have a lot to prove to them, and to myself. Even if I don't know exactly what that is yet.

There's nothing to do here, but I'm not complaining. I'm discovering the joys of being cut off from the rest of the world, with no means of communication other than an ancient portable VHF radio with zero range. If I see another boat, I can only talk to the skipper when we get within about five hundred feet. It's weird to not know anything that's happening in the world. All around as far as the eye can see, there is nothing but saltwater and sky, seagulls and fish. Out here in the middle of the ocean, I'm entirely at one with the elements. It's as if this were a different plane of space and time. I have no other care in the world than my sailboat and Monique. My family and friends are in my thoughts, of course; I love them, but I can't say I miss them. Since I left home, I've spoken to them a few times on the phone, but only rarely. Obviously, I'm looking forward to telling them all about the crossing!

DAY 13, APRIL 30

I just lost a big tuna. It was well hooked on the line, but it wriggled free as I was pulling it in. It was so big, there was nothing I could have done to hold on to it.

DAY 16, MAY 3

The conditions have been fabulous ever since we left Cape Verde behind. Today, we're flying the spinnaker.

The wind veered a little to the north around noon, so I've had to adjust my course to the south to stay in the trade winds.

This damn wind has picked up though, and the boat is going crazy. I hurry to pull the sails in, but I've already wasted too much time by grabbing my GoPro to try to shoot some footage. The spinnaker takes the opportunity to explode right where it attaches to the tip of the mast, and it goes with such a loud bang, I'm worried I've broken the mast. The spinnaker's in the water now, and I have to haul it back on board by hand. What a pain! I guess that's what I get for trying to film everything. I've learned my lesson.

I inspect the sail cloth and see right away that at the top it's torn to shreds. This time, my big rolls of Insignia repair tape are not going to cut it. The spinnaker is now sitting in a big useless pile on the deck. I'll have to get it repaired when we make it to the Caribbean. Until then, I'll just have to live without it.

I'm frustrated, but I'm not going to let this dampen my spirits. It could have been far worse if the mast had been damaged. You can sail without a spinnaker, but you can't sail without a mast; it'll just take us longer to get where we're going if we don't have a lot of wind.

The good news is that I just collected egg number 15 from Monique!

DAY 17, MAY 4

Since the spinnaker tore, I've been sailing wing-on-wing, with the genoa on the starboard side and the mainsail on port. When you're running downwind, you want to avoid having both sails on the same side, because the genoa will be behind the mainsail and won't catch as much wind. The only way to maximize your boat speed is to set the genoa on the opposite side of the mainsail, which maximizes the sail area exposed to the wind. It's not as fast as sailing under spinnaker, but it's also not as risky. It's easier, and the boat stays more balanced.

We're sailing with the automatic pilot, but won't be for much longer, not at the speed the batteries are draining. Something's not right. The weather's fine, and the solar panel should be generating a decent energy reserve. There's still a thousand nautical miles left to go until the Caribbean—but we're more than halfway there!

Night falls, and the sky is clear. The sun sinks into the horizon behind the last of the afternoon's clouds, splintering the ocean into yellow shards. I'm sure Monique can appreciate the beauty of it. She's standing completely still, and it looks like she's enjoying the show. I pet her on the back, and she hops up onto my leg, all calm and fluffy. Sitting on the edge of the boat with my bare feet dangling just above the water's surface, I steer with one hand on the tiller and scratch her back with the other.

"Life is good, Momo, isn't it?" I say with a smile.

Yvinec is sailing on a path of golden light that stretches from the hull to the horizon. All I can hear is the creaking of the boat. The sun is nothing but a tiny pinprick, waiting to be swallowed up into the night. It's time for Monique to say goodnight. She's always looking for something else to nibble on, so she carries out one last inspection of the deck before she goes to bed.

~~~~~~~

THE CLOSER WE GET to the Caribbean, the more squalls we sail through, sometimes as many as ten or fifteen a day. It's not hard to see them coming. The dark clouds seem to barrel right toward us, loaded with rain and blasted along by the wind. You never know whether the wind's going to gust thirty or sixty knots when they blow through. Most of the time, the gusts don't clock higher than forty. The squalls give the boat a good rinsing down and get rid of the salt that eats away at everything on board. That's not all: I collect the rainwater that falls on the dodger—the canopy covering the cockpit—to top up my fresh water provisions. It's so nice to take a rain shower too! After all the buckets of seawater I've poured over myself to stay clean, I've ended up as salty as a side of bacon. So when I see a rain cloud coming, I dash into the cabin to grab my body wash, scrub myself down using seawater, and wait for the rain to rinse me off. If the squall passes nearby instead of right overhead, I feel like an idiot, standing there covered in soap suds!

If a squall looks like it might be a big one, I don't take any risks. I pull the sails down completely to make sure they don't get damaged. As soon as the squall has passed, I hoist the sails again, and on we go.

DAY 18, MAY 5

Happy birthday, Mom! It might sound funny, but I don't actually know how old my mother is. I have no idea how old anyone is, really. As far as I'm concerned, age doesn't mean a thing. I either like people or I don't. I have no way of reaching my mom to wish her a happy birthday, and that makes me sad. But under today's date in my journal, even before I make a note of my position and boat speed, I write those words: "Happy birthday, Mom!"

DAY 19, MAY 6

The squalls keep coming, one after the other. I've turned up the collar of my storm jacket to shield my neck from the onslaught of water, blasting me like thousands of tiny needles. Monique doesn't like this at all. She scurries into the cabin to stay warm and dry, only to come back out on deck with every flurry of flying fish—blast after blast of spray will hit her, but still she'll stand there, hoping for another tasty treat to land at her feet. When a big wave breaks over the boat, I'll look around to make sure she's still there; if I can't see her, I'll start to worry. And just as I start to panic, she'll decide to show her face—dripping wet, with a flying fish in her beak!

DAY 20, MAY 7

I think the GPS is toast. I turn it off and turn it on again, but it's lost its signal. I wonder what's causing the problem. I'm lost in the middle of the ocean, alone on my little sailboat, somewhere between Africa and South America, with nothing to guide me. There's nothing but water all around. The old VHF isn't powerful enough to communicate with other boats, even if there are any out there. I'm not panicking, though. Panicking won't get you anywhere; it will only cloud your judgment. I'm not saying that I always stay calm in all circumstances, but I do my best to stay positive. The best way to find a solution is to believe in yourself, trust in your abilities, and look for the most logical answer; I approach life as a challenge—a series of obstacles to overcome, not to avoid.

Everything will be fine. Whatever happens, I have a dinghy, a paddleboard, and a windsurf board to keep us afloat. I'll check the compass to make sure we keep heading due west (270 degrees), and at night I'll use the stars. As long as we keep heading west, it will all be okay. The only risk is if the boat starts to drift off course without me realizing. If it does, we won't end up where I've wanted, but we'll still end up arriving somewhere.

When the sun goes down, I stand at the bow and gaze at the stars as we sail right toward Orion's Belt, heading due west.

DAY 22, MAY 9

Good news, the GPS is working again! I figured out what the problem was—corrosion on the external antenna had been causing a loose connection. I just had to shorten the antenna and the signal came back.

Despite the GPS being down for two days, *Yvinec* has stayed her course admirably well. Now we're only a few hundred nautical miles from the Caribbean.

"Look at that big boat, Momo!" I cry. It's the first container ship I've seen the whole time we've been sailing offshore. Finally, a sign that we're not completely alone.

We're heading into our fourth week at sea. If all goes well, in just a few days, we'll set foot on dry land. I've started thinking ahead. People have told me I won't have any trouble finding work in Saint Barthélemy, or St. Barts, as the island is affectionately known. But what kind of work can I find? And for how long—a couple of months, or maybe a year? I don't know anyone there, but that's not a bad thing; I love venturing into the unknown. Since I was eighteen years old, I've been showing up in new places without knowing anyone, and without any money.

It's a challenge every time, but I've always been lucky. I wonder how people in St. Barts will react to a guy from Brittany showing up on a rusty sailboat with his pet chicken. What if my luck runs out? What if I can't find any work? One thing's for sure, I'm not going to get very far with sixty cents in my pocket!

As the days coast by, my wanderlust grows. I haven't even finished this Atlantic crossing, but my mind is already wandering all over the world map. I've been giving serious thought to the idea of heading north to Greenland. If I did, *Yvinec* would need to be strong and well equipped to survive up there, and so would I. The bare minimum would be a heater and a dry suit. And how would Monique cope? Would she be able to handle temperatures well below freezing? They don't make down jackets for chickens, do they?

DAY 24, MAY 11

The squalls aren't letting up. It's blowing hard now, forty, maybe forty-five knots, and the wind keeps shifting from northeast to south. The self-steering is struggling, and I am too. I wish I could take off my storm jacket, but the rain is coming down in sheets. After a full night on deck, I'm exhausted. If the wind holds strong, we should make land in four or five days. I'm crossing my fingers. I'm itching to get off the boat now. I can't wait to have more than a few dozen square feet to move around in.

DAY 27, MAY 14

I can't believe my eyes! Something is taking shape in the distance. Is it a beach? It is! Land ho! We've made it! Watch out Caribbean, Guirec and Monique are here!

"Momo, we did it! I'm so proud of you!" I cry, jumping around stark naked on the deck.

Even though the crossing has gone relatively smoothly, I still feel this is quite an accomplishment.

Standing at the bow of *Yvinec* with Monique perched on my shoulder, I gaze out at the land that's now so close—it's not St. Barts. We're not there yet. It's the island of Barbuda, a little farther east. Overjoyed, I dash down into the cabin to grab my phone, which is plugged in and charging. I scramble my way up the mast to see if I can get a signal. I'm not holding out much hope, but you never know; the signal is always better higher up. Yay! It's working!

I call my father, the last person I spoke with before setting sail from El Medano, and the first person whose voice I want to hear when I make land. "Dad? It's me. I'm here! I did it!" I'm laughing and crying on the phone as I tell my father the good news. I've never been so happy in my whole life. There's just enough time for me to hear the pride in his voice before I lose the signal.

DAY 28, MAY 15

Twenty-eight days and twenty-five eggs after setting out to sea, we make land in St. Barts. Monique has really found her sea legs.

I have cell phone reception again, so I listen to the flood of messages in my voice mail. The first is from Gladys, my banker, who's also a friend. Twenty-eight days earlier, we spoke on the phone and she agreed to increase my overdraft. "I'll increase your limit, but only for a week, okay?" she said. "Not for any longer, because I don't want any trouble." I reassured her there would be no trouble; of course I would top up my account. I just neglected to say when. And then I set sail across the Atlantic. Oops!

It's just past six in the evening and it's already dark. I can see the lights of St. Barts twinkling in the distance. I don't have any marine charts on board to indicate the potential navigational hazards, so I'd rather wait until morning before making my approach.

When you're at sea for weeks on end, the fatigue creeps up on you day by day, but you keep on going. Now that the end is in sight and I stop to think about it, I'm exhausted. Sleep has been intermittent at best, because it takes a lot of concentration to stay attuned to the boat and the elements. As soon as the coast comes into view, you see the light at the end of the tunnel and all the accumulated fatigue hits you. That's the most dangerous time of all. You start to decompress, and you let your guard down, but you're not in the clear quite yet. Serious things can still happen. There are more boats around, and more importantly, there are reefs and sandbars to steer clear of.

These twenty-eight days at sea have taught me how to be at one with *Yvinec*—eating, sleeping, and breathing on the ocean waves, with the boat constantly heeling in the wind. I have learned to embrace my weaknesses, play off of my strengths, and even to predict the weather.

I know myself better than ever before. I could have felt dejected, complaining that I got soaked to the skin. I could have told myself it was too hard out there alone, or that I didn't have the maturity or experience to sail across the ocean, that this just wasn't something I was cut out to do. But that couldn't have been further from the truth. I've discovered that I love being on my sailboat. I love the feeling of solitude out in the middle of the ocean. And I know I want to keep going; it's as simple as that.

As the days have passed by, my determination to explore and to seek new challenges, each one tougher and crazier than the last, has only grown stronger. This journey has made me stronger too.

~~~~~~

"LOOK, MOMO, WE'VE REACHED the end of our journey! Isn't it beautiful? See the color of the water? Aren't the fish pretty?"

Yvinec is gliding through crystal clear water now. There are magnificent sailboats all around. And here I am, on my rusty old boat with my pet chicken!

This morning, I followed Monique's example and rose with the sun. It was shortly after five when I hoisted the sails. I'd thought we'd make land at Gustavia, the main town on the island, but instead we find ourselves sailing into a little bay named Shell Beach a little farther south.

Imagine my surprise to see the iconic black-and-white flag of my native Brittany, the *Gwenn-ha-du*, flying from the top of one of the sailboats moored in the bay! I can hardly believe my eyes. It's my friend Manu's boat! I had no idea he was going to be in St. Barts. What a joy to cross paths here, an ocean away from home! I drop anchor right alongside him. Too bad—he's not on board. I can't wait until he gets back, either; I have to go ashore and let the authorities know I've arrived.

As I beach my dinghy and set foot on land, I can't believe how many shells there are, stretching as far as the eye can see. On this beach, the shells are the sand. There are shells of all shapes and sizes, washing in and out with the surf. At the far end of the bay, steep cliffs of green plunge into the clear turquoise water. At the edge of the beach, there's a restaurant, the Do Brazil.

I stroll into the harbormaster's office in the marina. "Hi there! I've just crossed the Atlantic. I'd like to register my arrival," I announce, beaming from ear to ear.

The officials don't even crack a smile. "Alright, but it's eight euros a day to moor here," is all they say.

What the heck?

"But I'm not at the dock; I'm anchored in the bay!" I protest. "Why do I have to pay?"

"Well," they reply, "if you don't want to pay, then off you go."

Normally, it doesn't cost anything to moor outside the marina. At least, that's what I've seen everywhere else I've sailed. I've never heard of anything like this. And I don't have any money.

Maybe they'll accept payment in fresh eggs? Um, nope. This only makes them even angrier. "Look, that's just the way it is!" they insist. Talk about a harsh return to civilization!

Regardless, I use their computer to register my arrival. On the entry form, I list the registration number of my sailboat and her port of origin, my first and last name, and my passport number. As for payment, the officials are just going to have to wait.

When I get back to the boat, my friend Manu is back on his boat and waves at me as I approach. "It's just like being at home; you can't get away from these Breton flags, can you?" I joke.

To my surprise, Manu explains that some of the first Europeans to land on St. Barts were from Brittany and the neighboring French region of Normandy. I guess that's why its official name—Saint Barthélemy—is French! It looks like we're following in our ancestors' footsteps (or boat wakes)! As Manu and I catch up, I explain that while I'm here, I hope to meet new people, discover the joys of island life, find some work, and save enough money to get *Yvinec* ready for a winter in the ice.

After taking a couple of days to relax, I decide to look for a job. As I walk around the town, I see a young woman in the street loading flowers into a truck. Instinctively, I ask if I can give her a hand. It comes naturally for me to approach people, and, as luck would have it, she's also very easygoing. She asks me where I'm from, whether I know the island, and what I'm doing here, so I tell her.

"Listen, if you want to roll up your sleeves, I can find a quick job for you this afternoon," she says.

It's as simple as that! Before I know it, I have fifty euros in my pocket. That's eighty-three times more money than I had when I arrived. Not exactly enough to spruce up the boat, but it'll pay for one or two little things I need on board.

In the next few days, I meet a bunch of locals and chat with some people who are working the tourist season. Everyone suggests I ask around for work in the bars and restaurants. Apparently with all the tourists around, there are big tips to be earned.

I don't think anyone would ever call me talented in the kitchen. Other than making anything you'd like out of fresh eggs, my skills are limited to rustling up a dish of tuna pasta and reheating a can of ravioli. But when it comes to waiting tables, I think I can figure things out. And I don't generally have any trouble selling myself. I don't say anything too far-fetched, but I can lay it on thick when I need to twist someone's arm. When I was in Australia, I convinced people I was a fisherman, a stonemason, and a tiler, and none of that was exactly true. But when push came to shove, I managed to do the work.

I start by browsing the classified ads. I see there are lots of openings for gardening and landscaping work, so I make a few calls. One guy is looking for someone like me—who's just passing through for two weeks' work. We arrange to meet at

Le Select, the oldest bar on the island. He turns out to be very friendly and we chat for a while. When he asks me if I've worked in gardening before, I use my winning strategy. "Of course, I did that all the time back in France!" I tell him.

That seals the deal. It's a sweet gig, too; I'm going to be earning nearly 150 euros a day. Needless to say, I'm thrilled.

The sound of birdsong fills my ears as I make my way to work the next day. The sun is already hot as it sweeps its way over the red-tiled roofs of the houses, spreading its glow over the free-roaming iguanas that don't seem the slightest bit afraid of my footsteps. My new job is on the other side of the island, and it's a solid hour's walk to get there. I introduce myself to my new colleagues and hit it off right away with Andréa, an adventurous guy who's into sailing. It's not the most stimulating work, but at least we're outside all the time, going from one villa to another, each more impressive than the last. And from the garden, all of these fancy places have an amazing ocean view.

In the evening, before I head back to my moored boat, I always stop in at Do Brazil to chat with the friends I've made among the staff. One night, the manager David asks me, "Guirec, I don't know if you're interested, but I could use a helping hand on Sunday."

My gardening job is wrapping up the following Friday, so it's good timing. Without hesitating, I take David up on his offer. "No problem. I'm used to working in restaurants."

On Sunday morning, David clarifies what he's expecting of me. He's no fool. He knows I haven't done this kind of thing before, but he can see that I'm keen. When my shift is over, he's happy with how it went and decides to give me a chance. I walk away with a contract for a month's work.

It's pretty sweet to be able to ride my paddleboard to work. It only takes me a few seconds to paddle over there from the boat, but somehow I still manage to be late every morning.

As soon as I'm there, I set up the lounge chairs on the beach two by two, with a parasol and a little table between them. When I'm done, I help to set the tables in the restaurant. Barefoot on the beach, chatting to customers, I'm in my element. I point at my sailboat in the bay, and people are amazed to hear that I sailed here all the way from Brittany.

"All by yourself?" they ask.

"Not quite. Just me and my chick," I reply.

"Ah, your girlfriend?" they assume.

"No, an actual chicken!"

Soon the whole island knows the story of the young guy from Brittany and his pet chicken, and some people even swim over to the boat for a closer look. "How's Monique doing today?" they ask.

There are lots of tourists here, but there's something really friendly and genuine about the atmosphere on the island. Being here feels like being with family.

Once word gets out, the media soon come knocking at my door. *Ouest-France*, the newspaper from back home, prints a recap of our story and includes a link to our Facebook page. That leads to more and more people liking our page and following our adventures. I've posted a few videos from our crossing, and Monique is really starting to steal my thunder! There's nothing special about a sailor crossing the Atlantic solo, but there aren't many, if any at all, who've done it with a hen laying eggs on board!

When I'm working, Monique stays on the boat and wanders around on deck. To anyone who wants to see her, I say, "Be my

guest! Just swim out to the boat, climb aboard, and there she is!"
So that's what they do.

Here on St. Barts, just like it was when we were at sea, water
is a precious resource. There are no natural water sources on the
island, so the locals have to collect rainwater and desalinate the
seawater.

The scenery is fantastic and I'm definitely getting used to this
place. It's going to be hard to leave.

One day when I'm working at the restaurant, I meet Jean-Mi. He
runs CaribWaterplay, a small windsurfing center on Saint-Jean
beach, one of the longest stretches of sand on St. Barts. The
beach is right at the end of the airport runway, so it's quite something to see the planes flying in low over the sand. It's a tiny
airport, and the runway is only long enough for small planes to
take off and land.

Jean-Mi and I hit it off right away. It isn't long before he tells
me he's looking for someone to lend a hand at the beach. He
could see me giving windsurfing lessons. I couldn't agree more!
For once, I won't have to bluff my way into a job; windsurfing
is my favorite sport and my greatest passion. It's an offer I can't
refuse. "No problem. I'm used to teaching windsurfing back in
France."

My contract starts at the beginning of July.

It makes sense to move closer to where I'll be working, so
Monique and I sail around the island and moor in the bay across
from the windsurfing center. In principle, anchoring here isn't
allowed because the bay is on the flight path for the airport, but
we'll see what happens.

It's only a short sail away through shades of turquoise. The water is crystal clear, and schools of brightly colored fish and sea turtles swim around every hollow and every bed of seagrass.

It's a pleasure to be able to commute by paddleboard again every morning. And this time, it's even better, because Monique can join me at work! After a couple of weeks, I decide to ditch the paddleboard and take the dinghy to work instead. Momo and I beach the Zodiac on the sand right in front of the windsurfing school. Before I have time to disembark, she hops up onto the side of the boat and flutters down onto the sand, all by herself. I hop out too, and Momo waits while I pull the dinghy up a little farther onto the sand before we make our way into the windsurfing school together. She sticks to me like glue. If I walk, she walks at my heel; if I run, she runs right behind me! People are intrigued; Monique is a great conversation starter!

After a few days I find some planks of wood lying around and make a little coop for Monique on the beach, with a mesh door so she can't wander around unsupervised. I'm a little worried about stray dogs, so I want to keep her safe. When I do let Monique roam free, the tourists can't stop taking photos and bombarding me with questions.

It certainly doesn't take long for Monique to acclimatize. I want her to have just as much fun on the water as I'm having, and since they don't make life jackets for chickens, I'm going to teach her to swim. I carry her gently into the shallows, then set her on the surface and let go, making sure I stay within arm's reach. The first couple of times, she doesn't move a muscle and very slowly sinks into the water. She has to learn that it's in her best interest to move when her feathers are soaking wet. So I move away a little and call her. And when she understands that she has to pedal her feet, what do you know, she's swimming! It's as simple as that. Well done, Monique!

Life is sweet. I get to spend all day, every day, wearing board-shorts on the water or the beach, teaching tourists how to windsurf and paddleboard. It's paradise. And it pays well too. Jean-Mi is a pretty easygoing boss. He takes a relaxed approach to everything. When there are no customers, I get to surf a few waves or go windsurfing, if the wind is up. Then, as soon as I see someone walk up to the hut on the beach, I hurry back to shore to get to work.

The kids who hang around the windsurfing center soon adopt me. The regulars are Élie, Antonin, Noa, and Léo, who are all between eight and twelve years old. They live here on St. Barts all year round, and when they're not at school, they're down at the beach with me. We've become good friends. They love to swim out to my sailboat and play with Monique. The poor little thing, she never gets a minute's peace anymore! They teach her how to boogie board and how to ride a skateboard. Sometimes she grumbles a bit, but I can tell she really enjoys it! Often, the kids join us for dinner on deck, and we crank up the music. Sometimes there's a deafening din when the planes take off right over our heads; Momo doesn't care. Sometimes I take the kids out of the bay for a crash course in ocean sailing; one of them takes the helm while the others trim the sails.

I keep thinking about my crazy plan to sail to the North Pole and spend the winter in the sea ice. The idea is to drop anchor in a bay in Greenland as far north as possible, wait for the ice to form around *Yvinec*'s hull, and then live completely self-sufficiently, trapped in wintry isolation with no means of communication at all. I dream of ice fishing under the Northern Lights.

Here in St. Barts, my friends tell me I'm nuts. Especially when I tell them I'm taking Monique with me. "There's no way a chicken can survive up there in the freezing cold!" they say.

They can say what they like. If I'd listened to other people, Monique would still be pecking her way around a farmyard in the Canary Islands, and I would have had no one to talk to on my sailboat. Life would have been sad.

By mid-September, I've managed to put aside enough money to do my first round of work on the sailboat. It's off-season here now, and hurricane season, so it's a good time to think about heading farther south toward the Intertropical Convergence Zone, an area better known as the doldrums. Hurricanes don't tend to form there. Plus, I learn it will be cheaper to work on the boat down there; that seals the deal. This time, I won't be sailing solo; I'll have a solid crew by my side—Jonas, the guy I met in the Canary Islands, has just arrived from Costa Rica, and my buddy Andréa has some vacation time he wants to use. It's time to set sail and enjoy the ride!

We make the most of every moment and enjoy some sweet stops along the way. In Les Saintes, we pull up the swing keel so we can land right on Le Pain de Sucre beach. It's amazing; we can almost reach out and pick the coconuts right from the deck of the boat. On the island of Marie-Galante, we fish for lobster and are rewarded with a real feast. In Dominica, we go ashore and head into the jungle on an excursion up the Indian River.

We never stop for long in any of these places, but we savor every moment we're there. Soon Andréa has to say goodbye. It's time for him to head back to work in St. Barts. The time has flown by; it's October already, and there are so many amazing things to discover that we could cruise around here for months. But the time has come to find a place to get work done on the boat. Jonas is going to lend a hand.

On we sail, toward Martinique, then Saint Lucia and the Grenadines. We'd been advised to avoid Venezuela, because there's a risk we'd run into pirates. So we head to Trinidad instead. To ward off any bad luck, we decide to goof around a little. I tape a black patch over one eye, get Monique to perch on my shoulder, and try to strike a fearsome pose.

We make it to Trinidad without a hitch, hoist the boat out of the water, and get to work. We take everything apart and strip *Yvinec* down to a shell. Our first priority is the hull. There's a lot of rust, so it's going to be a big job. The corrosion is so bad, in fact, that in some places we have to cut holes big enough that we can stick our heads through the hull.

While we work, Monique gets on with her own simple life, roaming free around the boatyard. Soon everyone there knows her by name. Often, I find myself going from boat to boat looking for her. "You haven't seen Monique, have you?"

"Monique? Oh yes, she was here earlier; I think she went that way..."

We work like crazy, fifteen hours a day, sweating in temperatures over a hundred degrees. But I've never been more motivated to get a job done.

At night, we sleep on board the boat, perched in dry dock on her cradle. We have to use a ladder to climb up to the deck from the ground. Poor Momo is so disoriented, she's laying eggs all over the boatyard. One day, she decides to nest on the roof of a little golf cart, and often I find her in its glove compartment, sitting happily on her egg. In the evening, when it's time for her to go to bed, she climbs the ladder all by herself.

Our neighbors, Christian and Claudine, have a steel-hulled boat too. Theirs is named *Gadjo*. Christian shows me how to do a decent welding job; there are now more than forty holes in *Yvinec*'s hull that need to be sealed by welding sheet metal over them. It's starting to feel like we'll never get the job done, and I'm beginning to wonder how the heck we managed to not sink on our transatlantic crossing.

In Monique's honor, Christian paints a magnificent red-feathered hen on each side of the bow. It's the perfect opportunity to pull out my stencil so I can finally finish painting my sailboat's name on both sides of the hull.

I figure I might as well replace the anemometer, speedometer, and depth-sounder as well. I've already replaced the Plexiglas in the dodger to keep the cockpit dry, and I've even fitted a stainless steel roof to Monique's coop.

After a month and a half in dry dock, *Yvinec* looks newer and fresher than ever. It's finally time to put her back in the water. I've been looking forward to it, because it's not very comfortable living aboard a boat on dry land. The tourist season in St. Barts is starting up again, and I have a job to get back to at the windsurfing center. It takes us five days to sail back to Saint-Jean beach.

We barely have time to catch our breath before I start working again. Once more, I save every last cent to pay for the rest of the equipment I need for the boat.

More and more journalists are getting wind of my Atlantic crossing with Momo. After the *Ouest-France* daily newspaper, *VSD*, *France Dimanche*, and *Voiles et Voiliers* magazines; Europe 1 radio; and the *Thalassa* TV documentary team reach out to me for a story. All this exposure snags me a few local sponsors that are willing to help me on my way. In exchange for their contributions, I stick their logos on the boom and mainsail.

One day, I'm chatting on the beach with a couple of tourists who've been renting lounge chairs in front of the windsurfing center. The husband especially is curious about my plan to spend the winter in Greenland, so I invite him to come aboard for a visit the next day. We head out for a sail together and he bombards me all kinds of questions about *Yvinec*, taking a bunch of photos. When we get back to our mooring, he asks me, "If you had to switch boats, if you could choose any boat in the world, what would you choose?"

That's a strange question, I think. "I don't know," I reply. "Probably a boat with an aluminum hull."

"Okay, and how much does one of those cost?" he presses.

"Well, it's hard to say; it depends on the boat, I suppose," I stammer.

Then he guesses with an astronomical sum out of nowhere and asks me if that would be enough.

What's he getting at? I'm not sure I understand. Dumbstruck as it dawns on me what he might be saying, I stammer, "Sure, I guess that would cover it . . ."

It turns out that he's serious. He really wants to help. Somewhat awkwardly, I explain that I'm very attached to *Yvinec*; I saved hard to buy this sailboat. A rust bucket she may be, but I've risked my life sailing her across the Atlantic, and I'm not ready to let her go.

He seems surprised. I keep talking. (Always keep talking!) "That being said, my little boat could use a few upgrades."

"Oh, really? What do you need?"

"Well, a new engine would be great. A new set of sails wouldn't hurt. And while we're at it, maybe a new winch." So many things I'd just figured I couldn't afford to buy anytime soon.

"Listen Guirec, you're an ambitious guy, and your project sounds awesome. I really want to help you out," he says.

Wow, he is serious. And he wants absolutely nothing in return.

"Let's keep this between us, though," he insists.

I'm extremely grateful and will never be able to thank him enough. Of course, I'm serious about going to Greenland, so I'd be perfectly willing to set sail aboard a boat equipped with whatever upgrades I could afford to make. But thanks to this man's kindness and generosity, I'll be as well prepared as I can possibly be.

Around the same time, Monique and I launch our first crowd-funding campaign online, and we soon reach our goal. Once again, I'm very thankful to all the people who have chipped in to help us out on our journey.

In St. Barts there isn't really anywhere to tinker with a sailboat, so I head to Saint Martin, where I know I'll find a boatyard and all the marine supply stores I need. Once again, I have to take *Yvinec* out of the water. But it's nowhere near as big a job as the repairs in Trinidad were, and it's much more fun to be installing new equipment rather than fixing holes in the hull. It's out with the old and in with the new as I replace the engine, wind generator, sails, and GPS unit. I also splurge on a better AIS tracking system and an Iridium satellite phone.

To pick up the last pieces of equipment I need, and to see my family in Paris, I decide to fly back to France for a quick trip before I embark on my next big adventure. I'm also fortunate to meet up with the French adventurer and filmmaker Nicolas Vanier. He and I are acquainted and he has kindly agreed to give me some advice—and some extreme cold-weather gear. Nicolas gives me lots of things he no longer has a use for: a tent, snowshoes, parka, snow pants, winter boots, you name it—all designed to withstand the harsh environment of the North Pole. I feel proud that a man like him is willing to help with such generosity. Now all I need to buy is a dry suit and some serious sailing clothing. While I'm at it, I pick up a new laptop, some photo and video equipment, and a few hard drives. I've decided I want to make a film of my adventure and document it all with photos.

I also figure I should invest in a drone. Johann, a guy I met in Saint Martin, taught me how to fly one and told me how useful it could be for navigating.

The day to set sail again is fast approaching. I can't believe we're leaving this tropical paradise. A year ago, I sailed into St. Barts with no idea what was waiting for me or how long I would stay. The months have flown by. I've worked a lot and taken the opportunity to explore the Caribbean. I've also made some good friends, and I'm sad to be leaving them behind.

Space on board is even more limited now than it was before, and I have to clear out what I won't be needing in Greenland. I decide to keep my paddleboard, but I give all my other boards away to Élie and Antonin, my little island brothers. I'm really going to miss them. After an amazing going-away party on the beach, the time has come for Monique and I to embark on the next chapter of our adventure.

Monique explores the ice of Greenland

PART 2

~~~~

Hibernating in the Ice

O N JUNE 29, at six in the morning, Monique sings with the sunrise. I'm already up and out on deck, raring to go. I'm so keen to set sail, I haven't even finished putting everything away below deck; it's a hot mess inside the cabin. A white-tailed tropicbird glides overhead as I cast a final backward glance at the little volcanic rock of St. Barts, rising from the ocean with its palm trees and white-flowered cacti. It's time to head north, Momo!

My enthusiasm doesn't last long. The automatic pilot, one of the only parts of the boat I haven't replaced, gives out after only a few nautical miles. Typical! I end up spending a full fourteen hours steering at the helm until we make it to the British Virgin Islands. There I find an anchorage in a tiny, remote bay on the island of Virgin Gorda and try to see what the problem is. It looks like a hydraulic hose has worn out, but it's a very specific part, so I can't use just anything to replace it. I leave *Yvinec* moored in the bay and take the dinghy to the nearest port, where I order the part I need. I have to go to the neighboring island, Tortola, to pick it up when it arrives.

In the meantime, I'm horrified to see the boat moored next to mine catch fire—most likely because of a short circuit. But there's nothing I can do; the flames are already licking their way up the rigging. The sailboat sinks in a matter of minutes. The whole thing sends shivers down my spine. Luckily, there was no one on board. The moral of the story: always turn off the power whenever I leave *Yvinec*!

I don't waste any time when the replacement part gets here. I install it without delay and we keep heading north. Now the sailing is smooth. Monique has slipped right back into her old habits, standing on guard, waiting for unsuspecting flying fish to come her way. Unfortunately for me, there's no way I can fish right now, because we're sailing through one huge bank of sargassum after the other. This brown seaweed bloom is caused by nutrient pollution from the Amazon and Congo rivers; it's an environmental nuisance that has been plaguing the Caribbean Sea for some time. The seaweed floats and forms vast rafts that drift out to sea and are carried for thousands of miles on the current. As the warming of the climate intensifies, the seaweed thrives, and it smothers fauna and flora everywhere it washes up. I feel sad and powerless; humans are causing nature to go off the rails.

After nine days at sea, we have to stop in Bermuda to let a tropical depression go by. With an eye on my watch, I stop for as short a time as possible—exactly eighteen hours. I decide to make the most of the opportunity by changing the oil in my new engine, and filling up with diesel and fresh water.

And then onward I sail, heading for Halifax in Atlantic Canada. My buddy Andréa is going to meet me there. When I said goodbye to him in St. Barts, he was getting ready to sail off on an adventure of his own, but he ended up shipwrecked and lost his boat. So I suggested he join me for part of the journey from Canada to Greenland. We'll see how well Momo adapts to having a roommate for a few weeks!

Two days after I leave for Halifax, a storm whips the sea into a frenzy. For five whole hours I clench my cheeks (I won't say which ones!), pulling down all the sails and trying my best to make sure we take the waves at the right angle. Some of the biggest sets roll through at a solid thirty or thirty-five feet. My anemometer registers some gusts in excess of fifty knots. I don't think I've seen conditions this heavy before; the spray is blasting me in the face, and I feel totally wiped, even though the storm ends up being pretty short-lived.

The next few days are much calmer. As every new day dawns, the sea and the sun melt into one endless watercolor of pink, gold, purple, and blue. It's such a beautiful seascape, I could swear it was painted with a brush. Now that the fair weather has returned, I can fly the spinnaker again. Even though it's tricky to pull it down in time if a squall blows through, it's still my favorite sail. I love the pace we go when it's billowing over the bow. We cross paths with dolphins and whales—talk about an amazing experience! It's times like these that tell me I've made the right decision, going on this adventure. And Monique is still laying an egg almost every day.

As we get closer to Halifax, after fifteen days at sea and 1,600 nautical miles, it's starting to get colder, so I let Momo warm up inside the cabin. The fog rolls in as I steer into the long channel leading to the Port of Halifax. A four-knot current is running, there's next to no visibility, and container ships as tall as buildings are churning up the water. Nothing can stop these monsters of the sea; I find it very unsettling.

Eventually I make it to the dock in the marina, a little fraught. The customs officers come aboard and ask me a whole bunch of questions. When they see I have bananas with me, they tell me I'm not supposed to bring fruit and vegetables into the country, but they go easy on me. I figure I'd better come clean with them about Monique too. "Believe it or not, I have a chicken on board too!" I explain. They raise an eyebrow and ask if I'm pulling their leg. I show them the newspaper and magazine articles about Momo and me and, clearly amused, they advise me to keep a low profile, taking one of the magazines with them as a souvenir. Phew!

I make the most of the stopover in Halifax to buy the last few things I need: an extreme cold-weather sleeping bag, merino long johns, gloves, a winter hat, and a camping stove. That's everything I think I'll need to stay alive in extreme winter conditions. I also buy two forty-pound sacks of rice, and on my last day, I can't resist buying myself a sweet pair of backcountry skis! I figure I'll get some climbing skins for them when I get to Greenland; I've spent enough for now. Halifax is a very livable city, full of green spaces, and I've enjoyed my short time here. Andréa is on board with me now, so it's time to head off again.

~~~~~~

AFTER THREE VERY enjoyable days sailing together, we arrive in Saint Pierre and Miquelon, a tiny remote enclave of France off the coast of Newfoundland. The people there welcome us with open arms; everyone seems to have a smile on their face. A local film crew comes on board to interview us, and we're thrilled to see our faces on the TV news that night.

More daring than ever, Monique tries to jump from the boat to the dock, but she misjudges the distance and falls into the water with a splash. Before I've had time to strip down and dive in to the rescue, she's already swum her way back on board and perched on the tiller, looking a little bedraggled. I carry her into the washrooms on the dock and give her a nice, warm shower.

Our visit coincides with the Rock N' Rhum music festival, so Andréa and I are stoked that we get to enjoy the festive, easygoing atmosphere in Saint Pierre and Miquelon with the tunes of Breton rock group Soldat Louis filling our ears.

The temperatures are seriously starting to drop now. The time has come for me to build a coop indoors for Monique. I've found the perfect spot—right below the starboard berth. A half-day's work later, I call Monique over to check out her new pad. She tiptoes inside, looks around, shifts a few wood shavings on the floor, and lays down. Success! A year ago, if someone had told me I'd be building a chicken coop inside the boat, I would have screamed, "Never!" But it had to get done.

Next stop, Greenland!

It's hard for us to actually leave Saint Pierre and Miquelon. No one wants us to go! The local fishermen have given us plenty of fish and scallops to take with us, and even lobster—sometimes ten at once! I still don't have a working refrigerator on board, but in these temperatures all I have to do to keep things cool is open a hatch in the floor and put them right up against the hull. Because steel conducts heat, any food down there will stay at the same temperature as the water. It's a huge benefit.

Once the hilly landscape of Saint Pierre and Miquelon fades in our wake, Andréa and I find ourselves facing some of the toughest sailing conditions yet. The storms we encounter are the real deal; we feel we're running for our lives through the enormous breaking waves. Andréa is helping a lot, but I still can't bring myself to give up the helm. The temperatures are dropping even lower, and the rain is coming down in sheets. We're soaked to the bone and freezing our butts off. On the bright side though, the wind generator I installed in Saint Martin is going full tilt, so the batteries are always fully charged—the days are getting shorter and I can't count on my solar panels to generate much power anymore.

My water tank has sprung a leak, so we've lost all our fresh water reserves. We have to ration what little there is left, and it's complicated—not to mention unappetizing—to cook everything in seawater.

Three days away from Greenland, the night sky comes alive. Green, yellow, and pink veils dance over our heads, as if aliens were beaming holograms down to us from outer space. There they are! Not the aliens, the Northern Lights! This is the first time I've seen the aurora borealis. They're even more impressive than I had imagined. Andréa and I are lost for words. We stand there gazing up at the sky, as *Yvinec*'s mast seems to conduct this orchestra of light.

On August 19, the first iceberg finally glides into view. I'm speechless. It simply defies description. A mountain of sculpted ice surges forth from the royal blue ocean. I go so far as to nose the boat right up against the ice. What an incredible feeling! It's impossible to tell whether the ice is floating on the ocean or suspended from the sky; it's somewhere in between. The beauty of it all is captivating—but now that we're in iceberg territory, the stakes are a notch higher. The sailing is only going to get harder from here on in. I won't be able to let my guard down for a second.

Soon we find ourselves navigating our way through huge fields of floating ice that bang against the hull. There's something strangely magical about it, but I have to admit it's stressing me out. On the map, the south of Greenland looks like it's been torn to shreds. It's full of tiny holes, as if the coast were made of lace. There are islets as far as the eye can see, and we have to safely work our way between them all. I'm worried we might hit a reef; I don't have charts detailed enough to see where the dangers are. It's a good thing Andréa is here. He climbs the mast to make sure we spot the biggest chunks of ice in time. Sometimes he even launches the dinghy and sails ahead to make sure everything is clear. We're inching our way forward, and soon we're sailing up into a fjord.

The place looks different from how I'd imagined it. The landscape is more colorful, with gray rocks covered in yellow, green, red, and brown moss. It's still summer in the south of Greenland; the weather is milder than I'd thought. Monique is roaming around the deck again. The sea of ice is sparkling in the sun.

We've been sailing up the fjord for a few hours when the first antennas finally start to appear on the horizon. Then little houses of all kinds of colors come into view. They're staggered one on top of the other, like a cliff of stairs rising from the sea. We lower the sails and motor in the rest of the way. A few other boats speed past us, making big wakes that roll *Yvinec* from side to side.

Gently I ease us toward the shore along a channel that leads the way into the little port, through a mosaic of fishing boats at anchor. We have just arrived in Qaqortoq. We moor *Yvinec* at the dock, across from a fish-processing plant.

I tuck Monique away somewhere safe—by that, I mean I push her all the way to the back of her coop—and pile stuff in the front to hide her. I put on some music so no one will hear her if she starts to cluck. Before I jump out onto the dock, I warn her one last time, "Be good, Monique. Not a peep, okay?"

There isn't really a harbormaster's office here—not that we can see, at least. Everything is written in Greenlandic, with lots of *q*'s and *k*'s, and I can't read a word of it.

We eventually find a building that looks like a police station. Andréa and I introduce ourselves to two guys who clearly have no idea why we're here. One of them can just about string together a few words of English, so I explain that we've just sailed in from Saint Pierre and Miquelon.

"Well done," he replies. "Now, what are you doing here?" But after conversing for a while, I realize I was worried for nothing. Here, there are no official landing papers to fill out, and moorage is free in the port. Welcome to Greenland!

Qaqortoq is my first point of contact with the Inuit. By European standards, it's a small town, with around three thousand inhabitants. I happen upon a tannery, and it turns out it has a reputation—it's apparently the last place in Greenland that still buys sealskins from hunters to make fur products. I'm surprised I can't find any skins for my skis here. "No ski in Greenland!" people tell me.

When I return to my sailboat, some kids are fishing on the dock beside it. It's hard to communicate with them, because I'm speaking English and they're answering in Greenlandic, but soon we start to laugh together and I know we're going to get along well. One by one, the locals start to gather around us, asking questions in a mix of English and Greenlandic. When I tell them our story, they can't believe their ears!

In Qaqortoq, everything has to be imported, so it's all crazy expensive. I buy the bare minimum of food, a few fishing lures to get ready for the winter, and some diesel for the engine. An hour of Internet access costs the equivalent of eight euros. That's the price you pay for isolation; we're really and truly at the ends of the earth.

I'm going to need a gun. It's a good idea to have one to scare bears away, and if I have an unpleasant encounter, I might have to use it to defend myself. I don't really know how to go about getting a gun; I've never bought one in my life, and I don't have any kind of permit. As it turns out, that's not a problem, because weapons here are readily available to anyone. In the supermarket, the rifles are right next to the bakery department. And there's no shortage of them to choose from. I feel like an idiot standing in front of twenty different models of rifles. I randomly pick one and stuff it into my shopping cart with a few boxes of ammunition. I head to the checkout and walk out of the supermarket with a rifle under one arm and a French baguette in the other.

Three days later, we hoist the sails again and head toward Nuuk, the capital of Greenland. After Nuuk, I'm going to sail as far north as possible, as close to the Pole as I can, in search of a sheltered bay where I can hunker down for the winter. On the map, I've scoped out a place called Upernavik, a village in Baffin Bay surrounded by little bays and islets. I'm planning to take my time sailing up the coast, to get there at the latest by October 1, in time for the start of the Arctic winter.

For now, we're sailing between steep mountains that plunge into the water, pristine sandy beaches peppered here and there in their midst. Whenever we come across another boat, the crew wave and call out words of greeting I still can't understand. I simply respond with a big smile and yell "French! *Français!*" to which they laugh and smile in return. They know we're foreigners; when you're here on a sailboat, you've clearly come from somewhere else. Because apparently sailing is like skiing—no one does it in Greenland!

Suddenly it starts to rain and the fog rolls in. Enveloped in a misty veil, we forge ahead blindly through a cotton-wool seascape. It's magical and terrifying all at once. The horizon is a mirage. The depth changes rapidly and, before we know it, we're in some shallows. At times like this, I'm glad to have a sailboat with a swing keel, not a fixed keel.

When night falls, there is nothing. No human presence, no vegetation, only the ashes of the metaphorical fire in the sky with the occasional seal head, whale spout, or iceberg silhouetted against the horizon. At night, *Yvinec*'s wake shimmers emerald green as the Northern Lights reflect off the plankton in the water. Time seems to stand still.

We draw nearer to Ivittuut, a large village with around a thousand inhabitants, according to my map. We're hoping to find a place that's heated so we can warm up over hot chocolate and maybe have a bite to eat. But we don't see any lights on the shore as we approach.

We moor alongside an old ramshackle dock. There's something weird about this place. We soon see the village is empty. Heavy wooden planks are nailed over the doors and windows of all the houses. The streets are littered with animal carcasses and whale bones. This place is a ghost town. It's been left to ruin and everything looks like it's bathed in a strange kind of light. It's really creeping us out. Quickly, we make our way back to Monique and the boat. We leave the dock and sail away to moor in the next bay over, where it feels a little more welcoming. Only later would I find out that the village was officially abandoned in 1987 after the cryolite mine there closed down.

I've finally installed a stove on board. It's going to be our only source of heat. But it's not easy to get the temperature just right. It's so hot inside the cabin now, it feels almost tropical! That doesn't bother Monique at all. It doesn't take her long to understand that heat rises, and she finds herself a nice perch up by the ceiling.

We spend the night in Paamiut alongside a Greenlandic fishing boat equipped with an enormous harpoon at the bow for whale hunting. Yep, that's legal here. I'm torn between feeling sadness and respect for the traditions of these people whose survival depends on killing these mammals. Greenlanders essentially live off hunting and fishing. Unlike Westerners living in temperate climates, they can barely grow any fresh produce because their country is covered in snow and ice for most of the year—so they have to rely on what they are able to hunt and fish. From what I can see, they spend most of their time stocking up for winter. Marine mammal blubber provides valuable iron and vitamins and helps them to survive the extreme temperatures of the Arctic winter.

As we make our way out of Paamiut, we catch our first wild salmon! That bodes well for the winter. I gut the fish and cut it into meal-sized portions before stashing it in the "refrigerator" down in the bilge, which is actually more of a freezer these days, since the temperature has dropped to around freezing.

That night we feast on sushi, much to Monique's delight. Andréa and I share our favorite culinary techniques. I have to admit he's a fabulous cook; it's a real pleasure to have him aboard. He's the ideal kind of crew member, because he's pleasant to be around and always ready for anything. What's more, Monique seems to have adapted well to his presence.

After a week of sailing, when the tiny village of Qeqertarsuat-siaat comes into view, we're about halfway between Paamiut and Greenland's capital, Nuuk. As soon as we make land, we connect with the locals, who give us a tour of the village on their ATVs and take us out for a motorboat ride. As we power along, they peer through their ultra-high-powered binoculars at one uninhabited islet after another. We soon learn they're scoping these places out for deer hunting.

As we return to *Yvinec* and continue our journey north, we see a gigantic iceberg ahead. It has something of a bluish, transparent quality, and water is dripping from its surface. I'm hypnotized by the sight and want to get closer to take some photos. We throw out the anchor onto this icy monster and zip away in the dinghy to capture the scene up close.

But then, all hell breaks loose. I can see the iceberg shifting shape and it looks like the water is bubbling and swirling all around it. The nose of my sailboat is starting to pitch down into the water! Quickly, I abandon my quest to snap the photo of the century, and we hurry back aboard *Yvinec* before she sinks. The iceberg is flipping over! The deck is already pitching heavily as I dash to the front of the boat with my knife and slice through the anchor rope. As we break free from the sinking iceberg, the back of the boat slams back down to the water with a big splash. We motor away at full throttle and only just manage to escape in time before the iceberg goes under, sending up a huge wave that would have sunk us if we'd been any closer. Phew! That was a close call! I very nearly lost my boat.

Now that was a dumb idea! But I've learned my lesson. Iceberg Safety 101: always keep your distance! I should have read up on icebergs and known that before venturing into these waters. My ignorance very nearly cost us our lives and put an end to this adventure once and for all. Icebergs aren't anything to mess with. They might seem like mountains floating in water, but they can be far less stable than they look. I know that now.

Once our hearts have stopped racing, we find a place to moor the boat by a long, sandy beach. We all go ashore—Monique included—to stretch our legs and admire the scenery, which, surprisingly, looks a lot like Brittany and reminds me of home.

It's six in the morning on September 13, 2015, when we sail into Nuuk, twenty-one days after we left Qaqortoq. We've had some pretty hairy nights. We've had to fight against a strong current and headwind, and the swell has made it extra challenging to navigate our way through the floating islands of ice. The bigger icebergs show up on my radar just fine, but not the growlers— these chunks of ice are much smaller, but could still cause a lot of damage to the boat. In the end, we figured it would be safest to crawl our way along under engine power, using the docking light at the bow to give us a fighting chance of seeing them as early as possible. Needless to say, we didn't manage to get a lot of sleep, so we're relieved to be able to rest up a little here. Johann, my friend from Saint Martin, has come out here to join us for a few days. He's an expert drone pilot and I can't wait for him to teach me some aerial photography.

As luck would have it, we dock alongside a French Navy ship, the *Malabar*. She's a 165-foot oceangoing tug based in Brest, not too far from my little island in Brittany. What a nice surprise! That night, once Johann has arrived, we go aboard the Navy ship to shoot the breeze with my fellow countrymen.

Johann's brought the fair weather with him from the Caribbean, and we sail away from Nuuk the next day under sunny skies. We're heading for Sisimiut; that's where Andréa is due to take off a couple of days from now. At one point, we see a good forty seals swimming around the boat. I try to approach so I can film them, but they are camera shy; every time I turn the lens their way, they dive beneath the surface.

We only manage to cover thirty nautical miles the first day, because we find too many excuses to stop and capture images of what we're seeing. In spite of our vigilance, we end up bumping into a rock that's just below the surface and the impact knocks the swing keel up. Luckily, it's not as serious as we thought and there is no damage. That's what happens when you're trying to navigate without detailed charts; we're going to have to be even more careful from now on. I figure it's a good idea to reduce our boat speed. That night, we drop the anchor in a stunning bay dotted with little islets. I'm enjoying my friends' company. It's a real pleasure to share these magical moments with them, even though I'm keen to continue my journey solo once they go home.

The day dawns over a glassy sea—every sailor's dream. It turns out to be short-lived though, because the wind soon starts to fill in. The hours go by and we realize a storm is brewing. As the wind gets stronger and stronger, we gradually reduce sails until we haul everything down. We have to find a sheltered harbor to moor in, and quickly. But there's nothing nearby, so we have to keep on going. As darkness falls, we're relieved to be approaching a village. But the channel is tricky to navigate, and we have to weave our way through a narrow passage between the rocks. We're using what looks like a red navigation buoy in the distance to find our way, but it turns out to be a light in a window on the shore, and soon we find ourselves surrounded by rocks.

Eventually we manage to work our way out of this nightmare and spot the right path to shore. By now, the sea is in a state of frenzy, even inside the harbor. It takes us three tries to tie up *Yvinec* at the wharf. We tie her up with as long a line as we can to ease the strain and to allow for changes in the tide. The next morning we leave the dock early. The local fishermen try to talk us out of going to sea, but *Yvinec* can't handle another night of bashing against the wharf, and Andréa can't miss his flight. I stow the dinghy on deck and we bring everything that's lying around loose into the cabin.

With the engine going full throttle, our boat speed is barely half a knot. The conditions are chaotic, but we have to head off-shore, because it's too dangerous to hug the shoreline with all the reefs and rocks around. The waves are huge; some must be nearly thirty feet high. We try to make sure we stay perpendicular to the breakers, with the wind behind us. *Yvinec* tips onto her side several times, but always rights herself. The anemometer is registering gusts of sixty knots, stronger than we've ever seen. The cockpit has turned into a saltwater swimming pool, though way colder than anyone would want to take a dip in. Soaked to the skin and freezing, none of us are talking anymore. Johann goes below deck to warm up. I clock 16.4 knots surfing one wave, setting a new speed record for *Yvinec*. After thirteen hours of fighting the elements, gripping the helm for dear life, we eventually make our way into the harbor at Sisimiut and find shelter. The nightmare is finally over.

Inside the cabin, everything has been turned upside down. Monique's coop has sprung open and she is nowhere to be seen. We pick up the piles of clothes on the floor, and there she is—sitting on her egg! This hen of mine is unbelievable!

Andréa bids us farewell here in Sisimiut, his spirits buoyed by all the memories we've created. He's determined to buy himself another boat to replace the one that sank in St. Barts so he can set sail on another adventure as soon as he can. Johann and I continue toward Ilulissat, a sizable town (by Greenlandic standards) of around 4,500 people. This is my last port of call to stock up on supplies before Monique and I go into hibernation. The nights are getting longer already.

After a few hours at sea, the engine breaks down. Oh no, not now! There's barely any wind, but there's always a way to keep moving forward, even if it means launching the dinghy and using its outboard motor to shunt *Yvinec* along. The drone is coming in very handy. When we can't see any obvious pathway through the ice floes, we send it up for a bird's-eye view to help us find our way.

Coming into Disko Bay, we have to zigzag our way between some huge icebergs, some of which must be 150 feet high. With the memory of my last iceberg encounter still fresh in my mind,

I try not to steer too close. That is, until I spot an iceberg in the shape of an arch. It's too tempting. I can't resist the urge to paddle under the arch on my stand-up paddleboard. I pull down the sails, step into a pair of boardshorts, turn on my GoPro, jump onto the board, and start paddling. Meanwhile, Johann launches the drone and keeps an eye on my progress from above. It takes a while to paddle my way over there, but eventually I'm inside the arch, and the ice is just inches above my head.

When I look up, I can see some parts of the ice are crazed with thin cracks. Clearly, this little indulgence wasn't the smartest idea. Especially as I've gone out without any shoes, so I can't feel my feet anymore. I paddle my way back to the boat, and when I'm safely back on board, Johann and I look at the images he's captured. Sure enough, there's a big crack in the iceberg, and it could have collapsed right on top of me. Yikes!

It's early in the morning when we make our way into Ilulissat, after mooring overnight across the bay in Qeqertarsuaq to avoid sailing into the harbor in the dark—the wind was picking up, and it would have been impossible for us to navigate through the ice in the channel. The harbor is full, so we have no other option but to tie up alongside a fishing boat. With the engine out of commission, we have to use the dinghy to push *Yvinec* in toward the dock.

Ilulissat is the most touristy town in Greenland, because it's right across from the Jakobshavn Glacier, one of the largest in the Arctic. The glacier is also the reason why this place is sometimes so hard to access; a lot of icebergs break off from it.

Johann's memory cards are full of stunning images. But it's time for him to say goodbye, and for me to continue alone on my adventure. I'm already looking forward to seeing him again after the winter to tell him the rest of the story. That story begins now!

My number one priority is to get the engine repaired as quickly as possible. Fortunately, it's still under warranty, but parts need to be ordered, and it might be a month or more before they get here. The time is flying by; it's already the end of September, and I have no desire to spend the winter in the harbor at Ilulissat. Now the nights are very cold and in the morning the water around the boat is covered with a thin layer of ice that jams my rudder. To clear it, I have to break up the ice with a *touk*, one of the first things I've purchased in Ilulissat. It's basically a giant chisel—a sharp metal blade on the end of a long wooden handle. The Inuit use these tools to test the strength of the ice and make holes in it for their fishing lines.

In the daytime, I've been spending time in town while Monique stays tucked up nice and warm inside her coop. She's taken to perching barely an inch above the stove, so I'm worried I might come home to the smell of roast chicken if I don't keep her cooped up when I'm out.

While I'm in Ilulissat, I stock up on all the supplies I'm going to need to spend winter in the ice. Among the things I pick up are fifteen 15-gallon barrels, a few 5-gallon barrels, and six 50-gallon steel drums, all to fill with diesel. That'll mean I can carry over 500 gallons of fuel with me. Once the ice sets in around the boat, I won't be able to get any more supplies, and I know it will be vital to have enough to run the engine and keep the heating going, which will take a lot of fuel.

The engine parts finally arrive in mid-October. It's about time! I've been going crazy here in Ilulissat. The people here can't believe what I'm planning to do. They keep asking me all kinds of questions, but I don't have any of the answers.

"Where do you want to go?" they ask me.

"I don't know, somewhere up north," I reply vaguely.

To be honest, I'm getting a little worried. Now there are only two or three hours of daylight, and more and more ice is setting in each day. If I have to wait much longer, there'll be no way out of the harbor. From here, it's still 350 nautical miles to Upernavik, and the conditions will be extreme, to say the least. Sailing solo, this is not going to be a walk in the park.

On October 18, we're finally set to leave Ilulissat with a working engine and a deck filled with fuel drums. It's six in the morning when I get up and pull on my long johns and a sweater. Inside the cabin, it's pitch dark. That's strange; I should be able to see the harbor lights through the cabin window. I turn on the cabin light and, to my horror, I see that we're covered in a blanket of snow! I open the engine compartment, check the oil and water levels, and turn the key to start the engine, but nothing happens. Well, there's a click, but that's all. Seriously? Is this some kind of sick joke? I open the compartment again, tinker a little with the wires—and this time the engine fires to life! I tug on my boots and venture outside.

The tide is out, and the harbor is still frozen solid. On deck, none of the winches will turn and all the lines are stiff with ice. I have to use a big screwdriver to untie *Yvinec*'s mooring lines and set her free. Obviously, the rudder is stuck in the ice too, and it takes me a good while to smash the ice around it with a crowbar. Standing at the front of the boat, I use my *touk* to push us away from the dock. I shift the engine into gear, and we're on our way.

Is this really a good idea? I try not to think about it. I already know the answer to that question. For sure, it's a bit reckless, and more than slightly crazy, but after everything I've done to make it this far, I can't bring myself to turn back now.

As we get closer to the way out of the harbor, the ice is so dense it's impossible to get through. But suddenly, I see a big fishing boat nearby that is also leaving the harbor. With its powerful engine, it's blasting right through the ice. I wait for it to pass me so I can motor along in its wake. Unfortunately, it's a much faster boat than *Yvinec*, and by the time I come along with my little engine, the ice has already re-formed. It isn't long before we're trapped in a maze of icebergs and islands of sea ice. There's no way forward from here.

In the meantime, dawn has broken, and the low-lying sun is casting a surreal kind of light over the sea. In two or three hours, it will be dark again, and I won't be able to see a thing more. I climb up the mast and spot a clearing in the ice. It's already starting to get dark again, so now is the time to get moving. I set off on a northwesterly course, not really sure where it will lead. I manage to steer my way around the bigger chunks of ice and push the smaller ones away with my *touk*. By around four in the afternoon, I've made it across to Disko Island, on the west side of the bay. Just offshore, I drop anchor in a spot that's exposed to the wind. Throughout the night, I have to keep getting up to push away the ice that bumps against the hull.

By morning, there's a huge iceberg right alongside us. It must have been drifting along until it got snagged on the anchor chain. I have to let out a good hundred feet more chain so I can back away from the iceberg and pass it to starboard. I can't leave the helm for a second, and I make sure my *touk* is always close at hand. We motor on for a few hours before stopping again in a small bay a dozen or so nautical miles north of Saqqaq, the nearest village on the map. It's been forty-eight hours since I left the harbor in Ilulissat, and I've only covered around fifty nautical miles. I'm starting to feel discouraged. How can I keep going for another three hundred miles in conditions like these?

The next day, everything is frozen, even after the sun comes up. My lines are as stiff as rods, so I can't maneuver at all. Maybe I have to rethink this plan. To keep going in these conditions would be suicide. With a tear in my eye, I resign myself to turning around and heading south toward Saqqaq.

<hr>

I'VE BEEN STRUGGLING to make headway through the ice when, from out of nowhere, two fishing boats blast by at full speed, making *Yvinec* pitch and roll in their wake. There's no way I can keep pace with them, but at least I can follow the path they've opened in the ice. At last, the village comes into view. In the fading daylight, there's something comforting about the brightly colored little houses perched in the snow. Now I can see a tiny wharf, which looks like it's only about half the length of my boat, with a ladder leading down to the water's edge.

The mooring lines feel just as frozen as my hands as I prepare to dock. I'm certainly not expecting a motorboat to cut right in front of me like a reckless driver and swipe my parking spot from right under my nose—but it does. What a nerve! I shift the engine into reverse and wait for the skipper to unload his cargo. When the motorboat pulls away, I use my boat hook to help pull us in toward the wharf, with the wind in my face.

Two guys are standing on the wharf watching me maneuver my way in, making no effort to help. Seriously? They're just going to stand by and watch me struggling to keep my boat straight while I try to thread a mooring line as hard as iron through a ring right at their feet? I can't believe it.

I'm seething when I eventually manage to dock and one of the two men sidles over and asks me in broken English what I'm doing here. I'm used to being asked that question. So I explain that I've made my way up from Ilulissat and am headed north. He looks at me as if I'm from another planet. To prove that I'm not completely out of my mind, I pull out my chart and point to the village of Upernavik. The man leans closer, nods that he understands, then shakes his head.

"Dangerous! Much ice! Don't go! Impossible!" he insists.

Dangerous, impossible, much ice? Great, that's exactly what I'm looking for! The man listens as I explain the finer details of my plan, nods again, and turns to his friend. The two of them talk between themselves for a while, then he turns back to me and says very firmly, "Winter is too far along already; it's too dangerous. Why don't you stay in the village?"

I don't know how to tell them that spending the winter alone in the ice is important to me. I'm worried they won't understand. But from the disappointment on my face, they can see how much this means to me. They peer at my chart again, as if they're looking for something. Eventually, they point out two or three places, as if to say, well, if you really wanted to, you could go there, or there.

It's a relief to realize that all these two gruff men want to do is help me. Matias, the one who speaks English, works at the fish factory in Saqqaq. He'd love to help, I manage to understand, but he's not a fisherman and he doesn't know these waters very well. As we continue our conversation, more men gather on the wharf, and word soon gets around about where I'm planning to go. They all say the same thing: it's just not possible to go any farther north. It's far too dangerous.

I'm starting to have second thoughts. Maybe I shouldn't be so stubborn. It wouldn't be the end of the world if I stayed here instead. For once, maybe I should listen to other people's advice, even if I don't like the sound of it. If I run out of diesel in the next six months, I won't just be stuck somewhere; I'll have no heating either. I won't be feeling quite so clever then. It's already October 20; I've left it too late to get going. Already, there's practically no daylight. It's been one storm after another, and there's ice everywhere. What's more, because we're so close to the North Pole, the automatic pilot and compass aren't working anymore. My lines are frozen solid, and my winches won't turn. Much to my disappointment, the decision is out of my hands. I'm going to spend the winter farther south than I'd wanted, in the north of Disko Bay.

Once I'm back on board *Yvinec*, I moor in the bay in front of the village. Then I grab two of my fuel cans and go ashore with the dinghy. You can always find somewhere to buy diesel in Greenland. In this village, all I have to do is walk up the main street to find some. As I'm filling up my second can, a man on a snowmobile pulls up at the pump beside me. He looks to be about forty, and he speaks to me in such strongly accented English that at first I think it's Greenlandic.

"What?" I ask.

"Uno! My name," he repeats.

"Hi, Uno!" I reply. "I am Guirec, and I come from France!"

"*Tikilluarit!* Welcome! *Kaffe?* Coffee? My house! Come!" Uno insists.

"Oh, yes, nice! With pleasure! Thank you!" I reply.

How can I say no?

Whenever I'm invited somewhere, I don't like showing up empty-handed. I always try to bring something to give my host—but up here, it's not that easy to do. But then I have an idea—I could give him one of Monique's eggs! Freshly laid this morning too. Once I've taken the diesel back to the boat, I pick the freshest egg and carefully wrap it in paper.

Uno and his wife, and their daughter, who speaks very good English, welcome me with open arms. They are thrilled with the egg and highly amused when I tell them about Monique. They've never seen a fresh egg before, and they've only ever seen a chicken on TV or on their dinner plate!

Speaking of dinner, that's what the invitation to come over for "coffee" turns out to be. Here people always invite each other for coffee, even if that's the last thing they plan on serving. It's their way of saying "come over for dinner." Uno and I have a hard time communicating in English, but that doesn't stop us from striking up a rapport right away. With his daughter interpreting for us, we're getting by just fine. I tell them all about Brittany and how I crossed the Atlantic and visited the Caribbean. I explain how I came to meet Monique, and what my plan is for the winter: to spend six months in the pack ice, completely self-sufficient, with no means of communication at all. I pull out my chart and show them the places that Matias and the fishermen on the wharf pointed out.

"Why don't you spend the winter here with us instead, in Saqqaq with your boat?" they ask. "Won't you get bored out there all on your own? Don't you know there's nothing to do, and nothing to see? All you'll find is ice!"

How can I get them to see that the whole point of this adventure is to be alone and cut off from the world? I'm not afraid. I'm well equipped. I have my dinghy, a tent, a good sleeping bag, a dry suit, and enough drums to hold two tons of diesel. I'm sure it'd be amazing to spend the winter in a village in Greenland, but that's not what I set out to do. Not to mention the fact that I was planning to go much farther north. Already, it's hard for me to settle for Disko Bay. I know there's not much chance of me seeing polar bears around here, for example. I'm disappointed. Still, it could be worse. I could have been stuck in the harbor at Ilulissat, sandwiched between the motorboats and the fish factory.

Once he's grasped that when I set my mind on something I won't give up, Uno decides to help me. He and his fisherman friends are going to think of the best place for me to go. When I get back to the boat later that evening, I find Monique sleeping peacefully in her coop. After writing a few notes in my journal, it's time for me to go to bed too.

I'm exhausted, but I can't sleep. It's because of the dogs; they won't stop howling. They're purebred huskies—powerful dogs with a reputation for being the best sled dogs. The locals are so careful not to mix them with any other breeds that above a certain latitude, north of Sisimiut, travelers aren't allowed to bring dogs with them. In the village, all the huskies are chained up outside; none of them are allowed inside the houses. They are strictly work dogs, not family pets. This is hard for me to fathom, because in my experience, our dogs have always been treated as part of our family. But for Greenlanders, that would be unthinkable. When one of their dogs is too old to run fast enough or pull the weight of the sled anymore, the owners just part with it.

That first night, I feast my eyes on the icebergs all around and the Northern Lights that shimmer and sparkle over the village.

In the days that follow, I'm often invited over to Uno's for coffee. Using a little English-Greenlandic dictionary he has loaned me, I manage to string together a few sentences that make my new friends laugh out loud. With a few hand gestures thrown in for good measure, it isn't that hard for us to understand each other after all.

It isn't long before I know everyone in the village—all 150 of them, that is. Word soon gets around that I never accept an invitation without bringing one of Monique's eggs with me. And fresh eggs turn out to be remarkably popular here. They're a world away from any imported products the locals can find. People have even started to stop me in the street, asking, "Hey Guirec, any chance you could slip me one of Monique's eggs?" I wish! Monique only lays one egg a day. It's hard to keep everyone happy.

Monique is not enjoying life in Saqqaq very much. It's so cold outside that she has to stay in the cabin all the time. No one in the village has even seen her yet. But the children are curious. They soon persuade me to let them come aboard. They've never seen a chicken before, so at first they're a little wary. They look and they laugh, but they keep their distance. Lukaka, a boy of about eight or nine, has taken a shine to me and started to follow me everywhere. But he's still terrified of being left alone with Monique for even a second.

Lukaka soon becomes my best friend in Saqqaq. He won't stop talking, and because I can't understand a word he says, he draws in the snow to show me what he means. He takes me everywhere

in the village: to school, to church, to the "Commune"—
a community building where you can do pretty much anything,
from taking a shower to washing your laundry, playing a sport,
or making crafts—and to Pilersuisoq, the local grocery chain
store. Thanks to Lukaka, I get to see every inch of this tiny community, even the village dump! I'm amazed to see what people
throw away here. Even things that seem to be in perfect working
order—like washing machines and computers—as well as food
that's barely past its expiry date. One day, I even salvage a pack of
mini-yogurts! This place might be in the middle of nowhere, but
the consumer culture is firmly ingrained. As soon as something
breaks down, people buy a new one to replace it. They don't
repair anything.

Even if they wanted to, there are no electricians, stonema-
sons, or plumbers here. All the residents are hunters or fishers,
or they work at the fish factory, the school, the village hall, or
the grocery store. If they want to do something else, they move
to Ilulissat, Nuuk, or Denmark. There isn't even a doctor here.
When people get sick, they can find a few basic drugs at the grocery store. And if they need to see a professional, they have to go
to Ilulissat. In winter, when everything is frozen and the boats
can't go to sea, there's a helicopter shuttle that flies twice a week.

Uno and his friends have thought things over and come up with a
couple suggestions for places that would be sheltered enough for
me to spend the winter. Not far to the east of Saqqaq, just south
of a village by the name of Qeqertaq, I've pinpointed a spot that
looks promising, but I'd like to check it out before I make up my
mind. One morning, when Uno heads out fishing, he suggests
that sometime I go with him; once he's hauled up his line, we'll

take a quick detour past the bay on the way home. I jump at the chance of joining him, especially since rumor has it that Uno's the best fisherman in Saqqaq!

Until that day comes, I've been leaving Monique and strolling around the village, trying to converse with people without getting too much in their way. That's how I end up meeting Jonas one day when he gets back from seal hunting. I had never seen anything like it before. When I see him skinning and butchering the seals he had hunted on the ice, I head over to watch him at work. Nothing of the animal is wasted. Sealskin is used to make clothing, of course, but they find a use for the blubber, flesh, and guts too. I see how long and narrow a seal's stomach is when Jonas pulls one's out and proceeds to slit it open, clean it, and chop it into little pieces, to be kept outside all winter. Apparently, this is a local delicacy! Farther north, Jonas tells me, people even keep the eyes.

After school, there isn't much for the kids to do besides kicking a soccer ball around in the snow, so they often come down to the shore and wait for the fishermen. Sometimes they help them to gut the fish, and their reward is a piece of the liver. When the men are done cleaning the fish, the kids love to share the liver among themselves and nibble on it while it's still warm. They even offer me a morsel, dripping with blood.

"Guirec, Guirec, taste it! Come on, give it a taste!" they say.

The thought of it turns my stomach, but I can't bring myself to say no to them. It tastes gross. Like, really gross. Seeing me grimace, they burst out laughing, their lips red with fresh blood. As unappetizing as it may seem, I figure it's probably a healthier snack than the vast quantities of Haribo candies I've seen them wolf down.

I'm having a hard time stomaching the piece of raw liver when Jonas turns to me and invites me to join him for coffee. Sweet!

I dash off to take a shower first. In Saqqaq, there's no running water. Most of the houses don't have bathrooms, and people go to the Commune or the school to shower. Each of the washrooms has two showers, and people shower in pairs! The toilets are quite peculiar too. Because there's no running water or septic tanks, a big yellow garbage bag is put at the bottom of the toilet bowl. Once a week, an employee of the Commune comes to replace it with an empty bag and take the full one to the dump.

Jonas's place is a little yellow cabin on the water's edge. I knock on the door with one of Monique's eggs in hand. Like all the houses in Saqqaq, the windows have incredible ocean views, and I love that I can keep an eye on my boat from the living room. And like all the other homes in the village I've seen, the interior is both sparsely decorated and surprisingly well equipped with the latest technology—flat-screen TVs, laptops, and tablets. Apparently some eighty percent of Greenlanders have a Facebook account.

Dinner is served, and we sit down at the table. There's a dish of potatoes—that much I can see. But there are two other dishes I don't recognize. Jonas points at one and mimes a dolphin diving in and out of the water with the flat of his hand. I serve myself as small a portion as I possibly can. The other dish looks like some kind of meat. It's seal meat. Again, I barely put any on my plate. But Jonas protests with a wave of his hand and fills my plate a little too generously. How the heck am I supposed to eat all of that? I don't want to be rude, so I make an effort to finish my plate.

The seal meat tastes a bit like steak. It's not bad, actually. But I'm really not a fan of the dolphin. It's not my place to judge, though; hunting is a big part of the culture here. The land is not workable and pretty much all food has to be imported, so everything costs an arm and a leg. The menu might not be to my taste, but I enjoy listening to Jonas's hunting and fishing stories, so I stay for quite a while.

At around four the next morning, I meet Uno on his fishing boat and we head out for a day at sea. The previous day, he set a groundline with about 1,500 bait hooks at a good three thousand feet below the surface. If that sounds deep, it is. Back home in Brittany, the deepest you can fish in the English Channel is about three hundred feet. Every day, Uno brings in vast quantities of halibut, which he sells to a Danish company that has a warehouse in Saqqaq. The fishermen's catches are sent to Denmark by container ship, and eventually they'll find their way into fish-and-chips restaurants and other kitchens around the world. Fishing can be a very lucrative pursuit here in Saqqaq. And good fishermen can haul in a serious amount of cash. But wealth is not something people advertise around here. Everyone lives in the same way.

It's dark, it's cold, and there's ice everywhere. It's only November, but the fishing season is already drawing to a close. Everything stops at the beginning of December until the sea ice has melted in March or April. Today, as soon as the wind dies down, sheets of ice start to form on the water's surface. The ice doesn't faze Uno at all. He just guns the throttle and powers right into it. I'm not exactly faint of heart, but I'm worried he's going to tear a hole in the hull. Uno hits the gas with his formidable two-hundred-horsepower engine and launches the boat into the air, slamming it back down onto the ice to blast his way through. I have to hang on tight to avoid being thrown overboard. All the fishermen here do the same. Keeping their boats in good shape doesn't seem to be a priority for them. Every time they go full steam ahead into the ice, they just figure they're going to make it or break it.

This time, I'm pleased to say nobody's boat goes under. But Uno's line has gotten tangled with another fisherman's, and it takes a fair amount of time to untangle it. But the worst thing is that my new friend has to separate the fish out too: this one's mine, that one's his, and so on and so on. It's a never-ending process. Uno has no idea who the other line belongs to, but he still takes the time to put his colleague's fish back onto his bait hooks, one by one! The respect and solidarity among these fishermen is admirable.

Once Uno has figured out which of the fish are "his," he unhooks them from the line, guts them, and throws the innards overboard. Often, the circling gulls catch them before they hit the water. That day, he brings home a catch of over a hundred halibut. At last, Uno's work is done and we zoom away toward the bay I've been hoping to see.

The sun is up now, and the light is magical. Covered in a thin film of ice, the sea looks smoother and glassier than ever before. It's like a giant mirror. The bay looks well sheltered, and I think it will do the job nicely. In the distance, the nearest coastal village of Qeqertaq looks even smaller than all the other places I've visited.

When Saqqaq comes into view on the way back, the wind has died down and the sun is already setting. The sky is on fire and its reflection has turned the ice blood-red. The next morning, I decide to head back to the bay to stash my first couple drums of diesel. I can't fill them and take them all aboard at the same time because they'd be far too heavy for my boat. I figure I'll fill the other drums in Qeqertaq and use the opportunity to explore the village. On the way there, I see the sun's golden halo beginning to rise over the snow-capped peaks. But I can only glide so far into the bay, because there's a thick layer of ice covering most of it. Hugging the coastline, I try to forge a path as best I can, but the ice is so tightly packed I can't make it all the way to shore. Night is falling already, so I have no choice but to sleep here. I figure it'll be good practice for the winter ahead. The next morning, the ice stretches as far as the eye can see. The sea and the sky have blended into one another in shades of gray. The only sounds are my own breathing and the droplets of water dripping from the icebergs. As idyllic a scene as it is, I have no time to lose. I have to get to Qeqertaq.

Under engine power, *Yvinec* has no problem breaking up the thin film of ice covering the water's surface, and I'm zigzagging my way deftly between the thicker chunks. The engine is running at full throttle. It's important to keep the momentum going so we don't get stuck. At times it seems like the ice is a noose tightening around us, and I find myself holding my breath. *Yvinec* is really struggling to make headway. But after a few hours of slogging, we're finally out of the bay and motoring along nicely.

But it isn't long before we grind to a halt again. The ice is all around us now, stretching for miles in every direction. Qeqertaq seems completely inaccessible. I realize I have to turn around and head back to Saqqaq to fill up again. The path we forged yesterday through the ice is still there, so I know it's doable. The only problem is that the water intake that cools the engine keeps freezing, and ice is getting into its filter. If the engine isn't cooled, it might get damaged. What a pain! I have to stop about twenty times to clear the filter before I can set off again. I'm at my wit's end.

When I get back to Saqqaq, I have no idea what to do next. I can't see myself returning to the same bay. What if I get well and truly stuck next time? That's when I remember Uno telling me about another bay closer to the village, just a few hours away. I decide to change my plan and spend the winter there instead. I'll head over there as soon as I can.

Between the second and third week of November, I manage to fill all my drums with diesel and ferry them over to my winter site. Each trip takes anywhere between five and twenty hours, depending on the ice. When I get there, I unload my barrels and line them up on the beach, across from where I'm planning to drop anchor for the winter. By now, I'm starting to get to know the place a little. It looks like the bay is going to be well sheltered, and I'm happy with my choice. I can't wait for the sea ice to set in gradually around Monique and me. I'm looking forward to seeing *Yvinec* frozen into the bay for the winter. When I've finished transferring my fuel drums, I head back to the village one last time to say goodbye to everyone. *Inuulluarit, takuss'!*

I go online one last time and make my final phone calls to my loved ones: my mother, my sisters Maureen, Nolwenn, and Fantig, and a few friends. I'm going to miss being in contact with them, but this adventure can't wait any longer. I save my last phone call for my father. He gets a little teary, but he's very encouraging and tells me he has every confidence in me. We start hatching a plan for him to come sail with me for a week or two in the spring. My father isn't getting any younger, but he's in good health and he's a strong sailor. I'm over the moon at the thought of us sailing together.

Around six that evening, the time has come to cast off from our mooring. I can hardly believe it. Our winter adventure is beginning at last. The light of the full moon is reflected in the glassy sea. It's ridiculously cold, there's snow everywhere, and everything on deck is completely frozen. The mooring lines are so stiff I can't untie them; I have to pour boiling water on them to soften them up. I shift the engine into gear and *Yvinec* glides away gently. The lights of Saqqaq grow blurry in our wake before they disappear into the night. The ice is knocking at the hull, the Northern Lights are streaking across the sky, and billions of stars overhead are wishing me luck. I feel a flood of mixed emotions washing over me. I start talking to myself in front of the camera I've set up in the cockpit; out here I can sing, shout, and scream to my heart's content. "Well folks," I say, "I have no way to communicate with anyone, nothing but eighty pounds of rice to munch on, and we're going to spend the next six months living in this spectacular place in the most extreme temperatures imaginable, and I AM HAPPY! I hope I'm not making a grave mistake. Nah, don't be silly. You can't say things like that. Just go for it, man! Life's too short. You have to make the most of every second, because you never know what the future holds."

At that time, I didn't know it yet, but those words would turn out to carry a lot of truth.

We're gliding along beside icebergs. This is the greatest experience of my life. We won't be coming back before the end of May or beginning of June, when the ice has melted us free. Twelve hours later, it's still dark when we slip into the bay. Soon my Iridium satellite phone is going to power down and be out of service for the winter. I've got just enough minutes left on my phone plan to call my father and let him know I've made it here safe and sound. But it's too late back home for me to call him now, so I'll talk to him in the morning. It's November 25, and the winter starts now.

~~~~~~~

HAVE I REALLY come this far, almost within reach of my dream, for things to end here? I won't let that happen. Don't panic, Guirec. You won't get anywhere with your stomach tied in knots. Stay calm and think. There has to be a solution. There has to be a way. There always is. You have to keep looking ahead. Because even if the sun doesn't rise, there will always be another day. I'm going to make it through. We're going to make it through. Aren't we, Momo?

I'VE HEARD IT ALL about my plan to spend the winter up here in the ice. *It's madness. It's a crazy idea. You're nuts. You must have a death wish.*

I don't want to die. I've made a conscious choice to cut myself off from the rest of the world, and I'm well aware of the dangers. But I want to be reliant on no one but myself. These days, as soon as we run into the slightest problem, we pick up our cell phone and call for help, or we look online for an easy solution. We've lost the ability to think for ourselves and be inventive; take these modern conveniences away, and we have no choice but to redevelop these lost skills. Of course, I've thought about what would happen if I got sick. But I'll be careful to not take any risks and I'll take the time to think things through. I've been weighing the pros and cons for months, right up until the time came to cast off the mooring lines. And I haven't changed my mind.

When it comes to food, for a while I thought I'd be able to get by on whatever I managed to hunt and fish—as well as Monique's eggs, of course. In the end, I decided it would be wise to bring eighty pounds of rice—that's enough for roughly half a pound a day for six months—and a thirty-ounce bottle of olive oil. It'll make the rice taste better and stop it from sticking to the bottom of the pan. I have two bottles of shelf-stable milk left in the pantry, half a pat of butter, and a few jars of herbs and spices: bay leaves, rosemary, cumin, paprika, and coriander. That's all. And if I'm dying of hunger, there's always a hundred pounds or so of Monique's grain to keep me going. That's enough for her to live on for a year. I've tasted it, and it's not exactly appetizing, I have to say.

As for personal hygiene, I'll be happy with the bare minimum! When it's this cold you don't really sweat, so I figure I'll never smell that bad. It's not as if it's going to bother Monique, anyway. So it'll be no showers for the next six months—just a wipe with a wet washcloth, provided it isn't too cold inside the cabin. When I have to answer the call of nature, my bucket will do the job. I have no idea what I'm going to look like at the end of this adventure. There's already a little stubble on my cheeks that I have no intention of shaving off, and the same goes for my hair. I've always been clean-shaven and cut my hair short, so this will be a real change for me!

I'm not worried about fresh water, because there's no end of ice out here. People in Saqqaq stockpile the stuff. Whenever a chunk of iceberg washes up on the beach, they grab it. It's the purest water there is. Finally, I have vitamin D capsules to take once a month, and vitamin C tablets to take once a day. Those are to make up for the lack of fruit, vegetables, and sunlight.

If I run into big problems—if we run aground, or if I have to abandon ship and survive on land in temperatures well below zero—I have a waterproof grab bag filled with enough freeze-dried food for three meals for eleven days. If I ration myself, I can make it last nearly three weeks, which should be plenty of time to make it to the nearest village on foot.

Of course, I have no idea what lies ahead. But if there were nothing for me to learn and discover, what would be the point? I'm sure of one thing, that I will be a different person when I emerge from this unique experience. I'll have enough memories to last me a lifetime. I'm a little apprehensive, but that's all par for the course, isn't it?

It's ten at night here, and I need to get some sleep. Back home in Brittany, it's two in the morning, and everyone's been fast asleep for hours.

It's nearly eleven o'clock when I wake up. Looking through the cabin window above my bed, there's only a faint glow of half-light in the sky. That's the most I'm going to see of the sun for months. I'd better make the most of it while I can. Even the half-light only lasts a few hours, and it's getting shorter by the day. A month from now, there won't be any light at all until February. That's going to be a little hard on my morale.

I get up and go see Monique. She's already awake, and she's laid an egg! It's the very first egg of our new adventure. Out on deck, the thermometer is showing a frigid minus eighteen degrees Fahrenheit. Brrr! An iceberg has drifted in with the wind to keep us company. I hope it'll keep going and pass us by; if it comes any nearer and gets stuck, it's going to be a real headache.

But it's coming right toward us. Typical! I try to push it away with my *touk*, but it's not going anywhere. It looks like we're going to have to move out of its way. It had already crossed my mind to raise anchor and move to a more sheltered spot in the bay anyway. The electric winch won't work in this cold, so I'm going to have to haul up 180 feet of anchor chain by hand.

Outside, I can see a light in the distance. It's a fishing boat, and it looks like it's heading our way. As the boat approaches, I'm delighted to see Uno at the helm. I hadn't been expecting visitors quite so soon! Waving my arms wildly, I shout hello to him in Greenlandic: *"Aluu!"*

Uno pulls alongside and kills the engine. He asks me how I'm doing: *"Qanorippit?"*

I reply that I'm doing well: *"Ajunngilaq! Ajunngilanga, qujanaq!"*

He keeps on talking, but his words are lost in the wind. He puts his hand on his heart and shakes his head no. I still don't understand what he's trying to say, other than the fact that it must be something serious.

"Come aboard and tell me, Uno!" I call to him.

Once he's on board and has warmed up a little inside the cabin, he pulls his cell phone out of his pocket and shows me a screenshot of a text message. The message is for me. It's from my sister, Nolwenn. He gives me the phone, and I read the message. It's written in my own language, but no matter how many times I read it, I don't understand it. Because it doesn't make sense. Because it's completely unfathomable.

My father is dead.

It happened last night. While I was filming myself gushing that I was the happiest man alive, he was having a heart attack.

And now here I am, sitting on a freezing sailboat like a dumbass in the middle of nowhere, completely alone, with only a chicken for company.

Uno wraps his arms around me. He can't stay long. The weather is getting worse and he wants to get home before nightfall. He hugs me tight once more, then off he goes.

I watch the boat glide away, and Uno turns and waves to me one last time before he disappears into the mist.

Yesterday was the happiest day of my life. Today is the saddest.

Nolwenn's words keep echoing in my mind. I still can't believe what I read. An hour from now, maybe two, I was going to call my father. I was going to tell him again that everything I've been able to do is all because of him. My father was in good health. He and I were always close. He was the only person who believed in me and in what I wanted to do, and he was always the first person I wanted to share things with. And now, suddenly, he's gone.

The funeral is on Monday, three days from now, and there's no way I can be there. The next helicopter doesn't leave until Tuesday. I could put this adventure on hold and go home to grieve with my family. But would I ever have the courage to come back here? And wouldn't my father be disappointed in me if I gave up on my dream? If he could tell me anything from where he is now, I'm sure he would want me to carry on. I must live up to the hopes he had for me. I have to do him proud.

Crying won't do me any good, I tell myself. I have to keep going. I have no choice. I thought I'd planned for every contingency. But I had no idea that I'd have to deal with the worst news of my life on the very first day.

If I want to stay the course out here, I have to turn my desperation and anger into strength. I don't believe in coincidences. If my father passed away on the very day that I set out on this adventure, maybe it was so that he could keep me company. So he could stand by my side. Be there to support me. Maybe he was sending me a message. Okay, Dad, we're doing this together. I could sure use some of your energy, your courage, and your resolve to make it through this dream in one piece.

My father wouldn't have liked to see me fall to pieces. To busy myself, I feed Monique and cook myself a serving of rice for the day. Then I pull on some gloves and start to haul up the anchor so I can move *Yvinec* away from the iceberg.

Once I've moved the boat a short distance away, I call my sisters. I still have the few satellite phone credits that I'd been saving to call my father. I know it will have to be a brief conversation, so I've prepared a few words for them to read at the funeral. *Thanks, Dad, for everything you've always done for me.* But before I have chance to say it all, the line goes dead.

I hop into the dinghy and head ashore, where I walk until nightfall. Exhausted, I head back to the boat, eat my rice with Monique's egg from that morning, and go to bed.

When I wake up, my throat is dry, my eyelids feel like they're stuck together, and there's a big knot in my stomach. Everything from yesterday comes flooding back to me: seeing Uno put his hand on his heart and shake his head, reading that fateful message, hearing my sisters' words on the telephone. At one point I wonder whether I've dreamed all of this; I really wish it weren't true. And then I see the words I scribbled on a piece of paper, the words I wanted my sisters to read in church. This isn't just a bad dream. I'll never see my father again. I get out of bed and pull on some clothes, as if I'm on autopilot. Then I open Monique's coop. It does me good to see her going about her day without a care in the world. She's laid another egg and is pecking away at her grain. She comes over and steals some of my breakfast, then walks all over the iPad, making her little clucking sounds all the while. Life goes on, and I'm glad Monique is here to remind me.

I make the most of what light there is to go outside and get some air. The sky is still overcast. The west wind is still pushing the icebergs our way. I can hear them exploding like bombs in the icy silence. I have to stay on my guard and be ready to move again at a moment's notice. If a growler drifts too close, I push it away with my *touk*, and if it's too big for that, I try nudging it with the dinghy instead. Ice has started to form around the hull, and *Yvinec* looks like she's wearing a white skirt. I can't let the ice set in quite yet, because it would weigh down the boat dangerously. Sitting in the dinghy, I work my way around the hull, chipping away the ice with a plank of wood and a hammer, taking great care not to cause any damage. Out on deck, icicles are forming everywhere as the spray from the sea freezes midair. My sailboat looks like a ghost ship. Everything seems so surreal. The sea, the sky, the light, my boat, my father's death. I feel lost.

Inside the cabin, in spite of the heater keeping the temperature around fifty degrees Fahrenheit, things are starting to freeze too. Using my finger, I scratch away the frost that has built up around the window frames in the night. Anything in contact with the metal is freezing. It's only going to get worse in December, and even more so in January. Outside, the temperature might go down as low as minus forty degrees. I wasn't expecting things to freeze inside the cabin, so that's kind of a weird thing to get used to. I really can't afford to run out of diesel, so I don't want to push the thermostat any higher. Besides, fifty degrees is an average, not a consistent temperature inside the cabin. Because heat rises, there's a big difference between the floor and the ceiling. Down by the steel of the hull, the temperature is around thirty degrees, but up by the ceiling, it's closer to sixty. My feet are freezing, but my head's toasty warm! So long as I dress accordingly, I'll be okay.

NOVEMBER 30

Back home, they're burying my father at the local church. They're burying my father, and I'm out here, over two thousand miles away. The funeral is at 2:30 PM. With the time difference, that's 10:30 AM here. I want to be there for him, but I can't. What I can do, though, is pay tribute to him and say goodbye in my own way. So I get into my dinghy and weave a path through the ice. I pull the dinghy ashore and make my way to the foot of the mountain, and climb all the way to the summit. Up there, in a sea of clouds, I gather my thoughts. My father was a man of faith, a practicing Catholic, so I've climbed as high as I can to see him go up to heaven. There are a few words I want to say to him, just the important stuff. *I love you, Dad. Thank you for always believing in me. Thank you for telling me I could do whatever I set my mind to. Today's a really hard day for me, Dad. But I'm going to stand my ground when it gets tough, just like you always taught me. I'm not giving up. There's no way I'm giving up now.*

I'm mad at myself. Why am I here? So far away? Why didn't I spend more quality time with my father these last few years, while I still had the chance?

That night, from my berth inside the cabin, I gaze out at the stars through the window. Where I come from, we tell our children that the sky is filled with the spirits of those who have left us. After dark, they shine their love down on us, like billions of tiny night-lights. So I tell myself that my father is up there now, that he's watching over me, and that nothing bad can ever happen to me.

DECEMBER 4

Monique and I have been here for more than a week now, and the pack ice has shown no signs of setting in yet. At least the wind has died down a little; there aren't as many waves rolling in and breaking up the crust. There are plates of ice, covered in a fresh dusting of snow, drifting lazily across the bay.

Every day, sometimes twice a day, I go out to clear the ice that's formed on the hull. I've started to use a baseball bat to chip away at it, instead of the hammer and plank of wood. That way, the risk of causing damage to the boat isn't as high. When there's too much wind for me to work from the dinghy, I kneel on the edge of the deck and chip away from above. It's a royal pain in the ass. I'm fed up with this; it's high time for the pack ice to set in once and for all.

Until now, I've been spending most of my time moving the boat by raising the anchor and chain using arm strength alone, which is basically the same as maneuvering all eleven tons of *Yvinec* by hand, not to mention all the ice that's clinging to her hull. I'm all alone out here in the cold, the wind, and the snow—that often prevents me from seeing farther than thirty feet, running from one end of the deck to the other just to stay on an even keel. Otherwise, as soon as the anchor is raised, the boat will move, and not necessarily the right way; if I'm not careful, we could very easily run aground. Then I have to find a safe mooring. And then I have to set the anchor again, run out the chain . . . and if it's not my lucky day, I realize there's another iceberg to clear, one I hadn't noticed because the visibility is so poor.

All of that means I haven't had many chances to explore my surroundings. In this wind, I'm a little wary about launching the dinghy. If the outboard motor gives out, I might drift a long ways away from the boat, and then it would be "So long, Monique!"

When you have no way of communicating with anyone, it really makes you stop and think. Every time I'm about to do something, I have to envision the worst-case scenario. With no one to come to my rescue, there is zero margin for error.

We've gotten off to a rough start, but Monique is in top form and laying an egg a day, regular as clockwork! I've installed a light in her coop, which I turn off at nine each night. Because it's so dark outside most of the time, it would throw her body clock off-kilter if I didn't regulate her schedule. She would have no idea whether it was day or night, and I would say goodbye to my soft-boiled eggs! She doesn't seem to be suffering from the cold, even though I bet she didn't see much ice back in the Canary Islands! That said, the weather has been far too bad for me to let her go outside. I did make an exception, for just a few minutes, on the day of my father's funeral. Her coop was getting a little smelly, so I pulled on some gloves and changed her bedding.

Speaking of cleaning up, I've had an issue with my rice stash. Talk about an unpleasant surprise! I've been storing it all under the sink, and the sacks have gotten a little damp and torn. A good part of the rice has spilled out and fallen into the bilge. My two forty-pound sacks of rice are now eight pounds lighter; that means I've lost more than two weeks' worth of rice. I tried to recover the grains that were on the floor under the sink, but most of them were spoiled. I started by trying to pick out the good ones one by one, but then I ran out of patience and ended up pitching the whole lot.

Other than that, I've been keeping busy setting up my GoPro everywhere. When I'm not filming footage of the outdoor environment, the frozen boat, the icebergs, the chunks of sea ice floating around, I turn the camera on myself and talk to the lens about my day. It helps me to feel less alone.

DECEMBER 7

It's a beautiful day, so I take Monique out on deck for some fresh air—not for too long, though. Around noon, the daylight is weak at best. I launch the dinghy and grab an ice ax. I'm going on a mission to harvest a chunk of iceberg so I can replenish my fresh water reserves. When you're harvesting from an iceberg, you have to break it pretty high up—otherwise you'll be drinking saltwater. After a while, I find one I like. It only takes a short amount of work for me to chip away a chunk that will keep me with fresh water for a few days. Right as I'm steering the dinghy away though, a big piece of ice breaks away from the berg and falls onto the air chamber, which nearly capsizes us. Let's just say that somewhat dampens my spirits. I must have weakened the frozen giant by chipping it away with the ax. In future, I'll make sure I'm wearing my dry suit. It's a pain to put on and take off, but if I fall into the freezing water, it'll save my life.

Back at the boat, I put a chunk of iceberg into a pot, add a splash of mineral water, and put it on the stove to melt enough water to fill a few bottles. The rest of the ice can live outside on the deck until I need to melt more. Once night falls, the wind picks up. I'm trying to keep watch for icebergs, but I can't see a thing. As I sweep the beam of my flashlight over the sea, all it picks up are glimpses of rough, black sea, tossing chunks of ice around in every direction. Feeling decidedly on edge, I duck back inside the cabin, stuff T-shirts around the window seals for extra insulation, slip into my sleeping bag, and stay on the alert. It's really howling out there now. It's a full-on storm. In the forty-knot gusts, the shrouds that hold the mast upright are whistling, the halyard lines are whipping the mast, and growlers are knocking against the hull. Everything is vibrating and shaking. I'm on pins and needles.

The only good thing about this is that the wind generator is doing a great job of charging the batteries. That means I can plug my laptop in and put on a movie to help me relax. It's actually pretty cozy inside the cabin. We have heat, and we have light.

Monique seems quite content to scratch away at her bedding, never suspecting for a second that we might well end up ship-wrecked. If we do run aground, I know I'll make out all right with my dry suit, tent, and sleeping bag, but Monique would never survive out there in the cold.

I can't sleep. I'm on tenterhooks, listening for the slightest sound of something bumping against the hull. Is the storm over yet? Are we drifting? I've set both anchors and let out all the chain. But if an iceberg snags on the chain and adds its weight to the boat—if our weight goes from ten to twenty or thirty tons—the anchors won't hold fast. So every time I hear a bang, I freeze and hold my breath, hoping the anchor doesn't let go.

My GPS is too close to the magnetic pole to be a reliable depth indicator, the compass is going haywire, and on my navigation screen, the boat icon showing our position is completely upside down!

I manage to get an hour or two of sleep, and the alarm is what nudges me out of bed. I've been setting it to go off at ten in the morning to make sure I don't miss what few hours of daylight there are. It's snowed during the night, and the boat is white all over. Like every other morning, the wind has died off and there are patches of frozen sea floating atop the open water. Over-night, a huge iceberg has drifted near the boat. If the wind starts blowing again and turns west, it'll drag us onto the rocks. Obvi-ously, we can't stay where we are. The chain is clogged with ice, and I'm chipping it away with the *touk*. Every time I move the boat, I make sure to drop anchor again in at least sixty feet of water; that way, even if visibility is zero, I know I won't be too close to shore. The other danger with icebergs is that some of the part that's underwater might break off and suddenly shoot to the surface like a champagne cork. As crazy as it sounds, boats have been found shipwrecked before, with gaping holes in the hull and no one on board.

As the days and the nights go by, they're all starting to blend into one another. Still no pack ice. Days are spent dodging icebergs, chipping away ice, hauling up anchor chains and then pitching them overboard again a few hundred feet away. Nights are restless affairs with little or no sleep, spent listening for the slightest sound, feeling the vibrations of the boat, hoping the anchors are still holding fast on the seabed. I'm living in a real-life disaster movie. What the hell am I doing out here?

DECEMBER 10

My video camera is keeping me sane in my solitude. I've been spending more and more time confiding in it. It's been a rough night. A windy one too, as always. As I'm explaining out loud to the camera lens what a risk it would be for an iceberg to bang up against the hull again, there's a loud, heavy thud. I spring up and out of my sleeping bag and I'm out on deck in a flash— literally, I guess, because I don't even take the time to pull on a pair of pants. I'm standing there, half-naked in my boxers and slippers, shivering in the cold, and I can't believe my eyes. An iceberg has lodged itself right beside us, and in the swell *Yvinec* is now crashing repeatedly into it. I'm worried the hull is going to cave in; I know there are still a few weak spots in its side, even after the overhaul in Trinidad. I have to act fast. I have to pull up the anchor chain right now. I can't even see the end of the deck in my flashlight beam. With every ounce of strength I have, I haul up sixty feet of chain link by link. Fortunately it's enough for us to clear the iceberg.

My bare legs are numb from the cold. But I think we've managed to avoid the worst. Now all I can do is pray that this damn wind doesn't turn. When I'm back at last in the warmth of the cabin, there are stalactites dropping from my nose. It's 5:30 in the morning, and I'm absolutely wiped. I hope the hull isn't too badly damaged. The depth-sounder is acting up and must have taken a hit. For now, all I can do is wait for the dim light of day so I can head out again and assess the damage. So I pull on some socks, long johns, and a sweater, and I hunker down in my sleeping bag.

Even once I feel warm again, I can't sleep soundly, so I decide to go out on deck again to check that everything is all right. The iceberg is still there. It hasn't moved. It's about thirty feet away from the boat. But now there are lots more icebergs around as well. Jeez, they're everywhere. I don't like this at all.

Off we go again, this time to the other side of the bay. It should be more sheltered there. At least, that's what I'm hoping.

Here, we'll be sheltered from the west winds, which are the worst. They're the ones that send the icebergs into the bay and push us toward the shore. Now that we're safe, I have to get some rest. I've been keeping watch for several nights in a row. If things get even more difficult, I won't be in any state to manage. I have to gather my strength.

I keep waking up every fifteen minutes. My mind is still on alert, and I can't relax. So I grab my flashlight and head outside to get some air. And guess what? There's another iceberg beside us.

Seriously? Where the heck did this one come from? I can't believe what I'm seeing. And this one's a big deal. It must be at least fifteen feet high! All I want is a good night's sleep. Is that really too much to ask, just one night?

Yet again, I haul up the anchors and start the engine. It's 11:30 at night, and I've barely slept in the last two days. I can't take this anymore. It's all very well to tell myself that Monique and I will share some amazing adventures out here, but I can't see them happening anytime soon. I'm beginning to wonder what happened to all the fun we were supposed to be having by now.

It's past eleven when I poke my head outside the next morning. And the wind has dropped completely. What a relief! Finally I'm going to be able to head out fishing. I've been waiting long enough. There's more good news: my depth-sounder has started working again, so now I can keep an eye on the water level. It's dangerous for *Yvinec* to go any shallower than ten feet, because the keel might snag and we might end up running aground.

I put on my rice to cook and open up Monique's coop; then we have breakfast together and I get my fishing gear ready. It's not exactly warm inside the cabin. In the daytime, the temperature generally stays between fifty and sixty degrees Fahrenheit, but at night it can drop to as low as forty. I pull on my dry suit, grab my fishing line, hooks, and lures, jump into the dinghy, and off I go to catch my dinner!

Except I'm not going anywhere. The outboard motor won't start. And I'm not exactly a mechanic. Maybe it's a dirty spark plug? I lift the lid off the motor, take one of the plugs out, and—go figure—it fires to life. I put the spark plug back in place without cutting the motor, and give myself an electric shock. So

I turn it off, clean the other plug, and ... nothing. For once, the sea is glassy, and I could finally get out there and fish—but I can't. I'm furious. I don't want to take a chance and row the dinghy out there. It's too risky; I might drift too far away. And I can't see myself fishing from a stand-up paddleboard! In any case, I've missed my chance; it's already getting dark again. I climb back aboard the boat and admit defeat.

It's all very well to sever all communication, but I wish I had a weather forecast—at least then I would know what I was in for. I've had my fair share of surprises and setbacks. But I only have myself to blame; I wanted total isolation, and that's what I've got. It's the same with food. I've eaten nothing but rice and eggs for the last three weeks. Whatever possessed me to force this onto myself?

Wind, wind, and more damn wind is all we get for the next six days. When it blows from the west, it comes into the bay and causes chaos, with the rolling swell and the ice forming around the boat. Not to mention the constant fear that an iceberg will slam into us and tear a hole in the hull. I can't believe we're still afloat. It's surprising how well we're holding up. My father must be keeping an eye on us from up above.

When I check the condition of the hull, I see there's a fair bit of water in the bilge. So, I turn on the bilge pump and, dammit, it dies as soon as it gets going. I figure the drainage hole in the hull must be backed up with ice. I hop into the dinghy and tap away the ice inside the hole with a hammer and screwdriver. Then I turn on the pump again. Still nothing. I put on some water to boil and pour I-don't-know-how-many pots of steaming water down the hose. But it's still blocked. I give up. As the temperature keeps dropping, it's only going to get blocked again anyway. I'll take care of it when everything starts to melt in the spring. In the meantime, I'm going to have to bail out the bilge myself every day.

Just to recap, my father has died, it's dark all the time, I can't go out fishing, the weather is abysmal, there's ice everywhere inside the boat, the bilge pump isn't working, the outboard motor is toast—oh, and the sink drain and the bow docking light have gone kaput as well.

Thank goodness I have Monique. If there's anything that's keeping me going, it's her. We've built up a real rapport. She makes me laugh, as much as she gets on my nerves—it's maddening when she knocks over a glass of water onto my computer keyboard or when she takes a dump in one of my sweaters. When she does that, I give her a stern talking-to. I tell her I'm going to sprinkle her with cumin and bay leaves and eat her for dinner. "Mmm, you're going to be delicious," I say. I'm joking, of course. I'd be out of my mind to trade her company and her eggs for a chicken dinner or two.

To be honest, we don't quarrel too much. I've started talking to her. She's a better listener than my video camera. When I'm feeling down, I share my worries with her. I tell her all about the fishing trips I went on with my father when I was a little boy. And I tell her that will never happen again. Now, my father is with us, but we can't see him. Monique knows when I'm feeling sad. Animals can sense things like that. Better than people can. She talks back to me in her own way with lots of little bock-bock-bwawking sounds. Momo is my little ray of sunshine here on the boat. I don't know what I'd do without her.

I still can't quite believe my father is gone. I think it'll only sink in when the ice melts and I sail away from here. Or when I want to pick up the phone and call him. My sister told me he was in his car when it happened, in the parking lot across from his little island of Yvinec, waiting for the low tide so he could drive across. He didn't have the time to make it home to pass away in his happy place. Sometimes it feels deflating that he won't get to see what I've achieved, that I'll never see the pride in his eyes again. But I'm not giving up now. I'm going to keep on fighting.

For sure, I have my down days, but I'm still pretty happy out here. When the wind drops, when there's a bit of light, when the sea starts to freeze and I can see the bluish icebergs emerging from the mirror-like surface in the distance, it's magical. When it's snowed overnight, I wake to a dusting of white over the ice and the mountaintops, and the sky is a celebration of pink, orange, and yellow in watercolor. And on a clear night, the Northern Lights dance across the stars like ghosts in neon cloaks.

These last few days, my life has felt like a Hollywood movie. You know, one of those dramas about a prisoner in solitary confinement. For the first month or so, the guy spends all his time in a dark cell being mistreated, hit with a club, and having trays of prison food thrown in his face. Then one day, his cell door is thrown open and he gets to stretch his legs outside, feel the sunlight on his face, and eat regular food again. That's what it feels like for me right now. The nights are brutal and almost never-ending. I'm waiting for the pack ice to form so that I can leave the boat and go out fishing, and eat something other than rice and eggs. The sun will eventually come back again.

I'm trying not to think about food. I'll drive myself crazy if I start imagining a plate full of spaghetti carbonara laden with cream and bacon. I've been reading Otto Nordenskjöld's *Antarctica: Or, Two Years Amongst the Ice of the South Pole*, the amazing story of an early twentieth-century expedition to Antarctica, but I've been skipping the parts about the explorers divvying up their rations to stay alive. Just reading the words butter, ham, and bread is enough to make my head spin.

Sometimes, I worry I'm going mad. I'm talking to a chicken and grooming my facial hair with a fork. I do have a mirror on board, but I haven't been using it. Out here, appearance is the least of my concerns. Last night, when I was watching the latest video footage I've taken, I couldn't believe how different I look with long hair and my polar explorer's beard. The upshot is that it's keeping me warm. I've got a few chilblains on my cheeks, but the skin under my beard is just fine. All that fuzz makes for good protection from the elements. When I'm done detangling my beard, I throw any stray hairs into the stove, where they sizzle away and smell strangely appetizing, like roast pork. It's torture, I tell you!

It must be a little after eleven in the morning when I see it. Heading out on deck, I can suddenly sense something moving really close to the boat. Maybe it's just a chunk of ice. Maybe I'm hallucinating. I keep my eyes trained on the same spot, and again, there's a ripple in the water. There it is, a seal! With the cutest little round head and whiskers. Instinctively, I think "meat" and "dinner" and duck down into the cabin to fetch my rifle. When I come back out, the seal is still there. Just as it pokes its head out of the water, I tuck the butt of the rifle into the crook of my shoulder and take aim.

I'm about to pull the trigger. The seal isn't moving a muscle. It's just looking at me, not a hint of fear in its eyes. Its handsome face is right in my sights. I lower the rifle. I can't seem to think straight. I pull myself together, tuck the rifle into my shoulder again, and take aim. If I land this seal, I'll have enough meat for the next two months. But still the seal doesn't move. It could dive and swim away, but it doesn't. It just looks at me with puppy-dog eyes, and says, "Come on, you're not going to do that to me, are you?"

It really spoke to me, I swear.

I can't bring myself to pull the trigger. I'd never forgive myself. This is the seal's home. I'm the stranger here, intruding on its territory. I don't have the right to do this. Or the heart. No, I'm not going to do it. I let the seal swim away and put away my rifle. I'm really going to have to up my fishing game.

It's three in the morning and I haven't slept a wink. I don't get it; I don't usually have any trouble sleeping. Maybe a little music will help—a DJ friend in St. Barts made a playlist for me, so I put that on. These tunes aren't exactly lullabies—and electronic dance music isn't usually my thing—but it brings back memories of a place back home called L'Albatros. It was the first nightclub in France to have a rotating dance floor! I used to get a kick out of making all the girls think I was drunk, even though I'd never touched a drop of alcohol. My father used to joke that that was my only redeeming quality. My buddies would often ask me how I managed to have a good time without drinking. I swear I had just as much fun as they did, and the next morning I would always have a clear head when I went out to pull up my lobster traps.

In spite of being so tired, weary, and discouraged, and in spite of the blues that come and go, the time seems to go by pretty quickly. I don't really pay much attention to what day it is. I just check my watch to see what time it is to make sure I don't miss the daylight hours. It doesn't really matter whether it's Tuesday or Sunday, whether it's the fifth or the fourteenth of December. But still, I'm amazed when I open my laptop to see that it's December 19! Already? Christmas is six days from now, and in two weeks' time it'll be the New Year. I don't really know how Monique and I are going to celebrate. In France, we stay up late on Christmas Eve, so it'll be quite something to experience nearly twenty-four hours of nighttime up here. If only we could sit out on the pack ice, tucking into some delicious grilled lobster, but the ice around us is still moving.

I've managed to repair the dinghy's outboard motor, at least. I rubbed the spark plugs clean, checked the fuel level, put it all back together, and it fired up just fine. Maybe it was just too cold the day it broke down, or maybe there was too much salt in there. I have no idea. Either way, I'm very relieved. As long as we're in open water, that dinghy is crucial to my survival.

DECEMBER 20

I wake up at eleven in the morning and cast an eye out the cabin window as usual. Imagine my surprise to see a dull grayish film coating the surface of the sea! No, it isn't snow—if it were, I wouldn't be able to see anything out the window.

Outside, what I discover is an incredibly beautiful sight. The ice has formed around the boat and all the way to the shore, stretching as far as I can see. At last! This is what I've been waiting for! Finally, the pack ice is setting in. A whole month I've been waiting for this to happen, scanning the horizon, wondering when it's going to materialize, and, all of a sudden, here it is. It looks like we're going to get our Arctic winter at last! I can't believe how suddenly it's happened. Yesterday, there was only a bit of ice drifting across the bay. And now today, we're in a sea of ice.

I'm amazed to see this childhood dream of mine taking shape before my eyes. The pack ice seems to be getting thicker by the hour, as if by magic. I use my *touk* to check, and it's already a couple of inches thick. In three or four days, it should be solid enough for me to walk right out there. I learned the golden rule from one of the fishermen in Saqqaq: as long as you can move your boat, you can't walk on the ice. And right now, inside the cabin, I can still feel a swaying motion. At first glance, it might look like we're well and truly stuck, but if you look more closely, it's easy to see there's still some water between the hull and the ice. I guess I'll have to be patient a little while longer.

In the meantime, I just have to stay on board the boat and find a way to kill the time. I watch Monique poke her beak into everything—without finding a single thing to peck at. The poor thing! What's she going to do when I head out on the ice with my kitesurfing gear and my skis? Maybe I could bring her along for the ride? She did come windsurfing with me in the Caribbean. But this isn't the tropics; it's the North Pole.

What if I made her a sweater? Now there's a good idea to keep me busy! What could I make it with? Because obviously I don't know how to knit—and even if I did, I don't have any wool or needles. But I do have plenty of things that are already knitted— the toasty warm gloves and socks I picked up in Halifax. I wanted to make sure I had lots to keep me going, so I must have bought at least ten pairs of green woolen gloves. I think I can sacrifice one for Momo. I lay the gloves out on a chopping board, pick up a sharp kitchen knife, and slice the gloves open in two. All I'll have to do is stitch the pieces together, leaving a hole in the front for Monique's head, and another in the rear for her you-know-what. After that, it'll be easy for me to cut a couple slits in the sides for her wings. I've stitched sails back together, so I should be able to handle a job like this. But before doing any of that, I grab a tape measure and tuck Monique under my arm to take her measurements—like any good tailor would!

Chest circumference: twenty inches. Length: eight inches. Wing width: four inches. And with that, I set about making my chicken a sweater.

Let's just say this is more of a tinkering job than a work of haute couture. It doesn't look like much, but once Monique is wearing it, no one will notice the imperfections. And the main thing is that it will keep her warm.

It keeps me busy for quite a while. Getting her to try it on for size proves to be a little tricky at first. Then she relaxes a little and lets me pull in onto her. I manage to take a few very funny photos before she starts to contort herself and pick and pull at the wool with her beak and her claws. I end up taking the sweater off her back before she wrecks it completely. She's lucky I'm in a good mood today. But I'm not sure I feel like repeating the experience. Too bad. I thought she looked really pretty in her little handmade sweater. Plus, I've always thought redheads look good in green!

That night, for the first time since we arrived in the bay, I go to bed without a care. I'm looking forward to measuring the thickness of the ice tomorrow morning. But if there's one thing I've learned over the course of this adventure, it's to never cry victory. When you're up against nature, nature always wins. Nature always has the last word.

The pack ice only ends up holding for two days. The next night, the wind blows hard. Some of the gusts clock in at a solid thirty-five, even forty knots. From my berth, I can feel the boat shifting. The ice is damping the movement. It feels like we're stuck in mud.

The swell has started to form, and it's rolling beneath the thin crust of sea ice. The ice is starting to crack into big pieces. The motion of the waves is pitching the pieces up and down, and they're gaining momentum in the troughs between the peaks. The ice isn't very thick, so it won't do much damage when it hits the boat, but if a growler or a small iceberg were to hit the hull with the same force, it would be a serious problem. What am I supposed to do? There's still too much ice for me to raise anchor.

By the morning of day three, the wind has dropped a little. In the light of dawn, I climb up to the first spreader—a horizontal support bar about halfway up the mast. The view from up there is incredible. The entire expanse of sea ice has cracked apart. It looks like a giant jigsaw puzzle.

DECEMBER 24

The wind has started to blow again, and the pieces of the puzzle are jiggling around, bumping into one another like bumper cars at the fairground. These are hefty slabs of ice, nothing like the thin plates I saw the other day. Those would crack apart under the slightest impact. These are much thicker, and they're as hard as rock. Things weren't good before, but now the bay is a living hell. And *Yvinec*, Monique, and I are caught in the middle of it all. We could find ourselves crushed between two of these huge blocks at any time. That's the kind of risk we're running. The anchor chains are encased in ice and can't hold the weight of the boat anymore, not now that it's ballasted with all the chunks of pack ice stuck to the hull. We're drifting toward the shore. I can hear the chain groaning. I can feel the anchors slipping. The boat is definitely moving. Outside, the visibility is zero. The wind is howling a solid thirty knots, and it's blowing all the snow off the summits and sending it swirling around in squalls. Powerless, all I can do is glue my eyes to the depth-sounder and try to estimate how far away we are from the shallows. The needle is starting to go down, first from sixty-five to sixty feet, then fifty, and on it goes, until it reads twelve feet. It won't be long before we run aground.

It's time for me to put on my dry suit and grab my dry bags. In one of them is my survival kit, with the tent and freeze-dried food. I've filled the other with everything else I'm going to need: sleeping bag, camp stove, clothing, rice for me, grain for Monique, and headlamp, among other things. Then I sit down on the edge of my berth with the bags at my feet, hold Monique in my lap, and wait.

And there you have it: we've run aground. But we're not leaving the boat, not yet. We're still in the ice, and there's no water around us, so we're not sinking. That's the golden rule in the Navy: as long you're still afloat, you don't abandon ship. We're lucky our sailboat has a steel hull. If it were made of plastic, we'd have sunk by now. Yes, we've run aground, but at least we're warm and sheltered from the wind. I have no idea what's going to happen next. Unlike what most of us are led to believe, running aground isn't necessarily the end of the world. It all depends on the terrain—whether the bottom is rocky or sandy—the waves, the wind, the current, and the tide. I'm still waiting. Despite my natural optimism, possible scenarios start running through my mind. I imagine the water rising up to the cabin windows, or I envision the pack ice setting in again—blocking every way out of the cabin and trapping us inside the boat, or I picture the temperature dropping and the boat leaning over so hard the stove won't stay upright. Months later, the local fishermen are going to find a sailor and a chicken frozen to death.

Dark thoughts are the last thing you need when you're up shit creek. If you start to lose hope, that's when you're completely screwed. Success is dependent on attitude. You have to stay positive. Right now, the plan has to be to somehow get back afloat and get the hell out of here.

Holed up warm and cozy inside the cabin, Monique and I can hear the wind whistling outside. The boat heels to the side, then rights herself before heeling over once more. Everything is shaking. Books are falling from the shelves and dishes are rattling in the sink. Through the cabin windows, we see vast sheets of water and ice crashing over us. It's terrifying. The sound is deafening. It pains me to think what this is doing to the boat. I'm sure everything must be getting completely trashed.

In my lap, Monique isn't moving a muscle. She looks up at me, and I can tell she's worried too. She knows something isn't quite right. I give her feathers a gentle rub and tell her that everything is going to be all right, that we're going to be just fine. By reassuring her, I'm reassuring myself too. Oh, poor Momo, what have I roped you into? She'll never survive if we have to abandon ship.

We aren't completely out of luck, though. I get the sense we've managed to completely avoid the rocks, and we're resting on the sand. The next morning, that best-case scenario is confirmed. The wind has turned, and now, thanks to the high tide, we're afloat again. I fire up the engine and we motor away to cast anchor again in a good sixty feet of water. That night, when I'm lying snug and cozy in my bunk, I look out through the cabin window and smile up at the stars.

That's how Monique and I ring in our second Christmas together. Last year we were celebrating in St. Barts, and I was out on deck in boardshorts watching the spectacular fireworks. Today, we have nothing fancy to celebrate with. One of us is chowing down on his rice, and the other is pecking at her grain.

The year is nearly over. It's December 28. We've been here freezing our butts off for more than a month already, and there's still no pack ice to speak of. The wind keeps blowing all night long—that's more than twenty hours. The conditions just haven't been right for the pack ice to form properly. I can't leave the boat anymore and my fresh water reserves are running out. I've finished the container I keep inside, and out on deck, I have three chunks of ice left, which will keep us going for another week at most. We're going to have to resort to rationing. I could scrape up a bit of snow that's fallen on the deck, a couple of inches or so, but it tends to fly away with the slightest gust of wind, and it's not exactly the cleanest either.

Two days later, the sea freezes over again.

But then during the night, the ice breaks up, and I'm jolted awake by a bang, and then another, when it crashes against the hull. I'm not stressing out this time, though—there's nothing I can do, so I might as well wait it out. We're drifting, to be sure. Toward the shore, whether we like it or not. I check the depth-sounder. There's only three feet of water beneath the boat. Yep, we're beached. Again.

It's six in the morning on New Year's Eve and *Yvinec* is heeled over about forty degrees on her port side. The depth-sounder is telling me we're in forty-five feet of water, but still we've run aground. We must have drifted free from the shore overnight, only to hit a sandbar. The wind is blowing thirty knots, the water temperature is a frigid thirty degrees Fahrenheit, and the air temperature is minus twenty-two. With the wind chill, it feels closer to minus forty.

I'm powerless. All I can do is try to stay calm. Our fate lies in the hands of Mother Nature. We can only count on the wind, the tide, and the current to get us out of here. There's a lot riding on the strength of the boat too. Once again, I have the survival kit at the ready. I'm not sure we'll be quite so lucky a second time. Unless there are greater forces at work. I'm not usually a believer, but if the situation calls for it . . .

Out on deck, I can see big, fat snowflakes falling through the beam of my flashlight. It's so cold, I can't feel the tips of my fingers at the end of my gloves. We're beached about sixty feet from the shore. And there's a nasty-looking growler sitting barely six feet away. Maybe I can give it a push. First with one foot, then the other, I step out gingerly onto a slab of ice beside the boat. It seems solid enough to me. Hanging on to the edge of the boat, I inch my way around the boat, camera in hand.

Suddenly, the slab of ice I'm standing on breaks loose and starts to drift away. I only just manage to scramble back aboard in time. What a stupid thing for me to do. I really can't afford to take risks like that. Seriously—in these temperatures, if I fell into the water without my dry suit, I don't think I'd last very long.

It's New Year's Eve, and it's already midnight back home in France. Everyone is partying over there. I think about my family and friends, warm and cozy in their homes, popping champagne corks and having a great time. Cries of "Happy New Year!" must be ringing out in their living rooms, between their cell phones, and on the radios and TVs blaring away in the background. I wonder if any of them have spared a thought for me. I don't suppose they could imagine me sitting here in my bright orange dry suit, with my emergency grab bags at my feet, ready to abandon my boat for the umpteenth time.

For thirty-five days, I've been holed up in this damn bay with nothing to do but suffer my way through one ordeal after the other. I came out here to live a dream, and it's turned out to be a nightmare. I'm willing to make whatever sacrifices—and end up losing forty pounds if I must—but I don't want to lose my boat. My whole life is on this boat. This boat is the reason why I busted my ass halfway across the world and left my life at home behind when I was eighteen years old. I have this boat to thank for bringing Monique into my life. So please, whatever happens, don't let my boat go down.

I should have listened to the people I met in Saqqaq—Uno, Adam, Matias, and the others. But I had this idea in my head, and I refused to let it go. If I could go back now, I would spend more time asking myself the right questions before I took the crazy risks.

I think about my father. I've never been afraid of death—and I'm definitely not worried about it now that I know I won't be alone up there when my time comes. I'm not in any kind of hurry—I love life, and there are still lots of things I want to do and plenty of adventures I want to experience.

To pass the time, I decide to tidy up the cabin. When I come across some brightly colored paper garlands from St. Barts, I slip one of them over my head and another around Monique's neck, then I turn on the video camera and pretend that everything is okay. "Happy New Year, my sweet Momo!"

Outside, a snowstorm is raging. Things are no better or worse. We're still in limbo. Tomorrow's another day.

I've had a terrible night, constantly waking to the sounds of the boat bumping aground. Between nightmares and keeping watch, I've lost count of how many times I thought the hull had caved in under the relentless attacks from the swell. I might have worried *Yvinec* was a bit of a rust bucket, but she's turning out to be a tough one who can really hold her own.

This morning, the tide has come in, the wind has dropped, and my berth is quietly swaying. The boat isn't listing to the side the way it was last night, and I can feel a slight rocking movement. It sure looks as if *Yvinec* has righted herself. I tug a hat over my ears before I head out on deck. A good amount of the ice has given way to open water. The tide is high, and the wind has set us free. It's a miracle. I can pull up the anchor. And just like that, gently we glide away in the light of the Arctic dawn.

Today is January 1, 2016. And it looks like the new year is off to a good start.

~~~~~~~~~~

I CAN'T BELIEVE it's noon already! It was about time I woke up. Paranoid that we would start drifting again overnight, I eventually managed to fall asleep at around four in the morning. I haven't even unpacked my emergency grab bags.

Imagine my surprise when I look outside and see that everything has completely frozen again! The pack ice has formed, and it looks pretty solid. There's not an inch of open water in sight. It's crazy how quickly things can change. As soon as the wind dies, everything freezes. To top it all off, there's a brilliant blue sky. It's so beautiful; I think I feel happy at last! I don't want to get carried away, but I really want to believe the pack ice is here to stay. I think we've earned it.

The days are gradually getting longer. There's a little more light each day, but it's still a dim kind of light; the sun is nowhere to be seen. I'm beginning to think the hardest part of this adventure is behind me now. The darkest hour has passed. I've made it through the worst of the weather, the scariest icebergs, the sketchiest pack ice, the running aground, and the death of my father. Now it's time for the fun part. The sun is coming back, the ice is going to be solid enough for me to walk, run, and slide on—and steady enough for me to get the good nights of sleep I desperately need.

I gaze at the shore in contemplation. Over there, we were high and dry only yesterday.

The pack ice is getting thicker by the day. I'm going to have to do something about the dinghy. It's stuck in the ice, and with the pressure, the air chambers might explode. Until now I've been deliberately leaving it afloat, in case there was an emergency and we had to abandon ship.

Meanwhile, the inside of the sailboat cabin is looking a little the worse for wear. The ceiling liner has warped with all the humidity, so I'm going to have to tack it back in place.

JANUARY 7

This morning I wake to a kaleidoscope of color flooding the cabin with scintillating shades of pink, purple, and orange. When I stick my head out of the cabin window, I feel like I'm in the middle of a great big landscape painting. The whole sky is reflected in one vast shimmering mirror of ice. I hope I can capture the scene on camera; I'd love to have a photo of *Yvinec* with a backdrop like this.

I think the time has come for me to take my first steps on the pack ice! The temptation is too hard to resist. But I'm hesitant. The ice doesn't look super thick. I grab my *touk*, remembering the advice the fishermen gave me: if you can give it two hard hits without breaking through to the water, it's safe. I don't dare hit the ice too hard, but I think it'll be all right.

Trying to tread as lightly as possible, I take long, sliding steps to gently transfer my weight from one leg to the other. I can feel the ice shifting slightly beneath my feet. If it gives way, there's nothing for me to grab onto. There's a rush of adrenaline mixed in with the exhilaration of this all-new experience. I set up my tripod to capture some video of the scene while I take a bunch of photos with my DSLR camera. This feels like a special moment, and I get the sense that a whole different phase of my adventure is beginning. All my doubts have vanished into thin air, and I'm starting to think I could stay here for the rest of my life. It's as if time is standing still.

~~~~~~~

THE NEXT DAY, the pack ice has solidified nicely. The sky has turned a turquoise shade of blue, and so has the ice. Against the sea and the sky, the mountains are shining a brilliant white. There's a breath of wind, but the cold is bearable. The thermometer is indicating seventeen degrees Fahrenheit. This is Monique's chance to discover the pack ice for herself. It's a big moment for her, and for me!

I set her down on the ice and take a few steps back to film the scene with my GoPro. Tentatively, she puts one foot in front, then the other, holding it in midair for a second before she puts it down again. Intrigued by the ice, she starts to peck at it. Then there's a gust of wind behind her that puffs up her feathers like a spinnaker, sending her skating toward me out of control. And I burst out laughing.

Up until now, I've been too scared to fly the drone. I was worried I'd lose it if it ran into trouble in the heavy conditions. But now I can make the most of the nice weather to capture some aerial images. The view from up there is stunning. Plus, it's giving me some useful information about how far the pack ice extends and what kind of condition it's in.

I've spotted a small iceberg not too far away, and I'm going to try to head over there to harvest some ice and replenish my drinking water supply. Last night, we used the last few drops that were left.

I pull on my dry suit and, equipped with my backpack, ice ax, and *touk*, I tie a rope around my waist and pull the paddleboard behind me. Testing the ice with every step, I slowly walk over to the iceberg. The closer I get, the softer the ice is, and soon my *touk* is passing all the way through to the water. I try to use the paddleboard as a bridge, but it keeps slipping off the iceberg. It's so frustrating. It's only three feet away, just out of my reach.

Walking around to the other side, I can see a chunk of ice that's started to break off from the iceberg. I should be able to reach that with my ice ax. My only concern is that it's a little low—I hope it hasn't been blasted too much by the spray, otherwise the water might be too salty to drink when I melt it. The color seems a little dark to me, which isn't very encouraging. I taste it, but in the cold, it's hard to tell if it's all right. Whatever. I don't really have much of a choice, since it's already starting to get dark. I break the chunk into a few smaller pieces so it will fit in my backpack, and head back to the boat.

Back inside the cabin, I'm looking forward to melting the ice and cooking up a tasty plate of rice, with an egg on the side. I'm starving. It's done me good to get some fresh air and stretch my legs.

Verdict: the water is salty. It's gross. I guess I'll just be boiling myself an egg. In a pot of seawater. Yum—a nice, tasty, soft-boiled egg. Four and a half minutes, and it's done. I'll have to do without my daily portion of rice. Rice cooked in seawater is terrible. Believe me, I've tried it. Plus, it makes you thirsty. I don't have anything left to drink, and it's already dark.

Tomorrow, I'll go ashore and get some snow instead. Fortunately, Monique still has a bit of water left in her bowl. I'm hoping she's laid an egg, because I don't have any left in reserve. This morning there was nothing in her coop, but maybe she's laid one since—she does most days, but now not as predictably. I guess the lack of sunlight must be throwing her schedule off.

I've been topping up the heating tank with diesel every day, about two and a half gallons. I have to be just as frugal with fuel as I am with water. Right now, based on my calculations, I should have enough to keep the heat going until we're done hibernating.

It turns out Monique hasn't laid an egg for me today. Oh well—I guess I'll eat tomorrow instead. I'm hungry, but I'm also tired. As I get myself ready for bed, I think about an old French proverb that says "sleeping is as good as eating." We'll see if that's true.

Even though I've eaten nothing today, I still brush my teeth—with saltwater. It tastes really bad. Luckily, I still have a bottle of mouthwash. It stings my tongue a little, but at least it rinses the salt away, and it smells clean. I bought it for an abscess in one of my wisdom teeth—that happened just before we came into the bay for the winter, while I was shuttling my fuel drums from the village. I was in so much pain, I couldn't eat a thing. Apparently some sailors have gone so crazy with pain they've pulled out their own teeth. One of the solo sailors competing in the Vendée Globe race even stitched his own tongue back together when he sliced it open. Strangely enough, neither of those options sounded very appealing to me. Thanks to the antibiotics I had in my onboard first aid kit, the toothache soon passed.

I slip into my sleeping bag and close my eyes. Tonight, *Yvinec* is resting beneath a moonless sky.

In the morning, I have to act fast to make the most of the daylight and fetch some drinking water. The shore is only about three hundred yards away. It's a little overcast today, but the visibility is good. This shouldn't take me too long. I'm enjoying the exercise. It's good to be able to walk outside, breathe easily, and feel the wind on my face.

I'm nearly there. But before I reach the shore, there's still a short stretch of unfrozen water to cross. I hadn't anticipated that possibility. I leave the paddleboard out on the ice and, holding my backpack tight, I jump from slab to slab, just like I did back home on the beach when I hopped from one stone to another, trying not to get my feet wet. Except that here, the stones are moving—and the stakes are a little higher. But I make it to dry land safe and sound. This is the first time in fifty days or so that I've set foot on terra firma! I walk a good distance from the water's edge to find the best snow, well away from the ocean spray. And then, I stuff my backpack with big handfuls of it. I can see the first quarter moon in the sky now. The light is already getting dimmer, and it looks like the fog is rolling in over the ice. There's no time to waste. I haven't eaten a thing for about thirty hours, and my stomach is growling.

I make it back to my paddleboard after another intrepid balancing act across the slabs of ice. I drop the backpack full of snow onto the board, tie the rope around my waist, and pull it behind me like a sled. As I'm about to turn and walk back to the boat, I'm struck by the silence. I pause for a few seconds, *touk* in hand, waiting, listening. Between the ice and the shore, the sea ripples without a sound. And as I turn away from the shore and look out at the mist sweeping in on the vast frozen landscape, *Yvinec* is there, standing still in the ice—a familiar, reassuring presence.

Before I set off, I cry out, "Hey, Momo, can you hear me? I've found us some nice cold water. It's time for dinner! How about one of those delicious fresh eggs of yours?"

My voice echoes off the mountains on the shore. A bird—who knows where it came from—takes flight with a big flap of its wings. I've frightened it away. As I walk back to the boat, I hear nothing but the sound of my heavy breath, the weary crunching of my steps, and the scraping of the paddleboard on the ice behind me.

I've stashed a good amount of meltwater in the big blue container I always leave beside the stove.

I saw an animal running along the shoreline this morning. I zoomed in with my camera for a closer look. It was a red fox, with dark fur—just like the ones we see at home. I wish I could have gotten a little closer and made a new friend. Maybe he'd never seen a human before—when I called out to him, he sat down, looked over toward me, and ran off. I followed him for a long time with my eyes, until he disappeared behind the mountains.

Now the pack ice has set in, I'm hoping to see all kinds of animals: caribou, Arctic foxes, hares, and maybe even wolves. Most of all, I'm hoping to see a bear, even though I know I'd probably have to be much farther north for that.

I have a confession to make about my dinghy. I've done something really stupid. I was having such a hard time prying it free from the ice, I used a plank of wood to get some leverage—and ended up puncturing one of the air chambers. I'm furious with myself. I've tried patching it up, but the glue won't stick properly in the cold. I've given the outboard motor a cleaning, rinsed the dinghy with fresh water, deflated it, and stuffed it into the bathroom compartment I've been using as a storage locker.

Now I'm keen to free up some space inside the cabin, because I can barely move in here. I put my dry bags away, along with the tent, camp stove, and all my other survival gear. When I'm done, the port and starboard berths in the stern are packed full of stuff, and it's much lighter inside the main cabin. I've also freed up some space on deck by offloading the twelve drums of diesel onto the ice beside the boat. *Yvinec* is about 1,300 pounds lighter now! The ice is pretty solid and must be a good four or five inches thick—but to be safe, I've tied them up with a line. I've also offloaded the paddleboard and a few other odds and ends, to relieve some pressure and let the boat sit a little higher in the ice.

Now I can set about cleaning the hull. I have to give myself a kick in the butt, though; it's already four in the afternoon, and it's dark and cold outside. I heat a big pot of seawater, and then, for two solid hours in the light of my headlamp, I scrub, wash, scrape, and rinse away all the grime. When the job is done, the boat is squeaky clean all over. Now, I can fly the flag of my homeland with pride, and rest assured that I'll make a good impression on any fox or bear that happens to be passing by!

JANUARY 11

I can't find the words to describe the beauty of the landscape this morning. That's surprising, because every day now, I feel like I'm seeing the most amazing things I've ever laid eyes on. This is the first time it's snowed since the pack ice set in—just a couple of inches and a little contrast in the light is all it takes to wash everything in shades of pink.

This is what I came here to find. I think about all the people back home—commuting to and from work on the subway, sitting in traffic jams in their cars, and spending all day in front of a computer screen, and then I call out to Monique in her coop. "Hey Momo, life is pretty sweet, isn't it?"

I can see fresh tracks in the snow. Maybe it's a fox? Perhaps it smelled Monique and came over for a closer look. Whatever it is, I bet it's never seen a hen before!

I head back into the galley and cook up my rice for the day. Then I open up Monique's coop to discover a fresh egg in her nice, clean bedding. I fill her bowl with some well-earned grain, and to show my appreciation, I bring her outside with me for a breath of fresh air. Of course, I take a video of her walking in the snow. Her feet leave little imprints beside the fox's. Surely these must be the first chicken tracks the North Pole has ever seen!

Ah, the pack ice, the blue sky, the snow—and soon the sun will be back. All that's missing now is a nice, tasty fish.

Using my trusty *touk*, I make a hole in the ice, just the way the fishermen in Saqqaq showed me. The ice is rock-hard, and even after chipping away a good four inches, I still don't see any water. For sure, there's no risk of falling through it now. When I've finally made a hole about sixteen inches around, I drop my line into the water to jiggle for fish, like I do back home on my little island. All you have to do is jiggle the line up and down to make the fish think the lure is alive.

Barely five minutes later, I already have a bite! The fish in Greenland sure don't waste any time! That being said, this one's pretty small. And super ugly. A few seconds out of the water and it's already frozen solid. It reminds me of the ultra-venomous stonefish I saw in Australia when I was younger. It isn't exactly appetizing.

I can't risk poisoning myself out here on the ice, so I decide to use this as bait instead. I slice the fish into little pieces, and try my luck again. Eventually, I call it a day and head back inside empty-handed.

Normally I fall fast asleep as soon as I close my eyes. That's one of my strengths. But since we've been stuck in the ice, I've been going to bed early, around ten, and at three, four, or sometimes even five in the morning, I'm still wide awake. There's too much running through my mind. I'm already thinking about where I want to go next: the legendary Northwest Passage, which connects the Atlantic Ocean to the Pacific across Canada's Far North. It's only passable for a few weeks each year during the Arctic summer—the rest of the year, it's frozen solid. Plans are stacking up high in my mind. I'll need to fix up the boat; the hull is looking pretty battered. But I'm kind of short on cash. The great thing about being out here in the ice is that it's not costing me a cent! I'm also excited about all the fun things to do while I'm here: skiing, hiking, kite skiing, and snow windsurfing, just for starters!

A few hours ago I was exhausted, and now I feel ready to tackle a whole new day. What's going on? Ever since I set sail from Brittany two years ago, I've slept on my boat every night— without the slightest hint of insomnia. Now that we're encased in the pack ice, I've been able to get off the boat and work off the stress of the first few weeks, so that can't be the problem.

Come to think of it, maybe that's what's wrong: my boat is standing still. There's no motion, no rocking. It's as if I'm sleeping on land. I'm just not used to it anymore.

Almost every night, I get to watch a spectacular show through the cabin window as the Northern Lights dance and shimmer in long streaks of neon green across the sky. This is the North Pole version of a movie theater, and it's simply breathtaking.

For the last few days, sleep has been the least of my worries. The big problem now is the heat. The stove is puffing out so much smoke it's making my eyes water. That's not all: it's giving me a headache, it's making me cough, and the smell is unbearable. When the wind turned west, the stove hood blew right open with a bang that made me nearly jump out of my skin, sending flames licking into the air. It's happened a few times. It's dangerous, especially if it happens when I'm out and about. To be safe, I should be turning it off every time I leave the boat. The only thing is, if I turn it off, the cabin temperature drops by about ten degrees every hour. Tonight, I've had to turn it off and open the cabin window to get rid of the smoke. It's burning diesel, so it would otherwise be the perfect recipe to choke to death. Frankly, I'd rather be cold.

When I wake up the next morning, I manage to light the stove again without any trouble. This really isn't the time for it to break down! I don't think I'd be able to repair it. I don't have a single spare part.

It's been snowing nonstop for the last few days, but today the weather is beautiful. It's a great day for us to get outside and have some fun. Monique is perched on my shoulder, and we're looking out at the glistening snow-capped summits and the shadows beneath. The sun isn't far away now. Just a few more days and we'll be feeling its rays on our faces again. I've realized that not seeing the sun for a while can really get you down. If we climbed up the first hill here, we would see it, but I don't want to keep Monique out for long in this cold.

~~~~~~~~~

EVERY DAY I go out fishing, but I haven't caught a thing since I hooked that weird little fish the very first time. I've been using it as bait, but apparently, even its own kind don't find it appetizing. Still, every morning, even if it's windy or snowing, I prepare my lines with the greatest of care. I love the ritual. It reminds me of my life back home, on my little island. Then I head out onto the ice to dig as many as six holes. It's a long, exhausting job. I set one line per hole, and go back to the boat. I've given up jigging for fish for now, because after a while I find I can't feel my hands. When I go to pull up my lines a few hours later, the holes have already started to freeze over. So I have to dig again, just to get the lines out. And what do I always find? That's right—nothing at all.

Today, there's a stiff breeze blowing, but *Yvinec* isn't heeling over at all—because she's stuck in the ice, of course. It's a strange feeling, but it's also quite enjoyable. I can hear the wind howling and the shrouds whistling. The wind generator is going full tilt, and we've got thirteen volts of power output. It's a good time to charge my laptop. My AIS tracking system tells me there are two boats eighteen nautical miles away. This is exciting news! Through the cabin window I can just make out the lights in the distance. I turn my eyes back to the screen and click on one of the boats for more info. It's a seventy-five-foot fishing boat named *Aleqa*, moving at a speed of 4.9 knots. That's not very fast. There must be some ice out there.

It's kind of hard to believe: here we are, encased in ice, and, just a few miles away, there are two boats out fishing! There can't be much pack ice outside the entrance to this bay of ours. I'm tempted to call them on my VHF radio—for once, there's another boat within range. I bet they don't even speak English, but I haven't spoken to anyone in weeks, and I'm desperate to hear the sound of another human being's voice.

"*Aleqa, Aleqa?*" I call.

No answer.

"*Aleqa*, this is *Yvinec*. *Aleqa*, this is *Yvinec*. Do you copy?"

"*Aluu, qanorippit?*"

"*Aluu! Ajunngilaq!* Do you speak English?"

"A little . . ."

"Are you fishing?" I ask.

"Oh, we are trying to fish but too much ice, so we are returning to Disko Bay."

"Oh! What did you catch?"

The connection is patchy, so I don't hear the reply. Still, I'm thrilled to be in contact with another boat. English isn't my first language, or theirs, but we manage to understand each other and have a basic conversation.

"Can you see me with your screen? I am from France; I am *Yvinec!*" I continue.

"Oh, I can see you . . ."

"I'm staying here all winter!" I explain.

"Oh . . . You are to stay here for all winter?"

"Yes! Good! *Pik korik!* I can walk on the ice!"

"Okay. . . so . . . enjoy!"

"Yes, *takuss'!* Bye for now!"

I'm eager to get out on the pack ice with my sports gear, now that things have settled down. I need to keep myself occupied, and I want to have some fun. I take my stand-up paddleboard out of its bag, remove the fins, jump onto the board with a bit of momentum, and—wow!—I slide along the ice . . . for all of six feet. It's fun to mess around, but this isn't exactly the most thrilling of pursuits. How can I make it more exciting? I know; I'll tie a rope to the boat, lay it out on the ice as far as I can, carry the board to the end of the rope and jump on, then pull myself along the rope to gather some speed. Um, no. That's not very exciting either. I try to run with the board, then let it go and jump on as if I'm skateboarding. Nope, that's no good either. No power plus no speed equals no fun.

The time is starting to feel long. I can't wait to see the sun again. The darkness is getting me down. And I miss hearing from my family—my mother, my sisters, and their kids. I hope they're all okay.

JANUARY 19

I've climbed up the closest mountain this morning. I wanted to enjoy the view and take some photos. But I see a bad omen on the horizon: the sky is getting darker and darker. I have to scramble my way down as quickly as I can to take shelter. In a matter of minutes, the visibility might be reduced to zero, and I won't be able be able to find my way back to the boat if I'm not careful.

JANUARY 20

What I suspected was going to happen has happened. There's a massive storm raging outside, and the wind is gusting over forty-five knots. But I have to go out and check the state of the ice.

11 AM

The temperature has increased a few degrees. Some of the snow on the pack ice and on the deck has started to melt. The situation is alarming. The pack ice is rolling as the swell passes beneath the surface. If the wind picks up any more, there's a risk the ice might start to break apart. But I refuse to believe it. There's no way that could happen, is there? Surely it's thick enough. Plus, we've already had more than our fair share of storms and misadventures for the winter, haven't we?

12 PM

Tripod and camera in hand, I venture a short distance away to take some photos of *Yvinec*. The wind is swirling the snow off the summits. It's spectacular. All around it's a whirlwind of white. My boat is heeling in the ice. Its foundation is weakened. The wind is really howling now. It blows the tripod over, and the camera hits the ice. I take a few steps farther to capture the boat from a different angle. And it freaks me out to see the long cracks streaking across the pack ice. Tears of rage are welling in my eyes. This can't be possible. We must be cursed.

The visibility is now dropping dangerously. I can't even see the boat anymore. I take a few steps forward, hoping to see a little more clearly. And I breathe a sigh of relief when I see my own boot prints in the snow.

5 PM

I can't put on the heating because of the wind. The temperature inside the cabin is plummeting. It's about thirty-seven degrees Fahrenheit right now. I've insulated all the openings to stop the cold air coming in. My gloves are soaked through and my socks are nowhere close to drying. I'm feeling pretty sorry for myself. I boil some water to warm my hands.

My boat is shaking under the pressure of the ice. It seems the cracks in the crust out there are getting bigger. The pack ice is going to break up; I know it. I can't afford to waste any time. All my fuel drums are out on the ice. I have to haul them back on board.

I can barely stay on my feet, it's blowing so hard. I only just manage to avoid falling overboard. One by one, I haul the drums up onto the deck, just in time. It's a good thing I tied them up. The ice is slamming up against the hull all over now. Will the boat make it through another test of its strength like this?

7 PM

It's thirty-two degrees now—freezing point—and everything inside the boat is predictably frosty. We're trapped in a horrendous snowstorm. The pack ice is exploding into one giant jigsaw puzzle all around us. Sheets of ice are compressing the boat, and I swear everything is buckling before my eyes. The rumbling and the roaring is terrifying. Monique looks at me quizzically. My boat is suffering, and so am I.

The scene is nothing short of apocalyptic.

END OF DAY

How can I not find this completely demoralizing? We're back at square one. Things are just as tough now as they were a few weeks ago. Except this time, I'm in disbelief. How can *Yvinec* possibly emerge unscathed from this critical situation? I listen to the groaning of her steel hull as I imagine it buckling and warping helplessly in the ice. I'm really feeling her pain. My poor boat! She didn't ask for any of this. I could have made my life much simpler by spending the winter nearer to the village, closer to civilization. I would have still learned a lot, and I wouldn't have compromised my boat. But no, I chose to maroon myself here in the middle of nowhere, cut myself off from the world, and leave myself at the mercy of the indomitable Mother Nature.

Now we're surrounded by shifting slabs of ice. Earlier, I gunned the engine and tried to motor through, but it's no use. The ice is stronger than us. We've gone from having sixty feet of depth below us to just twenty. We're going to get beached, again! This will be the third time. I'm getting used to it. Running aground in Greenland in the dead of winter isn't so bad.

Inside the cabin, it's twenty-four degrees Fahrenheit—below freezing. I've pulled out my survival gear again so I have it all at the ready. I'm wearing my dry suit, steeling myself for the moment when *Yvinec* surrenders to the weight of the ice and the water comes gushing in. We won't stand a chance of staying afloat then. We'll have to hop, skip, and jump our way to shore across the floating slabs, and hope the ice doesn't give out. A fall would be fatal.

JANUARY 21

2 AM

I'm gutted. I had it all planned out. I was going to be spending five or six months on the pack ice this winter, and all in all, the ice has held for less than three weeks. Hurriedly, I start to disassemble some of the things on the boat, including the stove. I gather a few planks of wood together; I can always use these to build myself a shelter on the shore. I'll survive—I'm sure of it—but what about Monique?

In the early hours of the morning, the wind starts to shift to the east. It's a miracle. The ice is drifting out to sea now, and we're still afloat. I can't wrap my head around it. I thought we were done for. It looks like my lucky star is still with me.

Later, I'm able to lift the anchor and move the boat. I drop the anchor again in a more comfortable fifty-five feet of depth. We're going to be all right. This seems to be a strange kind of year, though. Maybe this is climate change at work. I'm curious to ask the people in the village what they think when I get back there.

JANUARY 29

It's minus twenty-nine degrees outside, and the pack ice has returned.

I still have an abundance of diesel in reserve, so I might as well use it. I've cranked the heat up to the max, and it's a balmy sixty-eight degrees inside the cabin now. It's a welcome change! I need to get outside and burn off some energy. I'm desperate to go for a run, explore on the shore, and do some more fishing when the weather improves. In the meantime, sitting in the cabin, I'm poring over my world map and plotting my next move. Monique is by my side, and I point to the Northwest Passage. I trace my finger along its length from east to west, from Baffin Bay to the Arctic Ocean, through the Bering Strait between Alaska and Russia, and down the Pacific coast from one country to the next: Canada, the United States, Mexico, Guatemala, El Salvador, Honduras, Nicaragua, Costa Rica—and onward to Panama, the Galápagos Islands, the Pacific Islands, and the Marquesas Islands. Ah, how sweet it will be to sail barefoot in boardshorts again under the blazing sun, catching fish with a troll line trailing in our wake!

But for now, we're in Greenland, holed up in Disko Bay, and this is the coldest we've ever been in our lives.

JANUARY 31

I'm melting my last chunk of ice. I won't get much more than half a gallon of water from it. I've scraped the snow off the deck too, but it's dirty and full of sand. All I can do is pour it through a bunch of old coffee filters and hope for the best.

After she's finished her grain, Monique pecks at the ground. She's pretending there's food there. It keeps her busy, and it's good for her morale. Sometimes I give her a bit of rice as a treat. Not too much though, because I'm worried I might run out. She doesn't have it easy on the boat these days, with the running aground, the cold, the storms, and all the rest, so I figure the least I can do is give her the scrapings from the bottom of the rice pot. I've been a little loose on discipline lately. She's been roaming freely, kicking wood shavings everywhere and trailing her droppings all over the place. At the moment, it's more of a henhouse than a sailboat!

In the early afternoon, I climb the mast to check how the pack ice is looking. I'm reassured by what I see. It seems to be setting in nicely. After ten days stuck on the boat, now I can finally walk out on the ice again. It's about minus thirty right now. It's light from nine in the morning to five in the afternoon, but the sun is still hiding behind the mountain.

I've decided to do some fishing. Still no success. Greenland is supposed to be a fisherman's paradise. I don't know what I'm doing wrong. I've tried everything: using a scoop net, jigging a line, setting a groundline, you name it. And still nothing. I have a net, but I don't know how to lay it out under the ice, and I don't want to catch a seal.

In these temperatures, Monique has to stay inside. If her bright red comb freezes, she'll lose it for sure. As soon as I set foot outside, my beard freezes up and icicles start to form at the tip of my nose.

From time to time, I've been writing in my notebooks—imagine my amazement when I'm rummaging around in the card table for a pen, and find a Kit Kat in there! I can't believe my eyes. It's by far the best surprise I've had in this whole journey to the frozen north. I'm so overcome with emotion, I get tears in my eyes. I'm over the moon. A candy bar! It must have been there since I set sail from Brittany, or maybe the Canary Islands. It's pretty battered and doesn't look like much, but after two months of nothing but rice and eggs, it's a gift from the sky.

FEBRUARY 3

This morning, I went out to pull in my lines, and as always, I came back empty-handed. Fortunately, it's a beautiful day outside. The snowy peaks glow pale pink in the early light, before flaming yellow and orange around noon. It looks like there's a line of fire smoldering just behind the summits. And then a blinding white semicircle of light slowly emerges from the fiery glow. Yes! Here it is at last!

I dash inside the cabin to fetch Monique. "Look over there, Momo! The sun's back!"

Monique is perched calmly on my shoulder, and together we witness the magical rising of the sun over the mountaintops. The first rays fill me with warmth inside and out. It's blinding, but I feel overcome with joy. It's so comforting and energizing to see the sun again. I sing at the top of my lungs and whirl around in circles on the ice, like I'm dancing around a campfire. At last, the polar night is over.

FEBRUARY 10

Since the sun came back, Monique has found a new spot to perch and cluck—just inside the hatch, at the top of the cabin steps. But in the last few days, she hasn't come out on deck. I get the sense she's brooding over something, and it's not an egg. She won't touch her grain, she isn't scratching at the floor, and she's been spending most of the time sleeping in her coop. This isn't normal. I'm worried about her. I don't like seeing her in this state.

At the end of the afternoon, I find her perched up high, on top of my books. She looks pretty cozy there and I don't want to disturb her. To make her more comfortable—and, I must admit, to protect my books—I roll up an old sweater and slip it under her behind, like a cushion.

That night, she falls asleep there with her head tucked under her wing. This is not like her at all. I hope she feels better tomorrow.

FEBRUARY 11

This morning, Monique seems to have perked up a little. She's spent all night up on her perch, and has managed to decorate a dictionary of mine, in spite of the sweater I put under her. I bring up her bowl to her, hoping she hasn't lost her appetite. To my great relief, she dips her beak right in and makes short work of her grain.

When I poke my head outside, I'm thrilled to see fresh snow. There's a stiff breeze blowing; I have to get out there and have some fun. The conditions are perfect to try some snow wind-surfing. I left my windsurf board behind with the kids in the Caribbean, but I can plug a windsurf rig into my stand-up paddle-board. Grinning from ear to ear, I set about rigging my windsurf sail out on the ice. I can't believe I'm about to try this. I feel a bit clumsy rigging the sail with my thick gloves on, and it seems to take me forever. When everything's ready, I attach a GoPro to the nose of the board, and it's time to get this show on the road!

Usually when I go windsurfing, I do a water start: I wade into the water, put one foot on the board and tread water with the other, and hold the rig in the air until the wind fills the sail and pulls me up onto the board. I guess I'm going to have to try a snow start here! I lie down on my back in the snow, holding the rig in the air, and I put one foot onto the board. The wind fills the sail and, as I'm hanging on to the boom, the power pulls me up off the snow just the way it should, but—instead of rising gracefully onto the board and sailing off into the distance—I'm catapulted over the front and land face-first in the snow, because the board doesn't slide at all; it just sticks to the snow and doesn't move an inch. Oh well! I might as well laugh it off and try again.

But after ten tries, I can't see the funny side anymore. Some-how, the snow is getting all mushed up and sticking to the bottom of the board. It's a real bummer. I'd been dreaming of windsurf-ing on snow for the longest time. But still, I have no regrets. At least I tried it, and it gave me something to do for a while.

When I head back to the boat, I feel exhausted from the exertion and all that time out in the cold. So, I decide to pamper myself with a little luxury: a shower!

I can wear the same pair of socks and the same pair of boxer shorts for days—merino wool is a wonderful material. Plus, I've barely been breaking a sweat, so my underwear tends to stay pretty clean. Well—I can't smell anything, anyway, and Monique isn't the type to complain. In any case, I'm sure I can't smell any worse than her bedding. I've been burning some scented candles too, and I've been dousing myself in fancy Nicolaï eau de toilette from back home every day and calling it a French shower!

Today feels like a special occasion. I put a pot of water on the stove to heat up and lay out a tarp to keep the floor dry. Then I dip my washcloth into the warm water and, standing on the tarp, I scrub myself all over with orange-blossom-scented body wash to get rid of the dirt. I draw the line at shampooing my hair— that would take too much water. My scalp can wait until I get back to Saqqaq. Then I rinse my whole body with warm water. Ah, what a treat this is!

I can't enjoy this for too long though; otherwise the cabin will turn into a swimming pool. I grab my towel and dry myself vigorously. It's a little chilly in here. The wind is finding a way in through the window and it's barely fifty degrees inside the cabin.

It feels great to pull on a clean pair of socks and boxers. These daily rituals we take so much for granted have become a distant memory out here in the cold.

Before I put all my clothes back on, I weigh myself. 163 pounds, says the scale. I've lost about 13 pounds in a matter of weeks.

This morning, the pack ice is covered in a blanket of fresh snow. Today's the day to try out my brand-new backcountry skis. I haven't skied in seven years. Back then, I was a bit of a daredevil. Today, I'm going to take it easy. Now would really not be a good time to wipe out and break a leg.

I load my ski boots into my backpack, strap my skis to the sides, grab my GoPro, and set off for shore. It's tough going, making your way up a mountain in the snow when you're as out of shape as I am. My lungs are burning, and the weight of the gear on my back isn't helping.

The higher I climb, the more spectacular the view gets. When I reach the summit, the beauty of the panorama really takes my breath away. The bay and the pack ice stretch as far as the eye can see, and the icebergs down there glint in the sun. I'm all alone in this vast landscape. It's a very moving experience to be standing on top of the world. Perhaps I'm the first human being to ever set foot on this land—who knows? I feel an immense sense of freedom.

It's time for me to pull on my ski boots, step into my bindings, and ski my way down. I have to be careful, because there are lots of icy patches among the pockets of soft powder. Regardless, this is a big moment.

When I'm back down on the shore, I flip the bindings into walk mode, freeing my heels so I can walk the last few hundred yards back to *Yvinec* on my skis. What a privilege it is to ski right up to my sailboat.

The next morning, I head out to set my fishing lines. Despite my continued lack of success, I'm not giving up. Across every hole, I lay a plank of wood to attach the line. At the end of the day, I'll come back out to break the ice forming over the hole. I really hope I'll catch a fish today. Just one . . .

The weather is stunning today. Not a single cloud in the sky. There's a plane up there, tracing a straight white line across the clear blue. Where has it come from? Where is it going? Inside, there must be two or three hundred people traveling to see their family and friends, sitting warm and cozy with an airline meal or a steaming cup of hot chocolate on their tray table. They might be gazing out the windows, marveling at the great white expanse, never once suspecting that a human being has chosen to hole himself up in the ice until Mother Nature sets him free again. Can they even see my boat from all the way up there?

It's a great day to ski over to the other side of the bay. I manage to cover a good mile or two across the ice before I see water. That's a little worrying. I take off my skis and inch my way closer to where the ice stops. If I fall into the water with ski boots on, I'll have a hard time getting out again. Two days ago, at least eighty percent of the bay was covered in pack ice. Now more than half of it has melted. I don't understand. It's still very cold. The waves must be eating away at the ice. I can't help but fear the worst if a big swell happens to roll in. I'm trying not to think about it.

Before I set out today, I turned the navigation lights on so I'd be able to get my bearings on the way back. I'm always worried that the fog or mist might sweep in suddenly, or that a snowstorm might blow through. If either happens, I might be steps away from the boat and walk right past it.

I head out one last time to check my lines. Still no fish. Six lines, ten or fifteen hooks, and not a single bite. Is this a joke? I feel deflated. So far, none of the things I've tried have worked.

I'm tired of waiting in the cold, with my beard and eyelids frozen over, for a fish that never comes.

Suddenly, I have a brain wave: what if I could fish from the comfort of my bed? I dig a hole in the ice right at the back of the boat, put a new line in the water, and set up a system of pulleys that carries the line down into the cabin so I can keep an eye on it from my warm, cozy sleeping bag. A little later, I'm toasty warm in my berth, line in hand, gazing out at the Northern Lights, hoping a fish is going to take the bait.

This morning, I get myself organized for a long walk to the other side of the bay. The snow is so deep, I sink in to my knees. The stuff gets into my boots, and soon I can't feel my feet. I know I'm a glutton for punishment, but the west wind blew hard last night, and I want to make sure the ice hasn't receded any farther.

Luckily, I was worried for nothing. It doesn't seem to have moved at all.

The next day, the wind is blowing hard again. Soon it's a full-on storm, and the snow is whipping at my face. The spinnaker halyard keeps whacking into the mast and it's making a hell of a racket. Monique doesn't seem to care though, and lays me a mighty fine egg. I head outside for some air and look out across the bay. This time, the ice is well and truly retreating. In a flash, I get dressed and grab my *touk* to venture out for a closer look.

There are pools of water all over the place! I can't help but feel demoralized. I test the ice, and it's still thick and solid. I'm a little perplexed. The sea temperature must have risen—I can't see there being any other explanation. I have to stop a hundred feet or so away from the water's edge. I can't go any closer; otherwise

I'd risk falling through the ice. I'd better turn around and head back; I didn't think to put on my dry suit. Back on the boat, I thought this might have been a mirage, but we are indeed surrounded by water.

That night, I toss and turn in my bed. The anxiety is tying my stomach in knots. The pack ice is twice as thick as it was last time we ran aground. I'm not holding out much hope for my boat if great slabs of this stuff come slamming into the hull. There's no way I'm getting any sleep tonight. Nightmare scenarios keep running through my mind. I have to go out there and check again, for the umpteenth time.

I turn the lights on at the top of the mast to help me find my bearings and off I go. I'm trying to stomp my feet hard into the snow to leave deep prints that will be easy to follow on my way back to the boat. It's minus thirty degrees outside, and with the wind it feels like minus seventy, or something crazy like that. If I lose my way, I'm done for. How many explorers have died just steps away from their tent? I can't see a thing, dammit, not even the sea. I turn around to follow my footsteps in the snow back to the boat, but the wind has already swept them clean. With the wind, the snow, and everything swirling around in the air like a fog, I've lost all sense of direction. I can't feel my face anymore. As the fear takes hold, the only thing I have to guide me is the wind direction. I'm trying to think. I must not panic.

At last, I can see the lights aboard *Yvinec*. With my head hunkered down, I trudge my way home. I can't afford to be taking risks like this. The next time I venture out into the void, I'll trail a lifeline behind me. Back on the boat, Monique is perched on the bookshelf, dozing peacefully, completely oblivious to the scare I've just had.

IT'S BEEN BLOWING for eight days without reprieve. The wind has turned east-northeast; curiously, it almost feels like there's some warmth to it. The ice inside the boat has melted; now there's condensation instead. That doesn't necessarily make it any more pleasant. Drops of water have been falling onto my sleeping bag all night long.

I've stored a few fuel drums on the shore, and now I have to go get some diesel from them. At this moment, it's too risky with the wind, but if the pack ice breaks apart and I end up stuck aboard my boat, I'm going to run out of my heating fuel pretty soon.

To pass the time, I've been looking at photos and watching videos of my family and friends, reminiscing about the good times we had back home, and rereading the letters they sent before I set off on my adventure. A little later, I watch a funny movie on my laptop, and it makes me laugh out loud. If there's one thing I've noticed about being alone, it's that my emotions are heightened. I often find myself bursting out laughing for no reason.

The wind has calmed down a little. I'm going to fetch some diesel. I put on my dry suit and, before I go, I grab my sled and a dry bag to bring back some snow. After walking a few hundred yards, I can see bare rock on the mountains. Clearly, the snow is melting because the air is getting warmer.

Lying in my berth, I can feel the boat moving. That's strange, because the pack ice is still there. The cold came back last night; it was about time. Yesterday, the ice that's holding the boat seemed to have weakened, and I was starting to see some water seeping up around the hull. Above my head, the cabin window has started to frost over, and the icy film is distorting my view of the world outside.

For a few weeks now, I've had to be frugal with toilet paper, because I'm down to my last few rolls. It's going to be tight. If need be, I do have a few newspapers lying around to use as backup.

FEBRUARY 26

As I open my eyes, a bluebird sky wishes me good morning through the cabin window. I can feel the sun's rays warming my face. We've lost another section of pack ice on the outside of the bay. The big melt seems to have started much earlier than usual. This was supposed to happen sometime around May.

My latest invention that was supposed to allow me to fish from the comfort of my berth unfortunately hasn't worked. I'm beginning to wonder whether there's even a single fish in this bay. It's either that, or I'm really bad at fishing. I've cut the bottom off a plastic bottle and replaced it with cling wrap; I'm hoping to use it as a spyglass. Kneeling beside a hole I've dug in the ice, I lower my invention into the water a little, and try to catch a glimpse of something down there. I think it's an ingenious system, but that doesn't mean it works!

There isn't enough snow to ski, and there isn't enough wind to go kite skiing on the ice. So I go for a long walk instead and take a bunch of photos. Then, to amuse myself, I kick a soccer ball around for a while on the ice, using *Yvinec*'s hull as a wall. The ball doesn't always bounce back straight, but running after it gives me a bit of exercise. A little later, I climb up the mast and start a conversation with an imaginary friend I've just conjured up. I ask him how long he's been here and how he's managing to survive, and I invite him over for a drink later, if he feels like it.

~~~~~~~~~~

THE COLD DIDN'T stick around for long. According to my thermometer, it's a balmy twenty-six degrees Fahrenheit right now, just a touch below freezing. Monique is perched on her little window ledge, enjoying the sun. I'm going to make the most of this beautiful weather to get some exercise and climb one of the peaks. Since I started this overwintering expedition, I've lost a lot of weight—more than twenty-five pounds. With this precarious diet of mine, I'm going to have to pay attention to my health and keep myself fit. *Touk* in hand, I venture out toward the shore. With these extra few degrees, I can already tell the pack ice isn't as thick.

Out here, there's nothing but the vast white icescape, the sound of my steps in the snow, the occasional Arctic hare, and a few caribou tracks. I stop for a moment to catch my breath and take in the spectacular view. It's so beautiful! I've certainly had lots of challenging times in the shadow of these mountains, but right now, this scenery is worth all the trouble in the world.

After a few hours of hiking, I head back down the mountain. Farther along, near the edge of the bay, I can see the pack ice comes to an end and gives way to deep blue water. I'm a little disoriented. I guess I haven't exactly followed the most direct route down. It must be around 4:30 in the afternoon when *Yvinec* comes into sight.

When I'm safely back on board, my legs are on fire, but I feel great. I've been cooped up so much these last few months; I've been long overdue to spend some time in nature and burn off some energy. I peer out the cabin window and see the sun disappearing behind the mountain.

February is nearly over. Tomorrow is the beginning of a new month, the fourth of our winter adventure.

MARCH 1

To start the month of March on a happy note, Monique has laid an egg in my sweater! So long as she keeps on laying, I'm a happy man. I love this rebellious "I'm going to lay wherever and whenever I want" streak of hers.

It's a few degrees below freezing today, and the sky is just as blue as yesterday. After the cold we've gotten used to, this feels like spring for us. I even go out on deck for a while in bare feet and nothing but my boardshorts! It's a great day to try out my slackline and play at being a tightrope walker on ice. I attach one end of the line to the boat and the other to a barrel that I've filled with seawater for weight and stability. I get up there with my boots on, but I can't take any more than three steps in the beginning without falling head over heels.

Monique looks at me mockingly. "I'd like to see *you* try!" I cry, picking her up and putting her down on the slackline. To my amazement, she perches there on the line quite comfortably without moving an inch. She has quite the balance, this hen of mine! I resolve to give it another shot. This time, I take off my boots so I can feel the line better. I put a mat down under the line so I won't fall barefoot in the snow. With some perseverance, I eventually manage to keep my balance and walk a few steps. I decide to call it a day before I lose all feeling in my toes, though. "See, Monique, it isn't that hard after all!" I joke.

I'm keen for Monique to enjoy some winter excitement while we're here. With the remnants of an old sled I found on the shore a few weeks earlier, I build her a fine carriage out of planks of wood and pieces of rope. In the beginning, she flaps her wings, obviously feeling a little out of her depth, but she soon gets used to it and seems to enjoy the feeling of sliding over the snow and ice.

At the end of the day, I head out for a run along the water's edge. I've been trying to make this a daily habit.

When I look at the photos I took the other day during my hike up the mountain, I barely recognize myself. I look like a caveman, and my face is an overgrown jungle. I've never had hair so long, and I've never had such a long, scraggly beard before. It looks like I've been rubbing engine oil into it. It's probably a good idea to give myself a haircut and say goodbye to the facial hair.

Obviously, I'm not very well equipped for this little beauty treatment. I have a pair of kitchen scissors and my Leatherman multifunction pocket knife, neither of which is exactly the right tool for the job. It's time to get started. I grab a big lock of hair, then another, but the scissors on the Leatherman are tiny and, at this rate, I'm going to be snipping away for days. I guess the kitchen scissors will have to do. I look at myself in the mirror and can't help but think that I look like a teenager who's trying to shock his parents. When I run my hand through the hair on the back of my head, I can feel some bare patches. Oh well. It doesn't matter. It's not as if there's anyone out here for me to impress. I use a razor to tidy up what's left of my beard.

YESTERDAY, WE CAME close to eating our first fish in a very long time! I caught a small skate. I was so excited, I put it back in the fishing hole with the hook in its mouth while I dashed off to fetch the camera. This was the first edible fish I'd caught in three months, so I had to capture the moment, didn't I? But when I returned, the fish had gone. I was so angry with myself. I missed what might have been my only opportunity to eat some tasty fresh fish. I don't think I'll be catching another one for a while.

But I'm not giving up. Hole by hole, I pull up the rest of my lines. Nothing. Until I get to the very last hole. There's something at the end of the line, but it isn't moving. I pull the line up, and there, all tangled up, I find two sea urchins! Two yummy sea urchins, fresh from the North Pole! I can't believe it. I'm beside myself with excitement.

That night, I scramble an egg for myself to go with the urchin meat. It's a small feast. I can't resist giving Monique a taste. There's no reason why I shouldn't.

It's been snowing nearly all night long. I still have more than half my diesel reserves left. There's no way I'm going to use it all, so I figure I might as well crank the heat up. It feels glorious inside the boat now; I could walk around naked if I wanted to!

Whenever the weather and the visibility will allow, I get out for a run, walk, or slide on the ice, and I dig holes. Today, the sun isn't far away. It's hiding behind a thin veil of cloud that's gradually fading away, with help from a gentle westerly breeze. At last, the conditions are right for me to try kite skiing. I've never gone kitesurfing on skis before. This is a first for me.

I pump up the air chamber of my kite, and off I go. This is working way better than my feeble attempt at windsurfing on snow! It's exhilarating to zip my way from one side of the bay to the other and sail upwind. The skis glide so well over this surface; they feel just like a board on the water.

Today is a new day, and I don't dare venture away from the boat. With all the blowing snow, I can barely see thirty feet in front of me. I'm starting to think about the next chapter of our adventure. When we get out of here, the boat is going to need a bit of work. I'll probably have to shore up in Ilulissat for a while.

MARCH 26

1 PM

Another storm is bearing down on us. I'm well aware that the pack ice is probably going to break up again. But this time, at least I have a few hours' notice to prepare for it. Hastily, I lift back aboard all the drums I've been keeping on the ice. The rudder is completely encased in ice, which is a huge problem. I can't steer the boat like this. It takes me hours and all my strength to smash it free with my *touk*. Meanwhile, the storm has been raging around me. I'm soaked, and I can't see a thing out here. I can feel the boat starting to move. I cross my fingers that everything is going to be all right. I sense this storm is going to spell the end of the pack ice this winter.

5 PM

It turns out I was right. This hibernation of ours is ending sooner than I thought. All around the boat, the ice is rolling, cracking, and smashing to smithereens. The wind keeps blowing harder and harder. Some of the gusts are blasting through at more than fifty-five knots! It's a good thing I've tied the dinghy, the paddleboard, and everything else up nice and tight. The pack ice has almost completely broken apart now, and in my heart, something has broken too. Just like every time a story has ended. I don't know if I'm sad or relieved.

7 PM

It's pitch dark. With a mix of fascination and dejection, I watch as the slabs of pack ice get blown away by the wind, one by one. *Yvinec* is free from her cage of ice. It's all over. I hope the anchor doesn't slip and get carried away in the ice and drag us ashore again. I check the engine over before I fire it up. No matter what, I have to be able to maneuver the boat.

MARCH 27

AFTER MIDNIGHT

I can hardly believe it. This isn't the same place anymore. But this is not the end of the story yet—a gigantic slab of ice has gotten stuck in *Yvinec*'s anchor chain, and it's holding us prisoner. It's giving the hull a real beating; it keeps banging up against the metal, and it's putting us in danger. Whatever it takes, I have to get us away from that ice. I hammer away at it all night long, nonstop, trying to get the ice to break away. Now the job is done. We're free!

We've been afloat in open water for a few days when I see another boat approaching—how exciting! Two of my friends from Saqqaq who were fishing in the area have come over to check on how Monique and I are doing. I invite them aboard for a cup of tea. I haven't bathed since I took my "shower" on a tarp on the cabin floor a good month ago. What can I say? I wasn't expecting company! Sitting in the cabin with our steaming cups of tea, we communicate the best we can. They barely speak a word of English, and I've forgotten the few words of Greenlandic I learned. I'm trying to find out whether there's still a lot of ice—*siku*—in the bay, and whether there are many icebergs—*ilulissat*—drifting out there. We laugh and somehow manage to understand each other using gestures and hand signals. What a joy it is to see human beings again, communicate with them, and hear voices other than my own! After a while, we say goodbye—or actually, see you soon, since I expect to be back in just a few days. *Aluu! Takuss'!* They've reassured me there's practically no ice left around Saqqaq, so it'll be smooth sailing into the harbor.

What do you say, Monique, is it time for us to get going?

APRIL 2

The sun is back, the ice in the bay has almost completely disappeared, and a gentle easterly breeze is beckoning us out to sea. The time has come. I feel a tug at my heartstrings as I pull up the anchor chain. Then I raise the sails and *Yvinec* glides away on the glassy sea. All being well, we'll be back in Saqqaq tomorrow.

I turn and look back at the shore where I went to gather fresh snow; I lift my gaze to the peaks where I feasted my eyes on this sky of a thousand colors and the pastel hues of the pack ice below. When we arrived here on November 25, I thought we'd be spending at least six months on the ice. But Mother Nature had other plans.

One hundred and thirty days and one hundred and six eggs later, we slip away quietly from this place that has been both an icy hell and a winter wonderland. I'm leaving a little part of me behind in this silent bay. Mere months have passed, yet I feel that something has changed. I think I've found what I came here to find: I've found myself.

Monique is the first hen in the world to have sailed the Northwest Passage!

PART 3

~~~~

The Northwest Passage

W HEN WE MOOR *Yvinec* at the dock, all the children in the village come running up to us. My buddy Lukaka and his friends hop right aboard and run circles around me, calling to Monique, who's perched up high, looking down in bemusement. They fiddle with my cell phone, iPad, and laptop, and seem to take great pleasure in starting up my dinghy, jumping in, jumping right out again and chanting "Guirec! Guirec!" Word of my return quickly spreads around the village. People are already inviting me to join them for "coffee" the very first night I'm back in the harbor. This generous welcome feels like a homecoming.

There's one thing I have to do before anything else though, and that's to head to the Commune and take a real shower. As the steaming water flows over my shoulders, I close my eyes and breathe in the sweet scent of the shower gel filling the whole room. I wish this moment could last forever! Once I'm squeaky-clean and dry and have pulled on some fresh clothes, I throw all my dirty laundry—clothes, sheets, duvet, and towels—into the washing machines. I can't help but appreciate what a privilege, not a mindless daily chore, it really is to do laundry. I've taken little conveniences like these for granted. Now they seem like a real luxury.

Before dinner, Uno sits me down for a good haircut. This is exactly what I need. I'm ready for an evening with company now. Life ashore seems delightfully civilized!

At dinner that night, I get to feast on my first vegetables in more than a hundred and thirty days! Zucchini, lettuce, tomatoes, corn, and potatoes, all flown in by helicopter from Ilulissat—it's an explosion of flavor for my taste buds!

I end up spending more than two months in the village. The weather has been improving day by day. The days have been growing longer and milder. I've been making the most of the opportunity to give *Yvinec* a good spring cleaning. It's also a good excuse to get rid of lots of things I no longer need that are just cluttering up the boat.

I've also been spending lots of time with my friends here. They've taken me dogsledding all around the area. I've gone halibut fishing with Uno and explored the wilderness with Adam. I've met Uno's nephew, Markus. He's the pride of the village; he plays soccer for Greenland's national team and lives in the finest house in Saqqaq. In the daytime, he goes fishing. In the evening, he trains in Ilulissat and has to endure a two-hour boat journey each way to get there. I've seen some of his matches on TV. I've been to countless birthday parties in the village as people celebrate with their doors open to all. You just go right in, feast on caribou and whale meat, enjoy a drink or two, chew on a little *mattak* (raw whale skin and fat), and then go on your merry way.

Immersing myself in village life and spending time with the people here has helped me to understand their way of living. Greenland is a very peaceful country. There are no police stations here. Most of the villages are very remote, so when they need it, people mainly rely on help from others. People will bend over backward to lend a hand. You might only need one extra pair of hands, but before you know it, fifteen villagers are there to help. And because there are no mechanics, plumbers, or electricians here, everyone is a jack-of-all-trades. The village of Saqqaq is like one big family.

Now that spring has sprung, Monique has started following me everywhere, and she's always surrounded by a swarm of playful kids. But the mosquitoes are the only swarm she's interested in. They're everywhere at this time of year, and Monique takes great pleasure in catching them mid-flight and devouring them greedily.

At the end of May, I sail back to Ilulissat to get my sailboat shipshape again. In the harbor, I very nearly lose Monique! While we're tied up alongside another vessel, she hops aboard the neighboring boat and goes exploring—but before she has a chance to hop back aboard *Yvinec*, the other boat goes out fishing! Luckily, the guys on board are kind enough to turn around and bring her back. They could very well have decided to eat her for dinner! It can't have been that hard for them to figure out who she belonged to and what had happened. There aren't exactly a lot of hens roaming around Greenland, and Monique has been quite the attraction here in the harbor!

Another day, she and I are out for a stroll around Ilulissat, and as we're walking past a school I happen to look up and see dozens of kids staring at us from the windows. The teacher opens the door, and Monique waltzes right into the school building as if she owned the place. The kids think she's hilarious. I lift her up to perch on the back of a chair, and say a few words of introduction: "I am Guirec, and this is Monique!"

"Moe-nique! Moe-nique!" they cry, as they ruffle her feathers.

It's not even the beginning of June, and the sun has stopped setting. In the evenings, it goes down slowly, casting an orange hue over the glassy sea, turning the mountains to gold—and then it bounces right back from the horizon like a ball of fire before beginning its long, steady ascent. The days are never-ending, much to the delight of the local kids, who often get to play soccer until one in the morning! It's hard to sleep.

I'm lying in bed, tossing and turning. Monique has certainly been a trusty companion for me, but sometimes I long for real human connection. I miss having someone to talk to. My phone vibrates. I'd forgotten all about it. It's Constantin, my eldest sister's son. Together with Théo, another of my nephews, we used to get up to all kinds of tricks. Once, when we were kids, we nearly set fire to the island back home. We were trying to make a campfire behind the house, but things got out of hand and the flames started shooting into the air! Luckily, the adults came running with a hose and buckets of water before the whole place went up in smoke. It's great to talk to Constantin; I can't wait to see these guys again.

Now it's time for me to get ready to sail the Northwest Passage in July. But there's a problem. I'm having some severe stomach pain. I usually try to tough this kind of thing out, but I realize this isn't going anywhere. I end up giving my childhood friend Maxence a call—he's a doctor now. He sends me off for some tests in Ilulissat, but the doctors there don't find anything. I suffer through a few more days, and then I call Maxence again. I'm bent double with the pain now. He thinks I'm showing the classic signs of appendicitis, so he tells me to get myself to Nuuk as quickly as I can. But I don't want to risk having surgery in Greenland. Plus, I don't have medical insurance, so it'd cost me an arm and a leg.

And so I book a last-minute flight to Paris, connecting through Copenhagen. Maxence is waiting for me at the airport to take me straight to the hospital, where they send me into surgery for peritonitis! If this had happened while I was stuck in the bay over the winter, I wouldn't be here to tell the tale. That's why most serious offshore sailors have their appendix taken out before they set sail on their first ocean voyage. The same goes for their wisdom teeth. Before I fly back, the doctors give me a complete checkup, and a clean bill of health!

I also make the most of this unexpected trip home to see my family. It warms my heart to be with them—but it does feel kind of cold and empty without my father here.

On July 12, I'm reunited with Monique, who's been hanging out with Julien, a Franco-Greenlandic buddy I met in Ilulissat. He's really pampered her while I've been away. I'm tired, but the North-west Passage can't wait forever. Two weeks after I get back to the boat, the conditions look favorable for me to cross Baffin Bay.

On July 31, at 11:05 PM on a mild, sunny night, I raise anchor and set sail with a heavy heart and a knot in my stomach. I'm turning the page on a long chapter.

When I made land in Qaqortoq nearly a year ago, I didn't think I'd be staying so long. I had no idea how attached I would get to this little country. I never thought I would find so many friends here—a real family—and I never imagined how hard it would be to say goodbye to them.

When I first set out on this adventure, I imagined that ice-bergs were static, placid parts of the winter decor. I thought the pack ice would stay as solid as a rock under a clear blue sky. And I figured every night I would sit back and enjoy the Northern Lights, shimmering way up high, as polar bears wandered by and seals with mustaches popped up to say hello. I had visions of feasting daily on fresh halibut and cod, and I imagined what it would feel like when it was all over and I made my first phone call home—to my father. I would have been the happiest and proudest man alive to tell him, "I did it, Dad!"

Today, I'm not quite the same person I used to be. I've had a lot of time to reflect. During these long months in the ice, I've learned to slow down, to think, and to ask myself a lot of existential ques-tions. There have been times when I've felt discouraged, but these have never lasted. And I've never feared for my life. But I have been worried that I would lose my boat—that was terrifying—and I have been worried that I might lose Monique. I've come to understand that I don't lack strength or courage.

With my father's death, I've learned the meaning of the words "never again." I have faced Mother Nature at her most hostile and endured the storms, the cold, the ice, and the snow—not to mention running aground with my boat. But I have always persevered, and I have never given up. That's not such a bad achievement, is it?

~~~~~~~~~

I'M NOT USED TO long stretches at sea anymore, and that's exactly what this journey is promising to be. All being well, I'll make it to Nome, Alaska, by the middle of September. That means spending a solid month or more at sea. Again, I've neglected to do some repairs because I don't have the money. I'm going to be sailing with no self-steering or automatic pilot. This close to the Pole, the compass components won't work, in any case. My charts are approximate at best, because there are no detailed charts for this part of the world. As far as communications systems are concerned, all I can count on is my Iridium unit. My buddy Johann in Saint Martin is going to upload the satellite weather records and ice charts for me. He's going to send me text messages and call me regularly to give me the most accurate GPS waypoints. The Northwest Passage can be a real minefield of pack ice and moving ice floes, so the more information I have to guide me, the better.

Before I set sail, I've replenished my water reserves. As for diesel, I had too much left after the winter, so to make the boat lighter I've left a few drums with people in Saqqaq. I've kept enough on board to motor through the dead calm seas that the Northwest Passage is notorious for.

Before they attempt the passage, most sailors make their way to Resolute, one of Canada's northernmost communities. There, they wait for the passage to open before heading directly south. Resolute is ten days from Saqqaq by sea. But there's a shorter route. I'd rather fork off to the south before getting to Resolute and cut through the Bellot Strait instead.

As I make my way northwest, I'm hugging the coast of Disko Island, not far from my winter bay. This place still feels like home to me. The sea is a mirror, and *Yvinec* is moving under engine power. I'm zigzagging between the icebergs with confidence. I'm in familiar territory. I've been rubbing shoulders with these majestic giants for a year now, and I've learned how to anticipate the way they behave and the way they drift.

As I leave Saqqaq behind, I feel like I'm neither here nor there; I'm treading water somewhere between the past and the present, caught between sadness and excitement. I've promised all my friends I'll return someday, but when?

Suddenly, I find myself heading right into a huge wall of fog. It's like sailing into a steam room, but colder. When *Yvinec* emerges on the other side, my clothes are soaked though and my mind is a little foggy, but somehow I feel cleansed of my sorrow. It's as if I've left the previous year behind that wall of fog. Uno, Adam, Lukaka, and the others; Disko Bay; my father's death—it's all dissolving in my wake in a swirl of memories that, as time goes on, will come to buoy my spirits and keep me moving forward.

Once we clear Disko Island, we're out in Baffin Bay. The wind is picking up, so now I can fly the sails. The sun is rising in the sky. It's the first day of August, and a new adventure is beginning. The sailing is smooth. I've got the wind behind me.

Suddenly, a big grayish spot comes into view ahead, right in the middle of the water. I check my charts, and I can't see any islands. Weird. Maybe it's a trick of the light. The blankets of fog hovering over the water are blurring the seascape. Only when I get within a couple hundred feet do I realize this is a massive wall of ice, not fog. It's a giant iceberg. It must be at least 150 feet high. I try not to think about the part that's underwater, which must be nearly ten times bigger than what's above the surface. I have to act fast. I fire up the engine and manage to change course with barely a moment to spare. Phew, that was a close call!

After that, I keep my eyes glued to the horizon and my hand on the tiller. Without radar to detect the icebergs, it's a good thing it's light enough twenty-four hours a day for me to spot them with my naked eye. I won't allow myself the slightest moment of rest. Sometimes, my eyes close by themselves for a few seconds, and I wake with a start when the boat turns into the wind and the sails start flapping.

Seventy-two hours with no sleep and no food is no fun at all. I have to stay at the helm and keep my eyes wide open to navigate the right path through the ice, to make sure we don't end up stuck in a dead end with no way forward and no way to turn around. And so I keep forging ahead.

I haven't slept in four days. I'm hungry. When I duck into the cabin for a moment to feed Monique, if I find an egg in her coop I cook it up quickly and eat at the helm. I'm shivering cold and I can barely feel my legs out here. Sometimes my vision gets blurry, and I'm not just talking about my eyesight. I'm losing my mind. I keep imagining someone else is on board. I look all over the boat, thinking someone is going to emerge and take over at the helm, but who? I'm losing it completely. Obviously, there's no one else on board; I'm all alone. What's happening to me?

I'm seeing things. I can see food right in front of me, a nice grilled lobster on a plate, just the way we serve it back home. I can see islands, mirages that disappear as soon as I draw near. I can see villages and boats, and I even hear voices. Or so I think.

These hallucinations are starting to really freak me out. I set a wake-up alarm and go inside the cabin to lie down for a while. To be safe, I heave to—meaning that I turn the boat into the wind, block the tiller, and backwind the genoa to keep the boat stable. But I can't leave the helm for too long, otherwise the boat will drift. I fall asleep as soon as my head hits the pillow, but somehow my mind is still alert, so this isn't exactly the most restorative of naps. My brain is in a fog and it's only getting worse. I'm so tired I don't know where I am anymore. I feel like I'm walking on dry land, and I'm about to reach the foot of a mountain. But I'm still on my sailboat, and this is an iceberg right in front of my nose. I snap into action and manage to tack just in time to steer clear of it.

After six days at sea in permanent daylight, and a hundred hours or so without sleep, I finally make it to the other side of Baffin Bay. Back in Ilulissat, the crew of a big container ship advised me to stop at Pond Inlet, a small community just south of Bylot Island, on the coast of the northern Canadian territory of Nunavut. They said not to worry about clearing customs, that the border guards were cool and wouldn't come aboard.

In a remote outpost like Pond Inlet, the customs office is usually just a little shack down by the water with no dock, nothing at all. I'm sure the officers aren't going to ask me any questions. I'll just get my passport stamped and be on my way.

Technically speaking, I should have applied for a permit for Monique weeks in advance. But I remember how accommodating the customs people were in Halifax. They didn't bat an eye when they saw Monique and found her highly amusing. Like Halifax, Pond Inlet is also in Canada, so I had no reason to believe that things would be any different.

I cast anchor in front of Pond Inlet. It turns out to be what we sailors call a rolly anchorage, which means the boat keeps moving side to side. But I'm in such a state, I swear I could sleep twelve hours straight on a block of concrete right beside a jackhammer. But first, I put some air in my dinghy and launch it, start the outboard motor, and head for land to get the formalities out of the way. When I make it to shore, the locals point the way to the customs office.

Two guys give me some papers to fill out while they ask me the usual questions. Where are you arriving from? What are you doing in Canada? Age? (Twenty-three.) Nationality? (French.) Am I traveling alone? (Yes.) Any fruit, vegetables, or plants on board? (No.) Any animals on board? (Er, no.) Any firearms? (No, no weapons.)

So far, so good.

And then, one of the customs officers turns to me and says, "Okay then, let's go take a look at your boat."

What? Oh, crap.

They pull on their life jackets, climb into my dinghy alongside me with their big steel-toed boots, and off we go. During the brief journey between the beach and my anchorage, I get myself tangled up in all kinds of lame explanations: *"I don't have any weapons as such, but I do have this thing a fisherman gave me to make some noise and scare away the bears, you know?"* They just look at me, wondering if I'm trying to screw with them. I'm skating on thin ice. What am I going to do? I know: when we get to the boat, I'll make sure I'm the first to go aboard. I'll go tuck away Monique somewhere discreet, and I'll find somewhere to hide my rifle.

But that's not how it goes at all.

When we get to the boat, Monique is roaming around on deck, waiting to welcome us aboard. Now the officers are looking at me even more suspiciously. I try my best to smooth the waters. I'm about to get out of the dinghy and go aboard with them, but apparently that's not part of the plan.

"You stay right here with my colleague. And I'll go aboard for a look-see," says one of the officers.

This isn't going to end well.

He goes inside the cabin and soon emerges with something in his hand. "And what is this, exactly?" He's holding my rifle.

What am I supposed to say to that? He doesn't lay a finger on Monique, but he passes the rifle to his colleague in the dinghy. He's also picked up all the bullets. There must be two hundred in all. I must have left all that stuff lying around on the card table. There's more than enough ammunition to riddle them both with holes. The two guys are playing tough and looking at me now as if I'm a terrorist. Back at the customs office, they put me in handcuffs.

This is getting serious.

"Your boat has now been seized by the Canadian government. It's no longer your property," they tell me.

Oh, great.

"You lied to us," they say. "You're going to be locked up until you get your sentence. If you're lucky, you get to pay a hefty fine, you get your boat back, and you turn around and go back where you came from. If not, we'll be putting you on a plane and sending you back to France."

I can't believe what I'm hearing. Oh please, not that. Not after all the trouble I've gone to. Not after a week of no sleep. Not right as I'm about to dip my toes into the Pacific Ocean after freezing my butt off in Greenland for a year. If I have to turn around now, it'll be the end of this whole journey. And I'll probably end up getting stuck in the ice again and have to wait for months on end before I can get going again.

I ask if I can make a phone call. Surely one of my sisters can help me find a lawyer, someone to get me out of this mess.

"No."

And with that, they take the laces out of my boots and remove the sailing-rope bracelet from my wrist and march me to a cell. There's a bench in there with a small mattress and a clean toilet. It's not exactly a five-star hotel, but I figure at least I'm warm and I can get some rest. Ever the optimist, I'm trying to see the positive side of the incident, but I soon feel disillusioned. It's actually freezing cold in this little shack of a building, and the guy in the cell next door, who's clearly drunk, won't stop yelling and banging on the wall. Sheer exhaustion eventually prevails, and I fall fast asleep.

When my jailers shake me awake, it feels like I've only just closed my eyes, but six hours have passed. They walk me to their office and pass me the telephone. On the other end of the line there's a friendly man, presumably someone quite high up in the diplomatic system, speaking to me in French. As well as apologizing profusely, I claim that I don't speak English very well and that I didn't understand the officers' questions. But most of all, I insist that I was at my wit's end after too many days without sleeping, and I wasn't thinking straight. I swear I don't mean anyone any harm, and I'm not intending to stay in Canada. I tell him my story—I'm just a young guy who's worked hard to buy himself a sailboat so he can live his dream of sailing the Northwest Passage to Alaska. I'm traveling with my pet chicken to brighten up my long, lonely days at sea. I'm an easygoing kind of guy. I'm not a criminal. While I'm making my case, I can hear him tapping away at his computer keyboard. He must have found either my Facebook page or my website—because all of a sudden, he becomes very amenable. All in all, he explains, what I've done is considered a serious offense and I should be punished—but this time, they're going to let it slide. Phew!

"Listen," he says, "we're going to let you go on your way down the Northwest Passage. We're even giving back your weapon, even though you don't have a permit for it. In these parts, you can't afford to mess around; you might need it for the bears."

The customs officers are clearly surprised and annoyed by this preferential treatment. "You don't know how lucky you are," they tell me. "This kind of thing never happens."

They wouldn't think twice about roasting Monique on a spit, I'm sure of it.

As relieved as I am, I won't be sticking around in Pond Inlet for long. There are no paved roads here. The village is a muddy and slightly run-down kind of place. The streets are studded with electric poles and lined with once-colorful wooden cottages that are now looking a little faded. Everything is so different from Halifax, I can hardly believe this is still Canada. Fortunately, wherever there are children, there's a spark of life. Here they brighten the streets with their laughter as they run, sing, and play ball. They keep following me around asking for candy. "Candy! Candy!" they cry. The locals are friendly and hospitable. They tell me my timing is perfect; the ice has just cleared, but it won't be long before it starts to form again. They give me some fish. It's something local, but I can't remember the name of it.

Now it's time to top up my fuel tank with diesel and set sail due north for the Bellot Strait. We're at 74 degrees of latitude—the furthest north Monique and I have ever been! It's three in the morning. The sun is low in the sky, and the sea is a millpond. We set off at a very gentle pace, under sail. I'll fire up the engine if we don't seem to be making any headway.

At the helm, I'm scanning the horizon with my binoculars, watching for the tiniest ice floe, hoping to catch a glimpse of a bear.

From time to time, I tie the tiller fast with a couple of lines so I can go down into the cabin and get some rest. But the boat won't sail straight, and I keep having to correct our course. So much for that idea. I'll just have to stay awake to keep us on track.

Now we're sailing down the coast of Baffin Island, almost in a straight line toward the Bellot Strait. I hope the strait is going to be passable. It's a shortcut, but it's also a bit of a crapshoot. It's very narrow and often choked with ice. It's basically a corridor, about twenty miles long and only a mile or so wide. That's why most sailboats tend to avoid it and head due south from Resolute instead.

But I have the weather on my side, at least according to the latest reports Johann has uploaded. The closer we get to the strait, the more ice floes I can see drifting our way. Not long after we left Pond Inlet, I was even able to fly the spinnaker for a while, but I've had to pull the sails down now. *Yvinec* is motoring along now, and I'm weaving my way through the ice.

If you want to sail through the Bellot Strait, you have to get the timing right. As well as the ice, there are very powerful currents to reckon with, which can run as fast as five to ten knots. It's absolutely imperative to have them on your side. And so I check the tide tables and try to time my approach so the outgoing tide carries us with it. It looks like I've calculated it correctly, and we're making good progress through the strait now. Under engine power, I'm guiding *Yvinec* gently through the ice floes. The scenery is spectacular, and the colors are as pure as the cool air I'm breathing into my lungs.

That's when I finally lay eyes on him. The king of the Arctic. All I can see of this majestic being is his head and his strong upper back. He's swimming quickly, right beside the boat. I didn't think he would come so close. As long as he doesn't try to climb aboard, I have nothing to fear. I figure he must have swum over from Prince of Wales Island on the west side of the strait. Maybe he's trying to make his way to the continent. He must be exhausted; polar bears aren't made to swim these kinds of distances. He must be searching for an ice floe to call home for a while. I really feel for him. As climate change advances, there's less and less ice out here, and bears have been spotted swimming longer and longer distances between landmasses. Sometimes females, with their cubs, die of exhaustion before they reach the ice.

I have my rifle in hand, just in case. I'm sure I could never bring myself to shoot the bear, but I might have to fire a shot into the air to frighten him away.

We make it through the strait without too much trouble—even though the current is so strong at times, it carries the boat sideways. I can't rely on the chart for navigation, so I have to climb up the mast to scope out the way ahead. This place is completely deserted, so it's really not the time to run aground. I'll never forget how the sky was set ablaze with the craziest of colors, all reflecting off the sea and the ice as we made our way through the last quarter of the strait at the end of the day—one of the most magical moments I've experienced since I left Greenland. In this wild natural environment, each and every creature has to fight for its own survival. Over there, on a sheet of ice, there's a group of seals, taking a nap in the soft evening light. They don't seem afraid at all. I figure there can't be many hunters around these parts—not human ones, at any rate. A little farther along, I see a bear devouring one of its own kind.

When we emerge from the Bellot Strait, I'd thought I would head straight for Cambridge Bay on the south shore of Victoria Island, but the sea ice is too thick. Instead, I decide to head due south and hug the Nunavut coastline.

As I'm dozing at the helm, I'm jolted awake by a loud crash. The boat has run right into a massive chunk of sea ice. It's jaw-droppingly beautiful, filled with hundreds of cavities that look like little swimming pools. It's indescribable. I have to take some photos of it. It seems like a good time to fly the drone. That way, I'll get a bird's-eye view and, hopefully, be able to spot a way out of this maze of ice. But no sooner has the drone taken off than it falls into one of the holes in the iceberg! Oh shit. I have to figure out a way to get it back. I manage to wedge the boat into a nook between two chunks of ice, so it's not likely to go anywhere. Then I gingerly step overboard onto the ice and hop my way from one floe to the next, taking care not to tread too close to the edges. Phew! My drone wasn't sitting too deep in the pool of water, so I've managed to retrieve it.

While I'm here, I realize this would be a great angle for capturing some images of *Yvinec* in the midst of this otherworldly seascape. I take a few steps back to get a better shot, which, with hindsight, maybe wasn't the smartest idea. Back on the boat, I climb to the top of the mast to take some wide-angle shots before we get out of here. The ice stretches as far as the eye can see. From up there, I see one giant plate of ice dotted with pretty turquoise puddles.

I've put the drone in a container of rice to absorb the humidity, but saltwater can cause corrosion, so I'm not certain I'll be able to save it. Fingers crossed!

We're at the 68th parallel now. As we make our way south, the sun is gradually losing a little of its sparkle each night. It's early in the morning when we approach the village of Gjoa Haven. This settlement was named by the twentieth-century Norwegian explorer Roald Amundsen after his boat *Gjøa*. When he attempted to sail the Northwest Passage in 1903, the ice set in around the boat, so he took refuge in a natural harbor not far from what was just a small Inuit encampment at the time. While he was stuck in the ice, Amundsen learned survival techniques from the Indigenous people, which would serve him well later on his expedition to the South Pole.

The Inuit name for Gjoa Haven is Uqsuqtuuq, but despite all my best efforts, I can't quite manage to pronounce it! I'm going to rest up here for a few hours, just enough time to get a good night's sleep and fill up with diesel.

The next morning, we get on our way and find ourselves gliding through a glassy sea. The water is perfectly smooth—other than the occasional ripple of a seal or whale cresting the surface. And speaking of whales, they're amazing! We've been seeing lots. Even narwhals—they're known as sea unicorns because of their long tusks. And I think a seal has adopted us. He keeps poking his head above the surface, disappearing, and reappearing playfully, clearly intrigued by our presence.

When I need to rest for a while, I lash the tiller fast with a couple of lines, and I fall asleep in a matter of seconds. Often it's the sound of a little explosion that wakes me, because we've just slammed into some floating ice. Even though I've reinforced the boat and welded some sheet metal to the bow for extra protection, the hull is still taking one hell of a beating. When I'm yanked out of a deep sleep, it takes me a while to remember where I am. Every time, I worry we've either collided with another boat or run aground on the shore. But it's just another sheet of ice.

There are no icebergs in the Northwest Passage. That reduces the danger, but you still have to keep your wits about you at all times. Icebergs show up on radar but ice floes don't, and there are plenty of those.

Since we left Greenland, we've covered 1,500 nautical miles. We're halfway through the Northwest Passage, just to the south of Victoria Island. I could take a little detour and stop in at Cambridge Bay, but I don't want to hang around. And because the forecast is good for the next few days, I decide to keep heading south. We've already descended a fair way in latitude.

After three days of smooth sailing, a depression is heading right toward us. Very quickly, the wind picks up, and soon we're sailing into a thirty-five- to forty-knot headwind. There's a big swell running, and the waves are breaking over the deck. It's a bumpy ride! I'm out of practice when it comes to navigating these kinds of storms. I've been sailing a zigzag course, tacking my way upwind the best I can, but it's slow going. We're barely covering twenty nautical miles a day—that's nothing. And I'm dead tired. I'm not sleeping, I'm not eating, and I've had enough.

Two days of this hellish weather, and I'm dead on my feet. I need some rest. So we sail into the lee of a tiny island in the middle of nowhere and I drop anchor for three hours or so. I manage to catch some rest, and then we continue on our way. I'm hoping to get to Nome in ten days. I get the sense that's going to feel like a very long time.

In the Arctic Ocean, all along the coast of this stunning part of Canada, the backdrop is more than just breathtaking. It's also a desolate, unforgiving, and inhospitable kind of place. There isn't a single tree in sight. It's as if no life at all could survive here.

On August 23, we enter Kugmallit Bay and I cast anchor in front of an Inuvialuit village by the name of Tuktoyaktuk— Tuktuuyaqtuumukkabsi for the locals! At the gas station there, I get talking to a friendly young guy named Richard, who asks me all kinds of questions. I tell him all about my adventures with Monique. He rallies around a few of his fisherman buddies with motorboats to help transport my fuel drums back to the boat. Of course, I invite them all aboard *Yvinec* for a drink and introduce them to Monique. Richard sticks around for a while afterward to chat. That's when it strikes me that it might be a good idea to get rid of my rifle before I enter the United States. After my misadventure in Pond Inlet, I really don't want to play with fire again. Plus, I shouldn't need a weapon anymore. And, who knows, I might even be able to get a bit of cash for it. So I ask Richard if he can find me a buyer, in exchange for a small commission on the sale.

Little did I know that Richard was the village dealer of anything and everything! "Listen, I'll take that rifle off your hands, okay?" he says. "I'll trade it for weed, alright? It's a killer deal, man. When you get to the States you can sell that for a decent profit, no problem. What do you say?"

Um, nope. I'm sure it's a killer deal, but other than an illegal firearm, a stash of cannabis is the last thing I want to be crossing an international border with. Plus, I've never smoked a thing in my life, not even a cigarette! And so I just smile and tell him I'm not interested.

"Okay, you win," he ends up saying. "How much do you want for it?"

We agree on a price, and he pulls a stack of bills out of his pocket and pays me right then and there in cold hard cash.

To thank me for my business, on the morning of our departure, Richard invites me over to his place for a breakfast fit for a king: bacon, sausages, toast, scrambled eggs, and orange juice!

Since we left Tuktoyaktuk, a good wind has been blowing and I've been flying the spinnaker a lot. This is what it's all about! On August 25, we pass Point Barrow, the northernmost tip of Alaska and the United States, leaving the Arctic Ocean in our wake. I can't believe I've come all this way without an automatic pilot! We still have about a week to go before we get to Nome, though.

For the last few days, we've had a few hours of darkness. I'm finding it hard to adjust. I've been loving these long, endless days, when the light dims without ever going out. It's sure made it easier for me to stay awake! We're sailing in the Chukchi Sea now, between Alaska and Russia. As we round Point Hope, a spit of land north of Nome, we're surrounded by whales. There are so many of them I don't know where to look, so I just point my camera everywhere and shoot. What's more, I'm well and truly spoiled that night as the Northern Lights dance across a magnificent star-studded sky. Past Point Hope, we sail into a monster of a squall, but I manage to navigate my way through it like a pro. As we approach the Diomede Islands, we're in the Bering Strait—the gateway to the Pacific!

And so, on September 1, 2016, after thirty-two days at sea and 3,400 nautical miles (nearly 4,000 land miles), after all the cold, hunger, and fatigue, we eventually cast anchor in Nome, Alaska, the official point of arrival for those navigating the Northwest Passage. We've done it! Dad, if you could see me now, you'd be so proud!

I know I'm not the first solo sailor to have made it through the Northwest Passage, but I'm sure I'm the youngest, and I bet Monique is the only hen in the world who can stake a claim to it!

Monique keeps warm in her haute couture sweater

PART 4

~~~

From Alaska
to Canada,
and Beyond

WHEN WE SAIL into Nome, I'm keen to get my passport stamped as soon as I can. After my last experience behind bars in northern Canada, there's no way I want to repeat the ordeal with the notoriously strict American authorities.

Once I cast anchor, I wait for the officials to motor over and come aboard, as that's the general rule when you're clearing customs in most countries. The next day, I'm still waiting. Burning with impatience, I decide to go ashore, hoping to speed up the formalities, but a fisherman I run into on the wharf tells me there's no customs office here. Good to know—I could have been waiting forever!

It turns out there are so few boats sailing through that the authorities wait until there's a handful before they send up an official from Anchorage, Alaska's largest city. But that might take a week or more, and I can't afford to wait that long—otherwise I might end up stuck here if some bad weather rolls in. So I decide to move on and deal with customs later. I have to admit, I'm glad I won't have to field any awkward questions about Monique up here.

Before I sail away though, I take the opportunity to explore the village. I might as well stick around for a day or two to catch my breath. With its one main street lined with wooden houses, bars, and saloons, it looks like the set of an old Western movie. As I'm walking around, I feel as if I've stepped back in time more than a century to the Gold Rush. Back in the late-nineteenth century, gold could be found lying on the beach, so the population skyrocketed as people flocked here for their chance to strike it rich. Although there are still a few nugget seekers around, most of the prospectors abandoned it years ago. There are missing-person posters on almost every electric pole I see. It looks like a guy went out for a run a few days ago and never came back. What could have happened to him? This seems like such a sleepy little place.

Two days later, as I'm about to raise anchor, I see a few guys taking the posters down.

"Oh good, so you've found him?" I ask.

Yes, they had found the guy—what was left of him, that is. The poor soul had been eaten alive by grizzlies, just outside the village!

Up until this point, all I'd seen had been some rather placid polar bears. Not once did I feel I was in danger in the Northwest Passage. But down here, clearly I have to be more careful.

In the village, incidents like this are rare, because the grizzlies tend to keep their distance. It's when you venture outside of the community that the danger increases. A bear can go from standing still to running thirty miles an hour in a matter of seconds! Bears might seem like heavy, clumsy creatures, but they are remarkably agile; they can easily climb trees and swim faster than you might think.

It's already September 6, and I really can't afford to stick around any longer in Nome, because some severe storms are headed our way. It's time to get out of the Bering Sea. Sitting north of the Aleutian Islands and south of the Arctic Circle, this is reputedly one of the most treacherous bodies of water in the world. In places, the seabed rises sharply without warning, sometimes throwing up monstrous waves.

Fishermen lose their lives here every year. Even in a storm, the fishing crews work relentlessly, in spite of the walls of frigid water crashing over their boats. They soldier on until they are satisfied with their catch. What's the big motivation for them? Alaskan king crab. They fish for them hundreds of feet below the surface. These giant crustaceans are prized for their juicy meat in fine-dining establishments around the world. They really are huge; some of them can measure over six feet across from leg to leg.

After three and a half days at sea, at last I'll be leaving these notorious waters behind me. But first, I have to make it past the Aleutians, a chain of volcanic islands. Basically, I have two options. One is to take the main route and stop in at Dutch Harbor, to the west; the other is to take the route less traveled, a shortcut closer east through False Pass, which would save me some time.

I don't have an Internet connection on board, so to help me weigh my options, I give my buddy Éric Dumont a call. He's a seasoned sailor who has finished two Vendée Globe races and has crossed the Atlantic at least fifty times. Over the phone, he tells me the precise route I should take, as well as the timing of all the tides and currents. But he also warns me there's a big depression heading our way. Sure enough, the wind soon starts to freshen. I run into trouble trying to reef the mainsail; the sliders are stuck and I have to climb up the mast to get them moving freely in the track.

The sensible thing to do would be to hunker down at Dutch Harbor and wait for the storm to pass. But I decide to try my luck and take the False Pass route instead—even though the charts suggest I shouldn't. I just want to get through this leg of the journey as quickly as I can.

The automatic pilot still isn't working properly. At 58 degrees north, we must still be too close to the magnetic pole. That means I have to stay at the helm for hours to make sure *Yvinec* doesn't veer off course. It's a brutal undertaking that makes my fingers ache, but I'm happy all the same, because I can see the islands emerging in the distance. As we draw closer, the mountains look like they're falling into the ocean. The scenery is nothing short of spectacular.

On September 9, we venture into False Pass. I have to wait until the tide is right, of course. The currents are always very strong in narrow passes like this. For now, the skies are blue and I'm enjoying the changing landscape. It's a mix of huge volcanoes and vast green plains. I haven't seen colors like these for a long time. We get a warm welcome from the marine wildlife as whales, sea lions, and seals come out to say hello. I even see a few sea otters swimming the backstroke. The water is brimming with life. I can feel my heart beating to the rhythm of the ocean beneath me.

Once we make it through the pass, we head due east and sail into King Cove just before nightfall as a depression barrels right toward us, threatening sixty knots of wind or more. We'll wait in the harbor for the storm to pass and be on our way again in the morning. It'll do me a world of good to have a quiet night without having to keep watch.

I go ashore to stretch my legs, and as I'm strolling around the village, a guy pulls over by the side of the road and tells me to watch out—because he's just seen a grizzly.

Oh great! It's pitch dark and I can't see a thing. I'd better hurry back to the boat; I haven't forgotten about the guy in Nome who went out for a run and got eaten alive. Seeing how freaked-out I look, the guy in his truck tells me not to worry. "Just walk along the water and you'll see a bunch of crab traps. If you see a grizzly, just climb up on those. You'll be fine up there. Have a good night!"

That's not very reassuring! Maybe I shouldn't have been so quick to get rid of my rifle.

The next morning, I set sail again. I'm eager to keep going east to Kodiak Island, where I can hopefully breathe a little easier and get some much-needed rest.

After three days of mostly smooth sailing, it's September 14 when we make land on Kodiak Island. This is the biggest island in Alaska, so going ashore here marks my return to civilization! It feels like the America I've seen in the movies, with men who look like hunters in blue jeans and plaid shirts driving big pickup trucks. Here, the economy mainly revolves around fishing for salmon, halibut, and king crab.

At the marina, I've been able to take a shower and do some laundry. I've also given the boat a good cleaning and installed a camping shower. It's basically just a showerhead attached to a plastic water pouch that heats up in the sun. What luxury I have to look forward to when the weather gets a little warmer!

On my first night in the marina, I meet up with the nice folks aboard *Bonavalette* and *Ratafia*, two sailboats I crossed paths with in the Northwest Passage. Over dinner, we trade memories from the last few weeks. None of us can quite believe that the challenges we made it through up there are behind us now.

Our only neighbors at our anchorage are the sea lions. It's crazy what a racket and a stink they're making! A whole colony of them have taken up residence beside the boat on one of the big log booms in the harbor. These huge creatures can grow to hundreds of pounds in weight. They don't seem fazed by humans at all. I guess their meat doesn't taste good enough for anyone to hunt them. When they're not snoozing, they spend all their time bellowing on that vast raft of theirs. Life is tough, eh?

It's September 23, and after a week enjoying this coastal forest scenery, the time has come for us to move on. Monique has a date with a CNN news crew in Seward, a short way farther north. Her life as a seafaring hen is already making waves around the world!

Just a few hours out of Kodiak Island, I can see the white sails of our friends aboard *Ratafia* flapping in the distance. They don't seem to be moving at all. As we draw alongside them, we find out their engine has broken down. There's not a breath of wind, and they're drifting in the strong current and a fair swell. We can't leave them adrift, so we give them a tow all the way to Seward, 160 nautical miles away.

Tying a line from the other boat's bow to *Yvinec*'s stern proves to be a perilous undertaking. We have to get the two boats as close as possible to one another while making sure they don't collide. Motoring against the current, we're making painfully slow progress as the boats pitch and roll in the swell. The automatic pilot still isn't working properly and often disengages. I have to keep making sure that my boat doesn't change course of her own accord, which does happen, and more than just once. One time, we only just manage to avoid a catastrophe when *Yvinec* does a U-turn and finds herself on a direct collision course with *Ratafia*. After a full day of this precarious navigation, my friends agree to join me aboard my boat so we can take turns at the helm. In the pouring rain, they launch their dinghy and shuttle themselves over to *Yvinec*. Soaked to the skin, they look like a pair of drowned rats. I can't help but smile sympathetically when I see what a sorry state they're in.

It takes us two days and two nights of towing to get to Seward. The air is damp and thick when we eventually moor our boats to the dock in the little fishing harbor. Alaska is a huge place and there's so much to explore, but I'm not planning on sticking around much longer. When Monique's interview is done, we set sail once more, heading for the Inside Passage, which I've been longing to sail.

But first, we have to cross the Gulf of Alaska. The sea is rolling with the wind and a dark line of mountains is slowly coming into view on the horizon. *Yvinec* is skimming gracefully across the water. Once in a while, a geyser spouts into the air; it's a killer whale on the hunt. The birds around here are savvy; they circle around overhead, waiting for a stray morsel. I can't take my eyes off a show like this, so I sit out on deck to enjoy it. At night, I watch the plankton shimmering in our wake and scan the sky for a glimpse of the Northern Lights.

It might look pretty calm out there, but there's actually a dangerous cross sea—when two swells coming from different directions intersect. I can't let my guard down for a second, because there are whole tree trunks drifting in packs alongside us, threatening to punch a hole in our side.

It's October 3 when we enter the Inside Passage. *Yvinec* is gliding gently through water as calm as a millpond, in the midst of tiny islands, beautiful bays, and spectacular fjords. The mountainsides are blanketed in pine forests, and so are their mirror images in the water. Eagles are circling playfully overhead. There's something intriguing, almost mystical, about this place. There's magic in the water too; dolphins are leaping all around the boat, and whale spouts keep erupting from the glassy surface.

The Inside Passage is a particularly tight and winding route, and it's notorious for its violent currents. As the tides come and go, water is flushed in and out of there by the mighty North Pacific. There's no way the engine or the sails can fight currents this intense, so we have to be flexible. When the currents are against us, we simply find somewhere to stop and wait until the time is right to move on.

We find ourselves casting anchor in front of remote cabins and deserted docks standing at the foot of towering mountains, smothered by the mist. Any rare locals we come across tend to sport impressive beards. They might seem gruff at first, but they're generally quite likable and welcoming. A few days later, we tie up at the dock in Hoonah, a small village on Chichagof Island. I still haven't officially entered the United States—there are no customs officials in any of the places we've been. But I'm hoping to get this formality out of the way soon; I don't want any trouble.

As soon as I've moored *Yvinec* at the dock, I notice a woman with long gray hair walking over. She has her hands clasped together as if in prayer, and the first thing she says is, "Please, don't go out after dark. And whatever you do, don't go walking alone in the forest."

It turns out that just the other day, a hunter had been mauled by a bear on the beach and had his leg muscles torn to shreds. Right as the bear was about to sink its jaws into his head, the friend he was hunting with fired his rifle and shot the bear, just in time.

"I'm glad you understand," the woman continues. "You take care now."

Okay, then.

The next day, I head into town to buy some groceries. I've been living off canned food for a while now, and I'm sick of it. There isn't much in the mini-mart here though, and since everything has to be imported, it's all crazy expensive. I ask the cashier for recommendations about what to do while I'm in town, and she suggests I pay a visit to Raino, who's apparently a living legend around here. I'm enjoying the scenery as I walk over to his place. There are only about seven hundred people living in Hoonah.

The town is a rustic kind of place with a real authentic feel to it. There is a paved road running through town, and it's lined with colorful wooden cabins painted pink, yellow, and green. The Indigenous Tlingit culture is ever-present here. Wherever I look, there seem to be totems and Indigenous artwork adorning the town.

Raino is standing out front when I walk up to his place. He's just heading out to visit a friend and drop off some fish he's prepared, so he tells me to hop in the passenger seat; we can chat on the way. As we're driving, we start getting to know one another, and I ask him a bazillion questions. There's something magnetic about this guy; it's as if he's embodying the whole spirit of Alaska. He's probably in his sixties, and he has a gentle, cheerful look about him. The two of us hit it off right away. I tell him that back home in France, I've been fishing since I was a little boy. It's one of my favorite things to do.

"I'll take you fishing tomorrow," he says.

Back at his place, Raino insists on loaning me his ATV so I can get out and explore the area. The trail is sandy and lined on both sides with huge, towering trees that almost block out the sky. A half-hour later, the landscape opens up and the trail widens as it leads down to the water. I can see a brown smudge moving on the beach—it's a bear! I grab my camera, but the bear is afraid and slopes away before I have the chance to take a photo.

I've been spending lots of time with my new buddy Raino. He's told me his life story. His father was an Indigenous Alaskan. His mother was Italian and immigrated to the States. Raino loves talking about First Nations traditional beliefs and culture. He reveres nature, animals, and his ancestors. As far as he's concerned, an animal never appears by chance. Its presence is always a sign.

Raino and I have been going out into the forest a lot. This is one of the wettest coastal rainforests in the world. When we're out there, we tread gently and speak in hushed voices, as if we're in a place of worship. From amid the lush vegetation, trees wrapped in lichen stretch up toward the sky. Creeping foliage cascades over branches to the thick layer of moss carpeting the forest floor. This forest is living and breathing in every shade of green, and I'm lost for words.

I've learned that Chichagof Island has the highest population of bears in Alaska. Chatting with the locals, I've heard all kinds of crazy stories about bear attacks: a dog that was eaten alive right here in town, a man who was mauled right in front of his house, and a kid who was hurt so badly he ended up needing two hundred stitches.

Although it's not always easy for humans and bears to coexist here, bears are protected animals in Alaska, and people in Hoonah respect them. Anyone who kills a bear has to explain themselves to the authorities. Often, attacks on humans are attributable to mother bears, who are notoriously protective of their cubs.

I've been going out fishing with Raino almost every day. The first time we went out, we caught a huge halibut. It must have weighed a good fourteen or fifteen pounds. Fish are so plentiful in these waters; the nets and traps we haul up are never empty. We've been talking a lot about our different fishing techniques and trading our favorite tips.

Often, we're out all day until the sun sets. I could never get tired of this landscape: the colors of the sky, the evergreen forests that stretch as far as the eye can see, and the gentle ripples on the glassy water as the whales swim by. One morning, we come across a doe that's swimming from one little island to another. I had no idea that deer could swim. The poor thing looks petrified. Sea lions are circling all around, trying to drown her so they can make a meal of her. Raino and I escort her to the shore, using his boat and dinghy to keep the predators at bay.

One of the things I love about Raino is that he's a hunter, but he has no interest in racking up trophies. Everyone here has a healthy respect for animals, and people only go hunting so they can put food on the table. What else can they do? There's only one mini-mart in town that sells a few basics at extortionate prices. For everything else, they have to go to Juneau—the closest city of any size—by ferry or air, which isn't exactly affordable either. And anyway, the goal of my journey is not to judge the people I meet, but to observe their way of life and learn from them.

Today is October 16, and it's snowing in Hoonah. Raino decides to take me out deer hunting. He tells me he'll carry the rifle to shoot the deer, and I'll hold another one to cover his back if there are any bears around. Out here, people always hunt with a partner for safety.

"Bears are highly intelligent animals," Raino tells me. "As soon as they hear a gun go off, they know there's going to be something to chow down on. So keep your eyes open, alright? Normally, if you're walking around somewhere there might be bears, you should make a lot of noise—sing, shout, whatever— to scare them away. Not so when you're hunting. If you do that, it's your target you'll be scaring away."

The trail cuts a narrow path between two embankments that obscure the horizon. I don't find this particularly reassuring. A bear could jump right out at us, and we'd never see it coming. We're creeping our way forward very gently. If there's the slightest snap of a twig, Raino turns around with a start. My heart is pounding in my chest. I feel powerless. I really don't want to have to pull the trigger.

Two hours later, we call it a day and return empty-handed. I have to say I'm relieved. I'm definitely more at home on the water among the whales and sea otters.

I've been joining Raino and his wife, Colette, for dinner every night. I feel like I've found a new family here. They've been taking care of me like their own son. To thank them for their hospitality, I bring them homemade French crepes. As we share the halibut we've caught—which is fried just like everything they cook—I tell them all about life back at home in France, and on my little island in Brittany, and how we love to eat grilled lobster and sea bass on a patio under the stars.

Raino keeps giving me gifts. It's gotten to the point where I daren't tell him I like something, because before I know it, he'll be giving it to me!

And if I find him eating something I'm not familiar with, he insists on giving that to me too. "It's all yours. That way, you get to taste it," he insists. Every time I go to his place, I come back to the boat with some sort of gift. He won't have it any other way.

"No, Raino, I'm only asking you what it is," I protest.

"Listen, just take it," he says. "It's all yours; I want you to have it."

I feel like I'm in my element here. I've even been thinking about spending the winter in Hoonah. I'd build myself a nice log cabin and spend my time fishing, like I would on my island back home. I'd spend my life on the water, at one with nature and the animals. I'd live the way the locals do. I'd be a happy man.

Thanks to Raino, I've learned a lot about the Indigenous peoples of Alaska and the pressure of American culture on their traditional way of life. Yesterday he introduced me to Yun, an Indigenous artist. The smell of wood in his workshop is fabulous. There are works of art everywhere in there: totems, paddles, masks, and canoes. Most of them are hidden beneath big sheets. Yun explains that this is to leave the spirits at peace. This man can work magic with his fingers. Yun lives in a tiny wooden hut that's so ramshackle, it's a wonder it's still standing. He greets me with words that belong to an ancient language, surely what people always used to speak here. There are masks all around his home. Suddenly, he pulls one of the masks over his face and starts to wave his arms around and chant in a language I don't understand. Then, in English, he tells me it is through art that Indigenous history and culture is passed down from generation to generation. Contrary to what many believe, totems are not used for worship. Totems are sculpted as a way of honoring ancestors, telling stories, commemorating great events, and symbolizing the clans to which people belong—in Hoonah, that's either the Eagles or the Ravens. Here, history is not recorded in the pages of a book, but in the carvings on a totem.

When the Christian missionaries came to Alaska, the Indigenous peoples were forced to turn their backs on their traditional beliefs, and a great many totems were destroyed. Today, there are a number of Indigenous associations, such as the one Yun is a part of, that advocate to preserve the rich culture and traditions of these First Peoples for the benefit of future generations.

As we say goodbye to Yun, I feel something in my heart I can't explain. This has been a unique and powerful experience for me, and I'm very grateful to Raino for making it happen.

I've been in Hoonah for over a month now. Winter is beginning to set in. I wish I could stay, but I can't. I still have a long way to travel.

As much as it pains me, I have to move on. I have to say goodbye to Raino, like I said goodbye to Uno a year earlier, not knowing whether we'll see each other again. Before I set sail, Raino insists on sending me off on the rest of my journey with a mountain of food. It's fresh, so I'll have to eat it quickly. He's put it all in a cooler, which is also a gift. Not to mention the delicious jars of canned salmon, venison, and wild mushrooms he's loaded me up with. He's even given me a big fishing rod and a bunch of hooks, bait, and a landing net.

Then, he invites me to follow him into his garage, where he keeps all the relics of his and his family's past. Like the bell from the boat that belonged to a buddy of his who was lost at sea. It's a garage full of memories.

Now Raino hands me the most magnificent paddle and says, "Here you go; this is for you."

The paddle has been carved and sculpted by Yun from a special kind of wood for me to hold on to my whole life. And Raino has asked the wise old artist to paint the story of his ancestors on there.

"You see, this is the story of my family. Now, my ancestors will be with you wherever you go. You are under their protection. As long as this paddle is aboard your boat, you have nothing to fear."

I feel overcome with emotion. I'm lost for words. Hanging on the wall at the end of the garage is a huge map of the world. Raino asks me to trace the route that I've sailed since I left home. He's going to trace the rest of my voyage on the map until I return to my native land.

When the time comes to say goodbye, he walks me to my boat. Together, we hang the paddle over my berth.

"Go in peace, Guirec," he says, as he envelops me in a huge bear hug.

Sometimes, it's really hard not to cry.

On October 31, I raise anchor and *Yvinec* glides away on a glassy sea. As we leave Hoonah behind in the fog, a pod of whales circles the boat in a magical dance. In the distance, through the mist, the trees are like huge spiderwebs. It's Halloween, and there's something haunting and otherworldly about the atmosphere. Everything seems eerie in the Inside Passage. The whales are not here by chance. They know we're leaving. They know Monique, *Yvinec*, and I might never come back here. And they want to bid us farewell.

~~~~~~~~~

AS *YVINEC* WEAVES her way stealthily between the islets, I occasionally catch a glimpse of a sea otter's whiskers; other times my eye wanders to a sea lion basking on a buoy or a bear fishing in the shallows.

Always to the rhythm of the tides, we've sailed into some of the villages along the way to replenish our water reserves and pick up a few groceries. After short pit stops in Petersburg and Wrangell, I'm getting a little tired of zigzagging through the fishermen's buoys dotted haphazardly across the middle of the channel—so one night on a whim, I drop anchor on the lee side of an island, where we'll be sheltered. There's a canoe on the beach, so I go ashore to investigate.

Soon I come across a cabin in the woods, and a man steps outside to greet me. His name is Eric, and he's been living here for a few years. He's in his sixties, but he looks thirty years younger. Eric invites me in for a chat. I learn he's essentially self-sufficient. He grows his own vegetables, generates his own power with a solar panel and wind generator, harvests rainwater, and even makes his own sparkling water to drink. For everything else, he gets by with the occasional trip into the nearest village. He also grows his own cannabis. Apparently it's been legalized here. Eric rolls himself a joint and invites me to share it with him. I've never been tempted to try marijuana, but if I were so inclined, now would be the time! At least his weed is homegrown and organic, so I know where it's from. I decline his kind offer; I don't need a joint to make me feel good! Eric and I end up spending the rest of the evening together. I tell him all about my travels, and he tells me all about living off-the-grid. The next morning, we meet at daybreak for a fishing session, and later I sail away with a hold full of shrimp.

A little farther south, I call in at the village of Meyers Chuck for a night. On the dock, I meet a fisherman who's eighty-five years old. He's just been discharged from the hospital. When he was out at sea, he fell overboard and his motorboat started to go round in circles. It ran him over twice, and the propeller sliced his chest open. He's lucky to be alive.

Out here, the closest villages are hours away by boat, so people have no choice but to stick together and figure things out for themselves. My new friend tells me there are only six permanent residents in the village, and visitors are rare at this time of the year. He invites me to join him and the rest of the village for dinner that night so I can tell them all about my adventures.

The next day, it's time to set sail again. Next stop, Canada!

Once we've emerged from the Inside Passage, we hug the Alaska coastline as we keep heading south toward the Canadian border. The water is littered with colossal tree trunks that bang into the hull with a dull thud. Poor *Yvinec* shudders with every impact. I'm feeling her pain. Hasn't she already suffered enough in the ice? During the daytime, I've been managing to steer around the obstacles, but things get much dicier after dark. I have to trust my reflexes to weave my way forward by starlight.

All in all though, I'm happy and my mind is at ease. When I look at the map and trace our route, I realize we've sailed halfway around the world! Where will we go next? There are so many possibilities to explore. As I let my finger wander over the map, I feel as free as the wind.

I check the GPS, and am thrilled to see we've crossed over the border. "Hey Momo, we're in Canada now!"

We're squeezing our way through some narrow channels between the islands and the mainland of the Canadian province of British Columbia. We have to wait for high tide. If we don't, we'll be fighting a current so strong we won't make any headway, even with the engine at full throttle. Sometimes, the water might look calm on the surface, but there are whirlpools sucking water beneath the boat, keeping it from moving forward. These are treacherous waters. If I fall overboard, I'll never be able to climb back onto the boat.

As Cape Scott comes into view, I'm itching to make land so I can start exploring. But I can't afford to let my guard down yet, because these waters around the northern tip of Vancouver Island are notoriously tricky to navigate, even for the locals.

I have a choice to make: whether I should sail down the east or the west coast of the island. I haven't looked into either of these options and end up deciding at the last minute.

"East it is!" I announce to Monique, as if I know what I'm talking about. We set our sights on the small town of Port Hardy. When we get there, I'll replenish my supplies and ask which places on the island I should try to visit. On my chart, I can see that this side of Vancouver Island is dotted with lots of small islands. That means it'll be sheltered, and we'll be sailing in calm waters, just like in the Inside Passage, but there'll be currents to take into account.

As we sail toward Port Hardy though, the tide turns, and suddenly we're fighting against a strong current. I fire up the engine, but still *Yvinec* is struggling along at barely one knot of boat speed. There's a lighthouse on our port side, but after two hours we still haven't passed it. *Yvinec* is running on the spot, so I decide to turn around. I'm not going to waste my diesel if we're not going anywhere.

And so, I decide to round Cape Scott and go down the west coast of the island instead. Off the cape, the boat is listing heavily in the howling wind and I'm having a hard time holding course. With the swell and current to contend with, it's all I can do to stop *Yvinec* from broaching. The last thing I want is for us to take a nose-dive. I know where we're heading, at least. On the map I've scoped out a sheltered place called Winter Harbour, and mercifully it's just a few nautical miles away, down at the end of an inlet.

After hours of challenging sailing, we finally make our way into the marina in the dead of night, soaking wet and very much the worse for wear. I tie *Yvinec* up to a decrepit old pontoon and nearly fall flat on my face when I step out in my rain boots. The old wood is as slippery as an ice rink! I shine my flashlight around, trying to get a sense of my surroundings, but all I can make out are the silhouettes of the trees, dancing in the moonlight. Never mind, it'll be light in a few hours. We'll soon see what this place has in store for us.

Like every time I make land in a new country, I have to complete the formalities for my entry into Canada. First thing in the morning, I make my way to the tiny shack at the end of the wharf.

There I find the village administrator—running on a treadmill. Without breaking pace for a second, she tells me there's no customs or border official here. I'm not surprised! The good news is I can complete the formalities by telephone. But the phone booth in the village is out of order, and there's no cell signal. It's a good thing I have my Iridium satellite phone.

A few minutes later, we've made our official entry. It doesn't get any easier than this.

When I tell the lady on the treadmill that it's all sorted out—she's still running, by the way—she says, "There are four of us who live here in Winter Harbour all year round. If you need supplies, you'll find the store at the end of the road. Don't go today, though; it'll be open tomorrow. It's only open one morning a week!"

Never mind, I'll go fishing instead! After all, there's nothing tastier than fresh-caught fish, right?

And so, in spite of the persistent drizzle, I set off to explore my new surroundings. I need to get some air. There aren't many places to walk around here. The ground is quite boggy, and so there's a boardwalk that people use to get around the village. The wind is rattling the shutters of the wooden houses, many of which have seen better days and have "For Sale" signs out front. Moss-covered walls and roofs with trees growing through them are signs that nature is gradually taking this place back.

As I explore, I see other structures that look perfectly well maintained; perhaps these are vacation homes that only get lived in when the weather is nicer. The fishing is so good here, people must come from far and wide. But clearly, there isn't much to do in the winter!

There's a storm blowing offshore, farther down the end of the inlet. At this time of year in the Pacific Ocean, the swells can be thirty feet or more. Now that I think about it, I'd rather take the inside route, down the east coast of the island. It'll be much calmer. But to do that, I have to double back and round Cape Scott a second time. As soon as the conditions improve, I'll set sail again.

The next day at the general store, the shelves are as empty as the village. In the freezer, there are blocks of butter and packets of bacon, and not much else. It's not exactly appetizing. I pick up a few bare essentials and head back to the boat. In the still water of the small marina, there are dozens of sea otters floating on their backs. They don't seem bothered in the slightest when I step onto the pontoon with my grocery bags.

Ten days later, there's a break in the weather, so I can finally leave Winter Harbour. The conditions are far better this time as I round Cape Scott. The weather is beautiful, and that buoys my spirits. I'm not really sure where I'm going now. I don't know what I want to do next. Everywhere I once dreamed of sailing—the Pacific Islands, Polynesia, Easter Island, Cape Horn,

Antarctica—seems to have lost its appeal. All kinds of questions are running through my mind. What should I do? Should I keep going and tackle the South Seas now, even though I know my boat isn't prepared for that? Would she hold up all right?

Or what if I called it a day and headed home? I could open a restaurant back in Brittany. I could live right by the water. I could fish, windsurf, and paddle to my heart's content. There's no need for me to sail around the world to be happy! More importantly, there's no need for me to impose extreme destinations on myself aboard my rusty, ill-equipped little sailboat.

I'm cold, it smells of damp, and the cabin is full of mold. I need to find a marina where I can lift the boat out of the water and tidy her up. I'm short on cash, but I'll find a way to make some money; I always do. I can't think straight at the moment. My mind is all foggy, and that doesn't bode well. I need to let in the sunshine again.

~~~~~~~~

NOW WE'RE IN Campbell River. A decent-sized town at last! With a huge grocery store, just like the ones I've seen in American movies. And, most importantly, an Internet connection. Going online is the first thing I need to do to start bringing in some money to fix up my boat. Thanks to social media, word has gotten out about Monique and our adventures. I post a whole bunch of photos and videos on Facebook, and soon I'm fielding inquiries from people who are interested in the media rights to my images. Of course, I'm no stranger to working out a deal. So far, I've been selling a few images each week; at this rate, it won't take long before I can start thinking about lifting the boat out of the water.

These photos and videos are also the building blocks for a project I've been working on with my long-distance girlfriend, Lauren, who's in Paris. Together, we've set up a nonprofit association to raise awareness about the beauty and vulnerability of our planet, especially among young people.

By February, I've brought in enough money to do the work I need to do on the boat. I've lifted *Yvinec* out of the water onto a cradle and have been spending my days welding, drilling, and sanding. There's a lot to do. The hull is dented all over the place and clearly weakened, and the anchor well at the bow is full of holes from hitting the slabs of ice up north and the tree trunks in the water down here. I'm going to have to reinforce it all with some new sheet metal. I've decided to make the most of the opportunity by replacing the nodes as well.

I've also installed a new arch over the cockpit, because the old one was being eaten away by rust. The new one is made of stainless steel, and it's designed so that I can hoist my dinghy underneath it while I'm sailing. Up until now, it's been on the deck, so I'll gain a lot of space on board.

I've been working like crazy. Inside the cabin, there's all the mold to scrape away, and the ceiling and walls need repainting. In the boatyard, I've made a couple of friends, who are lending me a helping hand—Emmanuel, who's a local, and Claude, who's from Quebec. Claude has even repainted the little hen at the bow, which the salty spray has weathered away.

At night, I've been sleeping on board, amid all the dust and dirt. There's no way for me to keep myself clean on the boat, because the water supply is disconnected. After a while, I get so fed up, I decide to treat myself to a few nights in a hotel room.

Obviously, you're not supposed to take a chicken into a hotel room, but I've come up with a solution. I simply hide Monique in a bag, making sure to leave a little opening so she can breathe. That way I can smuggle her into and out of the hotel, and no one is any the wiser. The place I decide on is one of those old-school hotels where you have to drop off your key at the front desk when you come and go. Sometimes, when I'm waiting for my key, Monique starts to fuss and wants to poke her head out of the bag. I have to keep my hand on the bag to hold her down and keep her hidden. But to express her discontent, she starts to make little bock-bock-bwawking sounds, so I have to feign a bad cough—believe me, a full-on coughing fit!—until I've retrieved my key from the desk.

To pay for *Yvinec*'s overhaul, as well as to sell videos of my travels to the media, Lauren has organized an exhibition of my photos back in France. And so I buy a plane ticket from Vancouver to Paris, leaving Monique with a buddy in Campbell River, and off I go. My photos of our hibernation in Greenland have been incredibly popular, especially those of *Yvinec* in the pack ice under a blazing pink sky. We've made them into posters and postcards. After the exhibition, I've brought in more than enough money to finish the upkeep on my boat and make the rest of my journey more comfortable.

On my return to Campbell River, my friend tells me Monique hasn't been doing so well. She might even be sick.

What? Momo can't be sick! She was the picture of good health when I left for Paris, so what possibly could have happened? I'm really worried. When I go to pick her up from my friend's place, Monique has lost weight, dropped a few feathers, and she doesn't seem quite herself. In the three weeks I've been gone, she's started to waste away like an iceberg melting in the summer sun. She won't eat, she spends most of her time sleeping, and there's a sadness in her eyes I've never seen before. She does seem happy to see me though, and when she's awake she won't leave my side for a second. I've brought her a few little presents back from France: some fresh grain, dried maggots, and a special mix of vitamins for hens. Little by little, her appetite improves, but this Monique isn't the bundle of energy I know and love.

There's no way we're going to sea with her in this state. I've heard about a vet, an American guy who specializes in treating birds—and especially hens. His practice is hours away from here, but I'd be willing to cross an entire continent to make sure Monique is all right. I make an appointment, and when we get to his office, the vet examines Monique and gives her a clean bill of health. There's no viral or bacterial infection. So what's wrong with her, then?

"She's depressed," the vet tells me.

Seriously? I remember, when I had to fly home to France for emergency surgery on my appendix, she seemed a little down when I got back to Greenland. But she soon bounced back, and I'd never given it a second thought. This time, though, I was away for longer. And it looks like Monique has really suffered in my absence. This might be a problem, going forward. What am I supposed to do if she can't live without me?

For now, though, she's here with me, and I'm not going anywhere without her. And neither is she.

I'VE ANNOUNCED ON social media that I'll be continuing my journey as soon as *Yvinec* is ready to take to the water again. Monique and I have hatched a plan. We're going to set sail for French Polynesia and its idyllic atolls. We could really see ourselves lounging around in paradise on the beaches of the Marquesas Islands, Bora Bora, Tahiti, and Mo'orea, and swimming in their clear turquoise lagoons. I've done a few interviews about the exhibition we put on, and used the opportunity to let people know where we'd be going next: first, we plan to sail from Vancouver to the Marquesas Islands, then spend the next four months exploring French Polynesia.

But at the beginning of April, I receive an e-mail from Lauren with a newspaper article attached. It's from the front page of a Tahitian newspaper, and it's dated March 29, 2017. The first thing I notice is the headline in big block letters: "Monique the Globe-Trotting Hen Not Welcome."

What?!? I keep on reading: "The globe-trotting French sailor Guirec Soudée announced plans last week to set sail for Tahiti in April. For obvious reasons around the restricted entry of animals to French Polynesia, and to ensure the island remains protected from sanitary risks, officials say the traveler's pet hen, Monique, is not welcome here."

The article ends with a sobering notice that "it is a criminal offense to bring in animals that can carry diseases." They're worried Monique is going to spread avian influenza. If we go there, I could face six months in jail and a fine of up to 3,570,000 CFP francs—that's almost 35,000 U.S. dollars! And Monique would be risking her life.

I guess we won't be going to paradise. Don't worry, Momo; I promise I'm not going anywhere without you anymore.

Well then, where are we supposed to go? There are only so many places to stop in the middle of the Pacific Ocean, and what if we're not welcome on any of the other islands either? But there's no point worrying about that right now—I have to finish the work on *Yvinec* before I can think about coming up with a plan B. Because without a boat, whether Momo is with me or not, I'm not moving an inch.

I'm still slaving away. It's starting to get warm out. At the beginning of May, I decide to rent a room from someone in town for a week or two. It's in an outbuilding at the end of the owner's garden, and it has its own shower. That way, I can get a good night's sleep and work harder during the day.

As spring turns to summer, my efforts are really starting to pay off. This boat of mine has never looked so good! Inside the cabin, there's now a brand-new gas stove, a rustic shower, and a usable toilet—what luxury! The repaired and freshly painted walls are as good as new. I've installed extra shelving and put in a new sink and countertop. It's all fitted out in pale wood, so it feels nice and cozy in there, like a cocoon. I've even managed to persuade a local grandma to sew me some beige curtains to hang over the little cabin windows! I've also replaced the batteries on the boat, which cost a small fortune. As for sailing equipment, I've repaired the electric winch, so I won't have to haul up the anchor chain by hand anymore. I've replaced the lines, bought new two anchors, installed a new VHF, put in some new solar panels, and set up a new mast for the wind generator.

Yvinec is now back in the water, tied up at the dock in Campbell River. She looks magnificent, and she's ready to set sail whenever I am. It feels good to be back on board my boat, and I'm starting to get the urge to sail again. It's summertime, and the Pacific wind and sea air are teasing me. The South Seas are calling my name.

Before I set sail for California and the destination I've chosen for my next epic solo journey—Antarctica—I decide to treat myself to a circumnavigation of Vancouver Island. I want to venture deep into the forests here in search of bears, wolves—maybe even a cougar. All from a safe distance, of course, because these creatures are just as dangerous as they are magnificent. People have been telling me, "By the time you've seen the cougar, it's already too late."

I'm seeing the dark, depressing villages I happened upon last winter come to life. Gone are the mossy docks, deserted streets, and abandoned houses lurking in the mist. The houses are now brimming with life and the boats moored in the marina are sparkling clean. There's a real summer vacation vibe. I'm lying flat on my stomach behind a rock, just waiting for a bear or a wolf to wander into the view of my camera lens. Black bears are everywhere up here, even along the paved roads.

I've just met a French guy named Damien. Like me, he's left everything behind in search of adventure. He's built himself a cabin by the beach, and he lives there year-round. Together— with Monique too, of course—we decide to set out on a three-day trek into the wilderness to immerse ourselves completely in nature, using a kayak to explore the coast. In the evening, we find a remote beach, go ashore, pitch our tent by the water, and light a fire.

We haven't seen any wolves in the forest, but we have seen lots of bears. Damien says they aren't aggressive. He tells me if they get too close to just clap my hands, and they'll go away. He seems to know what he's talking about. As for cougars, I understand they're a rare sight; the people here don't tend to think they're a real danger.

I have to keep an eye on Monique the whole time we're out here. Not so much because of the bears, but the bald eagles—as soon as she starts strutting around the beach, they spread their enormous wings and circle around overhead. Then there are the sea lions and seals to worry about, not to mention the foxes. The poor thing, she really hasn't had much fun since we arrived in Canada. There are too many predators. Whenever I can't carry her, I have to make sure she's safe indoors.

Before we round Cape Scott a third time, we call in at Hope Island, a tiny island of barely sixty residents, right at the very northern tip of Vancouver Island. I hop ashore and set off down a leafy trail lined with wildflowers. A short way in, I come across a sign that says, "Welcome to the Homelands of the Tlatlasikwala Nation." Oh, that's a nice way to be greeted, I say to myself. But then I see another sign just below the first, which seems rather less welcoming: "STOP: Authorized Persons Only Past This Point."

And then, the sign continues: "Hope Island is home to the Tlatlasikwala people. A Coast Guard station operated here from 1920 to 1988. In 1989, the federal government returned the land to the Tlatlasikwala Nation. The buildings you see are private homes. Access beyond is by invitation only. Thank you."

I can understand that the people here want their privacy. But honestly, I figure there's not much chance the place is overrun with tourists.

So I walk on past the sign, eager to explore this place. Right away, a bird swoops down from out of nowhere, heading for me.

"Hey! Watch it!" I wave my arms around to shoo it away, then laugh the whole thing off and keep on walking. But the bird isn't having any of it. It circles around and swoops in again, on the attack. Again, I try to wave it away with one hand and protect my face with the other arm, but it won't let up. The bird looks something like a small hen, with big feet and a crest on its head. Every time I take a step forward, it charges at me and flies in circles overhead, clearly trying to keep me away. This is one tenacious bird! I'm starting to question my judgment. Then I think about Raino and the basics of the Indigenous culture he tried to teach me. I remember what he told me about animals never appearing by chance, their presence always being a sign. And suddenly, it dawns on me: this bird is telling me not to go any farther. This is not my home, and no one has invited me here. Worse still, I'm a descendant of the white Europeans who colonized this part of the world and decimated the Tlatlasikwala people. So I give up. More awed and impressed than I'd like to admit, I turn around and make my way back to the boat.

My experiences farther down the coast turn out to be much more pleasant. I encounter lots of friendly people, former urbanites who have turned their backs on the consumer lifestyle and the modern comforts of city life to live in remote, isolated places on the beach or by the edge of the forest—just for a while, or maybe forever.

From one dock and pontoon to another, I gradually sail my way down the west coast of Vancouver Island. After Winter Harbour, I pass Cape Cook, one of the westernmost points in Canada, before stopping in at Kyuquot, Nootka Island, and Hot Springs Cove. From one place to the next, the sailing is smooth.

Everywhere I go ashore, I go fishing, swimming, walking around, and taking photos. I'm in paradise.

On August 3, I arrive in Tofino, a funky little surf town with cool cafés and restaurants that serve plenty of fresh fruit and vegetables. It's nice to eat something other than hamburgers for a change. The place is full of young surfers, and a fair number of Aussies and Kiwis. Tall and tanned with long blond hair, they look every inch the stereotypical beach bum. From morning to night, everyone here seems to walk around in boardshorts or wetsuits with a surfboard under one arm. Tofino is like the Woodstock of surfing. That's fine by me. I've been looking forward to getting back out there and catching a few waves. I haven't been surfing in ages.

The only problem with being in vacation mode is how easy it is to get used to. It's painful for me to wrench myself away from Tofino on the last day of August. I'm sure I could have settled down there quite happily for a while.

After six days of sailing with the wind behind me, I'm not far from the coast of California when my AIS system warns me of heavy cargo traffic heading our way at a speed of twenty knots. Their trajectory is a little concerning. I'm worried they haven't seen me, so I call them on the VHF to warn them that I'm here and to avoid a collision. Container ships are a very real danger dreaded by every sailor. From way up on the bridge, the captain might not even feel the impact of a collision. In the early hours of the morning, after a sleepless night, I can just make out a dark mass floating ahead of our path. As I move in for a closer look, I'm amazed to discover a slumbering whale that looks like it's sleeping at the surface. A little farther along, I can see fins cresting the waves. I can't believe it; these are the first sharks I've seen! They circle around as I approach, and trail away in my wake all too soon. I'm still reliving the moment when the silhouette of the Golden Gate Bridge emerges from the mist.

Yvinec is gliding along beautifully, all sails flying as we pass beneath this iconic steel monster of a bridge, escorted by a flotilla of container ships, other sailboats, and kitesurfers. Everyone raves about what a fantastic city San Francisco is. But I'm not really the urban type, so I have a hard time appreciating a city of this size, even though I'm sure its unique geography would be interesting to explore, and the eternal tug-of-war between fishermen and sea lions on the wharves would be fun to see. I don't feel like sticking around here for long. Everything is crazy expensive; even just a slip in the marina costs a hundred bucks a night. There's no way I'm paying that kind of money. This sailboat isn't a million-dollar yacht. I'd far rather head across the bay and cast anchor in Sausalito instead.

Making my official entry into the United States proves to be quite the challenge. There are no customs officials waiting to come aboard, so I have to go find them, and that's easier said than done. It takes me forever to find the right place, and no one seems to know where I should be going. I keep getting sent to one neighborhood after another and find myself taking the subway to the most far-flung parts of the city. Eventually, I find the right office and announce myself with all the necessary documentation. Not for the first time, I'm unsure whether I should declare that I have an animal on board. I know the American authorities don't mess around and it would be better not to lie to them. But if I tell them the truth, I'm worried things could go equally badly for me. And so I decide not to say anything, for the love of my dear Monique. I sure hope they don't decide to come aboard.

Suddenly the customs official, who's tapping away at his computer keyboard, turns to me and says, "Wow, this is incredible! I'm on your website, and your photos are superb." I should be flattered, but instead I feel sheepish. Here I am, trying to be discreet, but he's on my website, and he can obviously see photos of Monique too. It's only a matter of time before his mood changes; I just know it. But no, the U.S. customs official is calling his colleagues over to look at the images on his screen, and now they're chuckling and enthusing about what an amazing experience it all must have been.

Seriously, you can't make this stuff up! I was already imagining them slapping the cuffs on me and walking me to a jail cell; who'd have thought the long arm of the law would fawn over a bunch of pretty pictures? I can't wait to get back to the boat and tell Momo what just happened.

Before we set sail on the next long stretch of our adventure, I have to lift *Yvinec* out of the water again to give her hull a checkup and make sure it's as watertight as it should be. I'm heading for the most isolated region of the globe, where there are few, if any, places to stop over, so I'd better be well prepared. I've also done a lot of electrical work on board, both inside and out. At last, I have some proper lighting out on deck, so I won't have to use my headlamp anymore. Plus, I've invested in a satellite Internet setup worthy of a round-the-world racing yacht, with two antennas, a FleetBroadband s250 terminal (to make sure I have a proper data connection on board), as well as an Iridium GO!

satellite hotspot—so I can run a vessel tracker and get real-time weather reports. That way, anyone who wants to can track my position online at any time, even when I'm completely out of my depth in the middle of the Pacific Ocean! I've installed a brand-new automatic pilot as well as a new self-steering system. And that's not all—I've invested in a new radar system that will detect icebergs as we get closer to Antarctica, and I've replaced the genoa furler too.

I'm not quite ready to leave San Francisco yet, though. First, I'm going to give myself a few days to enjoy a classic American road trip. Who hasn't dreamed of driving a camper van through Yosemite National Park and down the iconic Highway 1 to Malibu, Santa Monica, and Los Angeles?

All feathers are on deck for the next day at sea!

Photo by Jean-Philippe Mériglie

PART 5

~

How Far South Can We Go?

O N THE MORNING of November 30, we pass below the Golden Gate Bridge once more, this time heading back out to sea. It's time for us to head toward the South Pacific! We're leaving civilization behind again, and we won't be back for a while. There are seven thousand nautical miles to cover if we want to sail all the way down the coast of South America to Ushuaia, on the southernmost tip of the continent—that's the same as three Atlantic crossings. If all goes well, that should be about two months of sailing. Unless something happens and we have to make land along the way, this will be the longest amount of time I've ever spent at sea. I feel a mix of excitement and trepidation.

Once we're out of the bay, I raise the sails. Right now, we're making good headway, doing five to six knots of boat speed in fifteen knots of wind. I've started out by sticking fairly close to the coast, but with all the fishing boat traffic to navigate around, I've had to keep watch on deck all the time. That soon gets tiring, so it isn't long before we head farther offshore.

Somehow, I've been feeling a little seasick. This has never happened to me before. But for months now, I've either been sailing inshore coastal waters, or I've been on land. I guess I've lost my sea legs. The swell is turning my stomach. It's a good thing I have an ace co-skipper on board with me. Life on *Yvinec* has turned Monique into an old sea dog. She takes everything in stride. No matter how high the swell is rolling, she moves to the rhythm of the boat, shifting her weight from one foot to the other. Just a few hours is all it's taken for her to get used to life on the ocean waves again and start figure skating her way around the deck like a pro. Feathers flapping in the wind, she's watching out for flying fish.

I feel like a rookie all over again. Even the slightest maneuver seems to take me forever to do. My spinnaker has torn, because I let it fall in the water when I was pulling it down. I'd better pull myself together, because where we're going, there'll be no margin for error. The Roaring Forties and Furious Fifties—famous for their intense windstorms—are notoriously challenging latitudes to sail through, and the legendary Cape Horn is sure to put me through my paces.

I'm lying in my berth, but having a hard time falling asleep. I've been feeling a little down, and there's no real reason why. I figure it's probably normal for me to feel this way; I am heading out on a very long and grueling journey. Or maybe I'm bummed because I'm not allowed to stop over in Tahiti with my feathered friend. It's so frustrating. We're going to pass right by, and because it's pretty much the halfway point on our way to Antarctica, it would be the perfect place to take a break.

My mind is still a jumble of questions, but I can't resist the idea of sailing from one Pole to the other and doing one big loop of the globe from top to bottom, finishing up at my little island in Brittany. If we make good headway and don't run into too many problems, I'll be back home in seven or eight months. It would be easier, for sure, to cut through the Panama Canal, but I'm thirsty for adventure. I'll save that route for another journey in my later years.

It's a dream to make land in Antarctica too, so I can go say hello to the penguins. But the icebergs down there are formidable beasts. And I'm going to be even more isolated than I was in Greenland, so I'd better not run into any big problems.

I'm sitting on deck, up at the bow. Gazing out at the sea, the sky, the moon, and the stars, I can feel the wind and the salt on my skin. I think about my father. I wonder where he is now, if he really is somewhere, and if he's found what he believed in so strongly. I figure that's part of the reason I'm feeling down—knowing he won't be there with his pipe and his hearty laugh to see me sail home. I've been trying to read, but I can't focus.

Now we're off the coast of Mexico, and I'm enjoying the tropical climate. It's been more than two years since I felt this kind of heat on my skin. I've been making the most of the conditions to put the finishing touches on the repairs I did in San Francisco. I knew I'd find some time to wrap up the finer details before we hit the livelier latitudes.

As we make our way south, images of what I imagine the Roaring Forties will be like keep looping around in my mind. The thought of it thrills me—and gives me butterflies in my stomach. On the one hand, I realize how incredibly lucky I am to be experiencing an epic adventure like this at my age, and on the other, I can't help but think it's crazy for me to be taking these kinds of unnecessary risks. I've been scaring myself reading books about skippers going through hell in the South Seas—boats capsizing, sailors going missing. Each book I read is more frightening than the last. Still, I reassure myself that I'm familiar with my boat; she's an extension of me, and together we'll have what it takes. Plus, I have Raino's paddle hanging over my berth, and right beside that, a photo of my father, who I know is watching over me. I feel protected.

As we sail closer to the equator, we've been encountering one squall after another. I can see them coming from far away. Whenever a low, dark cloud starts to take shape on the horizon, I reduce sail and take all the right precautions.

I also seize the opportunity to lather myself with soap from head to toe and wait for the squall to arrive and rinse me down with rainwater. Monique appreciates it, I'm sure. She looks at me as if to say, "It was about time; you were starting to smell!"

We're sailing close-hauled (pointing as close to the wind as possible), so the boat is heeling to the side and the waves are breaking over the deck. That means I have to keep the cabin windows closed, and the air soon gets stifling inside. *Yvinec* is starting to feel more like a sauna than a sailboat. I'm sweating buckets. It's so hot, it almost makes me miss Greenland! There's nothing more refreshing than seeing an iceberg right outside and a few growlers in the water! Monique seems to be desperate for a breath of fresh air too. She's been wandering around with her beak wide open and her wings spread all the time. The heat doesn't deter her from laying eggs, though; I'm pleased to say.

The sailing conditions are getting pretty frustrating. There are crosscurrents to contend with, and the winds are highly variable. Between the gusts, it's dead calm and the sails just flap. All we can do is wait for the next squall to bring some wind and fill our sails. When the wind does fill in, it's all or nothing. One time, it blows through and tips the boat, making all the books fall off the bookshelf onto my head, and another, it sends my dinner flying across the galley. Now the wind is blowing a solid twenty knots side-on. I've furled the genoa and reefed the mainsail for control, but our boat speed is only five knots. It's as if we have a stowaway clinging to the bottom of the hull. Maybe a whale has decided to hitch a ride with us; I guess I'm not the only one dreaming of the southern latitudes. We just have to grin and bear it.

After fifteen days at sea, we're entering the dreaded doldrums, an area right in the middle of the Pacific Ocean where the tropical air masses converge—and give sailors a real headache. As well as the weather conditions that have been pushing us too far to the west and halting our progress to the south, I feel like I'm caught in the *proverbial* doldrums. On board, it's been one disaster after another. The anemometer and navigation lights at the top of the mast have stopped working. My brand-new water tank has already sprung a leak, and all my fresh water reserves have spilled out into the bilge. The leading edge of the genoa has torn around the luff wire. And to top it all off, the gooseneck, the fitting that attaches the boom to the mast, has just snapped. That's a lot of things to go wrong all at once, and barely two weeks since the overhaul in San Francisco. I feel deflated. But I have to fix everything—and fast. I don't know where to start. But I do know I'm going to need a clear head, so I decide to get some rest before I do anything. A few hours of sleep are sure to help.

When I wake up, I decide on my priorities. The gooseneck is the most urgent thing to fix. I plug my welding machine into the generator, and before I lug everything over to the foot of the mast, I do a test in the shelter of the cockpit—because technically the generator isn't powerful enough for this kind of job. Phew, it works! But now I have to lug everything over to the foot of the mast. That's easier said than done, because this isn't a millpond; it's the middle of the ocean.

Once everything is plugged in and ready to go, I pull on a mask and gloves and get to work. I end up spending the whole day out there.

Things aren't working the way I thought they would, and it's getting dangerous. The waves keep splashing me, fireworks of sparks are flying in all directions, and I keep giving myself electric shocks. Eventually I manage to jury-rig something together, and with a sense of pride I reattach the boom to the mast. But in a matter of seconds, the weld fails. I scream with rage. My nerves are frayed, but I take a deep breath and try again. I grind away the broken metal and set about creating a new weld, but before I know it, the sparks have set the deck grip on fire. Now I'm swatting at the deck to put the fire out. Suddenly, I feel a shooting pain in my foot. A spark has gone through my shoe and burned me. I unplug everything, realizing it's madness to be messing around with this kind of equipment in these conditions. I was a whisker away from grabbing my survival kit and jumping into my dinghy in the middle of the Pacific Ocean to watch my boat—and Monique—go up in flames.

Deciding it's best to abandon the welding idea, I eventually manage to tie the gooseneck back in place with a bunch of lines. But how long will that hold? I can't sail into the Roaring Forties with a boat in this kind of shape. I have to stop over somewhere; that much is clear. But where? We're off the coast of Costa Rica right now, but more than four thousand nautical miles offshore! And even if I did decide that was a good idea, the winds are against us. Polynesia is fifteen days to the west, the way the winds are blowing. That would be the wisest place to go, but we're not wanted over there. I guess I'll just have to take my chances. Monique doesn't understand what's going on. She looks at me quizzically, with a hint of sadness in her eye. I don't know what's going on with this hen of mine. She's usually chirpier than this.

Today is Christmas Day, and what better present could I ask for than to cross the equator? This is a great moment and a first for *Yvinec*, Monique, and me. I feel a renewed sense of excitement. We've just crossed the invisible line that slices the world in two, and Monique doesn't seem to realize that we're bringing the dreams of my childhood to life. The globe I used to trace my finger around in my bedroom is now our playground. I can't believe we're now sailing in the Southern Hemisphere!

It's a special holiday, so I'm thinking about my family at home in France. Every year, my father would bring all eight of his children together at Christmas. Since I've been away, the family has grown even bigger, and I've never met some of my new nephews and nieces. My sisters are turning into mother hen types;

Monique's going to have some competition when we get home. I'm looking forward to introducing her to her new family and showing her around Yvinec, my island paradise. When I think about that, it buoys my spirits and keeps me going. But home has never seemed farther away.

A bird has just landed on the boat. It isn't a seabird, so where could it possibly have come from? There are no other boats around at all. The closest land is days away. I've put a few of Monique's grains on deck to feed our unexpected visitor. It's nice to welcome a new guest aboard. I try to approach, but the bird is afraid and flies a little farther away. In one of his books, the great French sailor Bernard Moitessier wrote about the little birds he would come across at sea, in the middle of nowhere. Lost birds, he used to call them. As I watch my little lost bird flit around the boat from one end to the other, it strikes me that I'm not so different, being so far away from my home, and my family too. The next morning, the bird has gone.

It's January 1, 2018. As one thrilling, adventure-packed year draws to a close, another great one is just beginning. We're slowly heading down toward Polynesia. I'd happily turn on the engine and motor for a while to get some miles under our belt, but when we left San Francisco, I was so eager to get going that I forgot to fill up with diesel. As a result, I've only been turning on the engine to recharge the batteries. I need to save as much diesel as I can for emergencies.

We're still having to sail due west to catch the wind. It's barely blowing at all—only about six knots—but it's better than nothing. In the night, I wake to the sound of seabirds calling. It's a sign we're getting closer to land. After a month at sea, that's reassuring.

When I get up in the morning, I see that these are white-tailed tropicbirds, with bright orange beaks and distinctive tails as long and thin as straw. In French, we actually call them "straw-tails." I open Monique's coop so she can see these beautiful birds for herself. I try to imitate their call and wave my arms to catch their attention—every time I come across another living being out here, I feel elated.

Monique is only laying an egg every two or three days now. That's not unusual; she's getting older.

I'm looking forward to rounding Cape Horn, checking out Antarctica, cruising back up the Atlantic, and sailing home to Brittany. I think about that little island of mine every day. Often, when everyone else in the house was asleep, I would sneak out of bed without a sound, pull on some shorts and a waterproof jacket, and venture out into the salty night with my fishing gear under my arm to flirt with the tide.

The winds are still carrying us west. If we're not careful, we're going to end up in Indonesia or Australia. It's time we started heading east again. But first, we have to set our sights on the nearest land. It's crucial that I find somewhere sheltered so I can do these essential repairs. When I check the GPS, I can see a tiny desert island that should give me the shelter from the swell that I need.

It's still 650 nautical miles away, though. That's one heck of a detour. When you go to sea, you should always expect the unexpected; when you run into problems, that's when the real adventure begins. In fact, I've made this my official motto: No problems, no adventure!

The wind is playing hard to get, and the water is a balmy eighty-two degrees Fahrenheit. I figure I might as well make the most of the chance to lower the sails and go for a swim with thirteen thousand feet of ocean beneath me. I've gotten into the habit of leaving about sixty feet of rope trailing behind the boat as a safety precaution, just in case I fall overboard. It also comes in handy when I want to go for a swim offshore, especially since the boat doesn't have a ladder.

There's always an element of risk when you're in the middle of the ocean. Even in the calmest of conditions, you never know when you might have to climb back aboard in a hurry. It's every sailor's worst nightmare to be floundering in the water, watching their boat sail off without them. I once heard a horrific story about an empty sailboat that was found with fingernail scratch marks all over the hull. The crew had apparently gone for a swim and forgotten to lower the ladder, and the gunwale was too high up from the water—so they had no way to climb back on deck. It gives me the heebie-jeebies just thinking about it.

Today, January 3, is my birthday. Monique has given me the best present I could ever ask for, a lovely fresh egg. Cracked onto a delicious French crepe topped with a candle, it sets the mood nicely for a little celebration. The next day, the wind veers north and freshens. Just what we needed! We're averaging seven knots of boat speed now. This is the fastest we've sailed since we left San Francisco. The swell is forming nicely, and sometimes *Yvinec* breaks the nine-knot barrier as she surfs down into the troughs. These are the thrilling conditions I've been missing for the last few weeks. I'm sailing wing-on-wing with both hands on the tiller. I'm hoping to get where I'm going before it gets dark, because

I don't have a detailed chart of the area, and I know these islands in the Pacific are all surrounded by reefs. The last thing I want is to run aground here.

As the sun goes down, I can finally see the mysterious island ahead. When we draw near, I slow our boat speed and climb the mast to try and find the channel with my spotlight. I hear the swing keel clunk against something, though, so I decide not to take the risk of going any farther right now. We'll cast anchor here tonight, and check things out properly in the light of day.

The next morning, I'm amazed to discover an island paradise surrounded by clear turquoise water. It's like a dream come true after forty days at sea. For three glorious days, Monique and I take advantage of a calm anchorage, sheltered from the swell, to focus on fixing up the boat. I want to make sure *Yvinec* is as tough as a tank for her journey to Antarctica, so I inspect and fine-tune everything on board. This is my chance to repair the navigation lights; disassemble, grease, and reassemble the winches; fix my water tank; and collect enough rainwater to replenish my reserves until I make it to Cape Horn. Most importantly, I attend to the most delicate operation of all, the gooseneck. This time, I manage to do a decent weld that looks like it'll hold up good and strong. I also go diving under the boat to clean off some barnacles and grime from the hull. While I'm down there swimming among the reef sharks, I figure I might as well catch a few fish too. Life is so sweet here; I feel like I'm in my element. It's frustrating to know that Monique and I can't go exploring all the other beautiful Polynesian islands. Maybe it's for the best, because I might never want to leave.

After I've caught up on sleep and enjoyed some sun, I hoist the sails again, and this little desert island tugs at my heartstrings as I watch it disappear in *Yvinec*'s wake. I decide to treat myself to a little pleasure by opening one of Raino's jars of canned food. It's delicious. I say a silent word of thanks to my friend in Alaska every time I savor one of his wonderful gifts.

I've found a new hobby: fly hunting! I have no idea where they're coming from, but flies have well and truly invaded the boat. There are hundreds of them! Monique is loving this, but I'm at my wit's end. It's hell. They're laying eggs all over the boat, and it seems new flies are hatching all the time.

The wind is out there somewhere. Farther south, the storms are rolling through one after the other. I'm almost looking forward to those heavy conditions that are going to push us all the way to Cape Horn.

In the meantime, I might as well put on my biologist's hat and collect some plankton samples with my special plankton net. Why, you might ask? Well, Monique and I have signed on with Plankton Planet, an initiative associated with Stanford University that relies on scientific researchers and pleasure boaters like us to gather data about plankton in the world's oceans. Plankton play an essential role in the survival of the ocean's ecosystems because they form the base of the whole marine food chain. Not only that, but since they contribute more than fifty percent of the oxygen in the earth's atmosphere, you could argue they are also essential to human survival as well. The problem is, in some parts of the world today, there can be as much as six times more plastic in the ocean than plankton. When this plastic breaks down into microparticles, fish can't tell the difference. It's horrifying when you stop to think about what that means. Our precious natural environment is vital to life on this planet. We marvel at its beauty and the resources it gives us, but we're also slowly killing it.

As the days go by, they're all starting to blend into one another. Today, I figure I might as well spruce myself up a little. But I mess up with the hair clippers, so I end up shaving all my hair off.

It's been nearly two months since we left San Francisco, and the farther south we sail, the cooler the temperatures have been getting. We're now at a latitude of 36 degrees south. This will probably be my last chance to take a shower for a while, so I make the most of it. I've prepared Monique's winter quarters inside the cabin. The wind still hasn't returned, but I can sense that things are about to get serious. We're bobbing up and down on a massive swell that's probably coming our way from the storms in the South Pacific. Here, the depressions can generate some mighty impressive swells that travel huge distances without losing any of their power—because there are no obstacles in their way. This phenomenon only occurs in latitudes as unforgiving as these.

I'm starting to get a strange feeling. I can't help but wonder whether we're being gently coaxed into the lion's den.

At the end of January, we venture into the Roaring Forties, and there's a depression just waiting to say hello. No sooner have we crossed the line on the map than it's blowing a solid forty-five knots with waves as big as thirty feet. I can hardly believe my eyes. It's like a big sign on the gateway to this latitude warning us exactly what we're getting ourselves into. According to the weather records, it's only a small depression, but it looks pretty darn intense to me already. I dread to think what the big storms will look like when we encounter them. It's challenging enough as it is for me to make it through this one.

I'm only flying the smaller staysail, but *Yvinec* is still blasting along at up to fourteen knots and even broaching a few times in the powerful breakers. I dare not leave the helm for a second. I'm getting some real adrenaline rushes, and I'm hanging on the best I can, trying to guide the boat down into the troughs as smoothly as possible. We eventually make it into calmer waters without any damage, but I definitely feel like I've been through the wringer. Inside the cabin, all the books on the shelf have flown across the floor, but Momo is safe and sound in her cozy coop, though she's covered in wood shavings from her bedding.

I've been trying to go barefoot around the boat as much as I can. It's my way of convincing myself that it's not as cold as it actually is. So, at night, I wear nothing on my feet, but I need a hat to keep my shaved head warm.

In the daytime, Monique is usually out on deck, but she's been getting a little too adventurous—especially since it's been raining squid! They've been washing over the deck whenever a wave hits the side of the hull, and Monique just jumps right onto them. I'm worried she'll go overboard if I don't coop her up safe inside.

Now that I can take stock of this first depression, I figure I've fared pretty well. Out here, things can very quickly go catastrophically wrong; no matter what communications devices I have on board, there's no one to help if I get into trouble. We're not far from Point Nemo, the most remote spot in the ocean;

nowhere on Earth is farther away from land than this point on the map. I find that completely mind-boggling. A profound sense of solitude has come over me, and I'm trying to put it out of my mind.

It's not easy to make the tactical choices to get out of this area as quickly as we can. We need to be carrying enough sail to make good headway, but we don't want to be overpowered and end up wrecking the boat. We have to pace ourselves, as the great Moitessier would say.

I'm in good spirits, though a little nervous. Life on board is going well. Monique is sliding from one side of the cabin to the other when she isn't safely tucked up in her coop. She doesn't seem to be faring too badly on these ocean roller coasters. I've been giving her double rations to get her ready for the colder temperatures. These days, she's eating a gourmet blend of oyster shells for calcium and dried insects for protein, as well as a little more grain than usual. Meanwhile, because I'm mindful of the need to save water, I've been eating things that need less water to cook. For example, instant ramen noodles use less water than pasta, so I've been working my way through one packet of those after another. The canned food I bought in the States is pretty unappetizing—nothing like the kind of stuff you find in a French grocery store. Thank goodness for instant mashed potatoes. I've come up with some pretty inventive culinary creations. One of my favorites is beans in maple syrup on a bed of mashed potatoes. I'm sure it'll be the next big thing in fancy restaurants.

The wind has died completely now, but the swell is still pitching and rolling the boat around. At night, the sails are flapping so loudly it's unbearable. I'm desperate to get some sleep so I can gather my strength and tackle the next storm. We're heading too far west, but if I veer east the wind will be right behind us. I'd have to pole out the genoa to keep it filled, but with this swell that would be too much of a pain. And so I give up on the idea of poling out the genoa and running with the wind, and decide instead to zigzag my way downwind toward Cape Horn, which is still two thousand nautical miles away. I don't really have any other option; I have to keep making progress, whatever it takes. Tonight, I find myself in awe at the spectacular sight of an enormous moon right over the bow. It's lighting up the entire surface of the water and is surrounded by a halo of color, like some sort of rainbow. I've never seen anything like this before, and it takes me a while to tear my eyes away from it.

Whenever I can find a little downtime, I read a few more pages of Bernard Moitessier's account of his journey to Cape Horn. He set sail from Tahiti. It took him eleven days to sail from the Roaring Forties to the cape. In his book there's a detailed map of the route he took, so I'm trying to sail the same course as best I can. I like the idea of following in the wake of a great seafarer like him. Guys like him didn't have a GPS to guide them. All they had to navigate with was a sextant. Without any weather reports to go on, they had no idea what they were heading into. I figure they must have been pretty ballsy back then to do this kind of thing.

For sure, I crossed the Atlantic without any kind of weather forecast, but after I left the Caribbean, my buddy Johann would always send me a weather report by text message every two or three days, and I made do with that until I got to Alaska. Now I have an Internet connection, which has revolutionized the way

I sail—even though the forecasts are only really reliable within a three-day window.

I'm trying to get some sleep—which is a pretty rare thing right now—when all of a sudden I hear the wind cranking up another notch or two. I need to go put a third reef in the mainsail, I figure, but the genoa should be fine as I've reefed that down a lot. Then, just as I'm getting dressed to go out on deck, I hear a sickening boom.

As I dash out the hatch, I can see right away that the genoa has come completely unfurled. In my mind, it's already torn to shreds, especially since there was already a small tear I tried to hide. I scurry to the front of the boat as the waves keep breaking over the deck. Dammit, the furler line has snapped. I have to feed another line through the genoa furler drum, and fast. I try to ease out the genoa sheet but then it starts flapping all over the place, and the forestay starts shaking so hard that the whole rigging is moving now as well. I'm terrified we'll get dismasted; that would be a total disaster. I steer downwind as much as I can, but it's not enough.

The wind is so strong now, I have no choice but to roll in the sail by hand, and that takes every ounce of strength I have. The whole thing seems to be taking forever. It takes me back to the times I had to haul up 250 feet of anchor chain during the storms in Greenland. Once the genoa is safely furled, I quickly put a third reef in the mainsail.

After that, I can't stop shaking. It takes me a while to calm my nerves. I've given myself a good scare with this incident, but somehow I've managed to escape unscathed.

Today, I saw my first boat down here! It was a big container ship, far away in the distance. But still, I was happy to know I wasn't completely alone in these unfriendly waters.

It's February 12, and now there are only 1,050 nautical miles between us and Cape Horn. We're covering about 130 nautical miles a day and averaging about five and a half knots of boat speed, which is pretty decent for *Yvinec*. We're entering the Furious Fifties now, and the purity of this seascape is surreal. This is what total isolation looks like. But there's a big depression coming from the west, and it's headed right for us. Because of a connection problem, I haven't been able to download the right weather record, but it's imperative that I have the right information to plan my next move. There are only two solutions, as far as I can see. One is to stay here and wait it out, but I don't like the sound of that. The other is to steer more southeast than south, which would take us nearer to the coast, and that's what I decide to do.

The wind is starting to freshen already, so it won't be long before the storm is upon us. I'm just about to lower the mainsail when, suddenly, a huge breaker slams into us. The wave knocks *Yvinec* all the way onto her side so the mast hits the water, leaving me floundering at the helm, clipped into my lifeline—thank goodness—in the trough of a forty-foot swell. I have to get to the foot of the mast and lower the mainsail, or we're going under. But the mainsail won't budge. I have no choice but to climb the mast and yank the cloth down by hand. And so I clamber up, yank the sail down with all my might, and slide down to the deck in a flash, petrified I'm going to be thrown overboard or the automatic pilot is going to disengage. Before I know it, we're back in the game and huddling head-down against the storm. The wind is really howling now. It's gusting sixty knots. I'm at the helm, holding on with white knuckles. I'm trying desperately to stop the boat luffing toward the wind every time we surf down the swell. That's how boats end up capsizing in seas as rough as this. When we hit the trough of each wave, we're briefly sheltered from the wind, so the boat bobs straight upright—only to be thrown onto her side the other way by the next wave that comes along. My hands are like Popsicles, and I'm struggling to stay warm in my dry suit and merino underwear. I can't take this anymore. I'm sailing bare-poled, and even the lazy bag that sits on the boom feels like too much sail to be carrying.

After I-don't-know-how-many interminable hours, the wind finally starts to drop, and I feel like I've been to hell and back. *Yvinec* has really done me proud, righting herself like a fearless warrior every time she's been knocked down. She's even tougher than I thought. I thank my lucky star, and give a nod to my father. I know he's up there somewhere, watching over me.

Meanwhile, Monique's latest egg has smashed inside her coop, and she's eaten it raw. That worries me, because she might acquire a taste for it, and that would spell the end of fresh eggs on my plate. She's tried this trick before, and I had to sacrifice an egg from my stash, empty it out, and fill it with mustard so she wouldn't be tempted to do it again. I guess I'll have to chalk this one up to exceptional circumstances.

In three or four days' time, we should be at Cape Horn. And I've just seen my first albatross! I've been dreaming of this moment.

The albatross is the king of all seabirds, and the emblem of the Southern Seas. I've heard some of them can have a wingspan as large as ten or twelve feet. That's how they're able to fly so far from land. It's magical to see this bird embracing the swell and gliding over the water with the lightness of a cloud. It seems like it never has to beat its wings. I'm so spellbound by the sight of it, by the time I think to grab my camera, the albatross is already gone.

We're sailing a due southerly course now, in line with the coast, about sixty nautical miles offshore. There's still a fair amount of wind and swell.

~~~~~~~

EIGHTY DAYS AT SEA, and the problems just keep on coming. The genoa furler is well and truly out of commission now. This time, it's the drum that's smashed to pieces. That drives me crazy, because I replaced the damn thing in San Francisco. I knew I needed a bigger one, but I let the guy in the store talk me into getting this one. "Oh, no, don't worry," he'd said. "Trust me, this is the one you need. It's smaller, lighter, and tougher, you'll see." Yeah, right!

It's crazy cold already, and I know the worst of the temperatures are yet to come. But there's no way I can light the stove in conditions like these.

It's February 18, and we're only two hundred nautical miles west of Cape Horn, at 56 degrees of latitude. But I'm still stuck in the doldrums with boat trouble—now the engine won't start. I'm sure the fuel tank must have taken on seawater. Without an engine, there's no way I can fight my way against the wind and current along the inshore channels to Ushuaia, which is still four days away. The engine is indispensable; it's too dangerous to try to get there without it. I'm going to have to give up on going to Ushuaia. Even the thought of this decision makes me feel sick—that's where I've been planning to rest up and get the permissions I need to go to Antarctica. I've even made a contact there who's agreed to look after Monique while I'm on my little expedition. I'm tearing my hair out—well, what's left of it anyway, since I shaved it all off. I've all but run out of fresh water, my food reserves are too low to last very much longer, and my boat is limping her way along without a genoa or an engine. It's vital I make this stopover.

My only choice is to continue heading south and keep a low profile. I won't go ashore with Monique, but I do need to find a sheltered spot so I can tinker with *Yvinec* and catch my breath after these last few weeks. On the map, I can see what looks like a nicely sheltered bay on a little island just north of the Antarctic mainland. Deception Island, it's called. That couldn't be more apt, because the French name for it translates to "Disappointment Island"!

We pass Cape Horn on February 19, but we're too far away from land to realize it. We can still say we're Cape Horners, though! I'm so proud of Monique, my little adventurer. She's the first chicken to round the mythical cape. But we still need to keep our wits about us. The Screaming Sixties are just around the corner.

Now we have to cross Drake Passage, which separates Cape Horn from Antarctica, and that won't exactly be a walk in the park. This is where the Pacific, Atlantic, and Southern oceans all come together. It's like a funnel, and it's notorious for being one of the trickiest bodies of water in the world to navigate. In some places, the seabed can rise from ten thousand feet to less than a tenth of that depth without warning, throwing up massive waves if there's a swell running. I'm trying to find a way across that won't put us at risk as the next depression creeps in. I've turned on the radar, and all my senses are now on high alert, because we might come across an iceberg at any time. Every twenty minutes, I check the radar screen. I'm not getting much sleep, unlike Monique. We're not going very fast with the current against us. But the gusts keep coming, one after the other. The wind will suddenly jack up from thirty to fifty knots in a matter of seconds, then drop right back down to twenty. It's exhausting.

It's February 23, and you could cut this fog with a knife. Deception Island is just a stone's throw away. I've inflated my dinghy and gotten it ready to launch—I don't have an engine, so I might need it to shunt *Yvinec* along. I spot an iceberg drifting right toward us, just in time to steer clear of it. At last, between two lines of swell, I see land emerging from the fog, like a mirage in its snowy blanket. And then, what do you know, a little tail breaks the surface right beside the boat—my first penguin! Welcome to Antarctica! This scenery is like something out of a movie. I'm thrilled to be here.

We've sailed the length of the Pacific and made it all the way through the Roaring Forties, the Furious Fifties, and the Screaming Sixties—though I'm tempted to call them the Sickening Sixties, given the conditions we had.

Deception Island is part of the South Shetland Islands archipelago at the northern tip of Antarctica.

The water temperature in this part of the Southern Ocean is a frigid thirty-five degrees Fahrenheit. As for the air temperature, I'd rather not know. Frozen to the bone, my fingers red and numb, I cast anchor.

Antarctica is simply indescribable. I can hardly believe my eyes. We've made it to the end of the end of the world. Here, it's Mother Nature who rules the roost. There's a real sense that people are only visitors here, and that's the magic of the place. I can't resist the temptation to take a closer look. So I make a very gentle approach in the dinghy, taking care not to disturb the wildlife. Off on the shore, penguins are standing around chatting in their top hats and tails beside sunbathing sea lions. This is another childhood dream come true for me. I'm like a kid in a candy store, taking photos of everything I see.

I can't lose sight of the task at hand, though. It's time to see what the problem is with the engine. As I suspected, seawater has gotten into the diesel. I'm not surprised; the boat has been more of a submarine these last few weeks. I've had to dismantle the engine to clean all the parts, and I've pumped all the water out. And I've lit the stove again. It was about time; things were starting to freeze inside the cabin.

A friend back home has messaged me to let me know that a French cruise ship is calling in here in the next few days. She suggests I get in touch with the captain, so I do. I explain that I've run into difficulties and that I'm in need of water, diesel, and food. Not to mention that I'm in a hurry to get going before the peak of the storm season hits. The captain invites me aboard, and it turns out this isn't just any ship. It's a luxury ocean liner. This is a floating palace and they've rolled out the red carpet for me. Fresh fruit, vegetables, bread, pâté, cake, and the list goes on. What a banquet! I feel so privileged and moved, I find myself wiping tears from my eyes. These kind souls have bailed me out in the blink of an eye by giving me fresh water, diesel, and provisions.

Now I'm waiting for a favorable weather window to head back to sea. It might be a while, because the conditions are very unsettled right now.

On March 3, it's time for me to say goodbye to Deception Island. I miss this place already, and I haven't even left yet. I do find myself wondering what would become of this continent if climate warming were to speed up dramatically. It's with a heavy heart that I sail away from this unforgettable land.

We haven't gone very far when we decide to stop in at King George Island because the forecast is calling for a series of storms. My eyes are glued to the radar screen. Here, there are huge ice floes drifting in packs. I have to stay as alert as I possibly can. Once we've sailed into the shelter of a bay, I drop the anchor and let out as much chain as I can for safety. Hmm, that's strange. According to my GPS, *Yvinec* should be high and dry, but there's plenty of water under the boat. Turns out it's not a mistake. This used to be part of the island, but with the effects of climate warming, chunks of the once-permanent sea ice are breaking away faster than the maps can be updated, and that's very disconcerting.

Now there's a snowstorm raging around us. The wind is howling seventy knots, and it's a frosty five degrees Fahrenheit out there.

Yvinec has turned into one giant ice cube. Monique and I are huddled around the stove, waiting for the storm to pass. The next day, I venture out on deck and start scraping away the snow and ice that have encased the boat. A little later, I see two Zodiacs approaching. If these are soldiers wanting to see my permissions, I'm screwed. They pull up alongside *Yvinec*, and I flash them my best smile, trying my best to tell myself everything is going to be all right. Monique is all tucked up in her coop, out of sight and not making a sound. I've even put on some music too, just in case. These guys are Argentinian soldiers, as I suspected, but they don't ask me for my papers, and they don't come aboard. They're actually very friendly, and they're here to invite me to visit their base. Politely, I decline their offer; I'm trying to keep a low profile. They insist, but I explain that I don't want to leave my boat. They ask me what my name is, and if I'm on Facebook. I tell them my name is Greg, and I'm not on social media. Now that my mild moment of panic is over, I enjoy chatting with them. It turns out these poor guys have been posted here for fifteen months straight, away from their wives and children, and they're finding it lonely. As they're leaving, they call out, "We're having a little party on Saturday night. Come join us!" I wish I could say yes, but I have to decline their invitation. The sea won't wait.

As soon as the weather eases, we go on our way. We can't afford to hang around any longer. There are too many storms blowing through, and we have to get out of here. We're still in the Screaming Sixties. The icebergs here can be enormous.

Today, the weather is beautiful. Before I sail too far away from the coast, I take a few moments to slow down and glide through a sea of ice. I reach over the side of the hull and lift some of the nicest blocks on board. I can melt these over the next few days to keep my fresh water supplies topped up. Later, we find ourselves approaching a gigantic iceberg, where a colony of penguins are putting on quite a show. They're sliding and diving all over the place. Anyone would think they were enjoying a day out at a theme park. Monique and I would love to join them, but it's best to keep our distance. Instead, I launch my drone and capture the whole scene on camera.

It's nighttime now, and we've covered another 150 nautical miles. I'm inside the cabin when I hear a strange sound, like nothing I've ever heard before. I hurry out on deck in a panic. That was crazy—where the heck could it be coming from? And then I hear the powerful blow of a whale's spout, mere feet away from the boat. Inside the hull, the whale song is amplified as if it's coming through a speaker. The whale seems to want to follow me for a while, so I decide to spend the night out on deck to keep it company.

The next morning, the spinnaker is flying as we approach Elephant Island. I feel overcome with emotion to think this was where the British explorer Ernest Shackleton and his crew aboard the *Endurance* were shipwrecked more than a hundred years ago. They sought refuge on this island, and in nothing more than a modified wooden lifeboat, Shackleton and a handful of crew members set out for South Georgia Island, 1,400 nautical miles away—coming back later to rescue the rest of his crew. The whole story is simply extraordinary; I choke back a tear imagining what it must have been like to get shipwrecked here back then.

The whale is still here. I'm sure it's the same one. I think it's adopted me. I'm hoping it will follow me for a good while and keep the icebergs out of our path! At the end of the day, a magical sunset puts on an amazing show. Here I am, floating in the middle of the ocean, watching the sky fade from blue to orange and then to red, as the clouds turn pink. And I have a whale for company. There's something comforting and reassuring about hearing the gentle blowing of its spout. It helps to remind me I'm not completely alone out here, and, somehow, it almost feels like being with family.

Today I'm sitting down to a gourmet meal. Thanks to the generosity of the cruise ship crew, I'm tucking in to a delicious plate of buttered potatoes and terrine. It's like I've died and gone to heaven.

There's a depression passing over us. I'm trying to hold as northerly a course as I can. Logically we should be trying to steer clear of this weather, but if we do, we'll be headed right into the ice. It's just dawned on me that sailing up the Atlantic isn't going to go as smoothly as I thought. It's too late in the season.

Even when the wind eases, it's still blowing from the north, so we're sailing upwind. *Yvinec* can only point as high as seventy degrees into the wind, and we're only doing five knots of boat speed at best.

It's close to freezing inside the cabin. I wish I had a layer of feathers like Monique to keep me warm.

It's March 14, and I think I'm hallucinating. It's pitch dark and we're somewhere between Elephant Island and South Georgia Island—when suddenly I see land on the radar screen. Is it an island? No, that's not possible; it isn't on any of the maps. I soon realize that it isn't an island—and it's drifting right toward us! I can't believe my eyes. According to the radar, this thing covers more than a hundred square miles. That's more than twice the size of Paris! This monster chunk of floating ice is fifteen miles long, and the danger is real. Wherever there's sea ice, there's debris breaking away and drifting in the wind. I can't let us get trapped here; I have to act fast. I'm going to skirt this floating behemoth to the north. But to do that, I have to zigzag my way upwind one tack after another, for what feels like an eternity. At daybreak, I get to see the ice monster with my own eyes. It's one huge wall of ice that fills the entire horizon. I can't see the end of it. It's stunning to see, but what a nightmare. On I battle until the following evening, and it's not until I've tacked fifty nautical miles to the north that I get to leave this ghostly floating monstrosity in my wake.

It's March 16, but it feels like Groundhog Day. Yep, there's another wall of ice on the radar screen. This one's smaller, but it's still a big deal. And there's another complication—a storm is approaching from the north. I can't skirt around this huge iceberg in time before the storm hits. That would be suicide—I would be putting myself in the worst possible place in the middle of the night, and I would lose too much time. The only option I have is to bear downwind as fast as I can and take the risk of slaloming my way through smaller icebergs and growlers. The wind is starting to pick up already, so the race against the clock has started. I have to make it out of that minefield by nightfall.

By the end of the day, I've somehow managed to navigate my way out of this hell. Right now it's pitch dark, and the drifting island of sea ice is five nautical miles behind us. But the wind is still howling, and it's getting stronger and stronger; the shrouds are whistling as it hits twenty, thirty, forty knots, gusting fifty. I'm beating a hasty retreat from the storm, headed east-southeast, with no sails flying at all. The sea is in a state of fury, and I'm on high alert. I keep ducking my head into the cabin to check the radar screen. There's no way I can set the self-steering or automatic pilot in conditions like these. The waves are interfering with the signal, and we're surfing down the wave faces at crazy speeds—sometimes reaching twenty knots or more.

Suddenly, a blob appears on the screen, real close, and the blood freezes in my veins. This is the nightmare scenario I've been dreading: finding ourselves on a collision course with an iceberg in a sea like this. If we crash into it at this speed, we'll sink in the blink of an eye. I'm really worried, because I can't see the damn thing. Standing on deck, I point my flashlight around, desperately trying to catch sight of it. There it is! I give the tiller a hard shove to luff us into the wind, kill our boat speed, and avoid a collision. But now we're standing still, facing right into the waves. The icy breakers are whipping at my face and chilling me to the bone as I try my damnedest to steer clear of the iceberg, hoping with all my heart that my lucky star is watching over me.

Phew! I manage to avert disaster, but only just. I'm on tenterhooks. I can't afford to fly much sail in a storm like this, but I need to generate some forward momentum. I end up hoisting a handkerchief of a staysail to try and sail close-hauled to the wind for the rest of the night without picking up too much speed. It's a relentless battle against the breakers as they batter the boat one after the other. I have to keep ducking into the cabin to warm up.

I can't hack it out here all night long. I'm just at the foot of the cabin steps when a rogue wave, way bigger than all the others, slams into us with a deafening crash.

Inside the boat it's a disaster area. There's a mishmash of cereal, pasta, and books floating atop all the water that's just flooded down the cabin steps. I'm wading through it all when I see my NAVTEX marine-safety information screen is dead. Oh, great. Out on deck, it's even worse. The bow rail has been ripped clean off, taking my paddleboard and emergency anchor with it. And to top it all off, the gooseneck has sheared off again. I'm screaming with rage. Enough is enough.

Eventually, the day dawns on March 17, bringing an end to this nightmare of a night. The wind has dropped, and I'm headed for South Georgia Island. I need to stop there to pull myself, and my boat, together.

As I arrive in the lee of the island, sheltered from the wind, I start up my Internet connection. To my despair, I find out I'm not allowed to stop here. Since I left Deception Island, the Antarctic authorities have warned the other islands around here that I visited without a permit. What, so I'm an outlaw now? Why are the odds stacked so high against me? I never imagined I'd run into so many problems down here with my harmless little hen. Once more, we won't be able to make land in a time of desperate need. I have to take some kind of refuge in order to repair what I can.

I may not be able to cast anchor, but at least I can lie hove to, pointing into the wind in these sheltered waters, and take the opportunity to clean up, do some repairs, and weld this damn gooseneck together again. I've turned on the heat inside the cabin. Believe me, it's not a luxury. I have to dry my things, and a good blast of heat certainly won't do me or Monique any harm. There's no time for me to rest, though. I can't afford to stick around.

We're still in the Furious Fifties. Another storm is coming (just for a change). We're reliving our experience in the Pacific, but in reverse. The depression is bearing down from the north and is expected to veer west with a vengeance.

It's three in the morning, and I've been at the helm for seven hours straight amid a seascape that's nothing short of apocalyptic. I can't keep my eyes open. I'm soaked to the skin and frozen to the bone, and every monstrous wave is out to finish me off. I've lost all sense of danger. All I can think about is the cold and fatigue I'm feeling. My head is spinning, and my fingers won't move anymore. Eventually I decide to go down into the cabin. I have to take off my wet clothes. I have to get some kind of rest. Please, can I just have fifteen minutes to close my eyes? Is that really too much to ask? Then I'll be good to go again, once more unto the breach.

I've just collapsed in my bunk when I feel the boat nose-dive and accelerate in a never-ending, dizzying surf down a monster of a wave. It's already too late, I know it; the automatic pilot is going to disengage. Then everything turns upside down and I'm thrown from floor to ceiling and back again. Everything crashes down on me—mattress, books, the whole shebang. I'm holding my breath, and it's as if time has stood still. Are we right side up, or upside down?

I pull myself to my feet, and I'm standing on the floor, not the ceiling. Thank goodness—we're upright! But there are more waves coming, so I have to get out there and take the helm as quickly as I can. What about the mast? Have we lost the mast? As I scramble over the mess of clothes, dishes, flour, books, computers, and hard drives that are strewn all across the floor, I can hear Monique squawking. Oh good, at least she's still here with me!

The hatch won't open; it's stuck. The dodger—the canopy that sits over the cockpit—must have shifted backward onto it. And so, I press my nose to the cabin window and look out. Hallelujah, the mast is still standing! I push and push with all my might, and the hatch eventually opens far enough for me to squeeze my way out. It's like the end of the world out here. We're still on a roller coaster of massive waves, and everything on deck has disappeared, even the flooring. All the lines are trailing in the water, and one of the solar panels has been torn half off. The dodger is hanging on by two measly screws, another sheet of Plexiglas has bitten the dust, and the railing stanchions are bent. I grab the tiller and take control, then I pull all the trailing lines back aboard.

Once the worst of the storm has passed, I sit Monique down in my lap and feed her the dried insects she loves to wolf down. I'm completely wiped, but I keep playing the whole thing out in my mind. Did we roll all the way over, or did we turn turtle and bob back up again? It doesn't really matter. It's a miracle we're still alive after capsizing in these conditions. But this poor boat of mine is in a very sorry state indeed. Trying to make sense of what happened, I think about my father and Raino's paddle, wondering whether they had a hand in the series of events. It's about time all these storms stopped battering us, otherwise there won't be much left of my dear sailboat.

It's March 29, and the conditions are calmer at last. Now's my chance to fix the dodger back in place. I really don't want to lose my only shelter out here on deck. It's only a temporary fix, but

I manage to rig up a system of straps and lines to hold it down tight. My Internet connection has been offline since the boat went upside down, but at least I still have my satellite phone.

There are more depressions in the forecast already. At these latitudes and at this time of year, I shouldn't expect anything less. The swell is still enormous and keeps on breaking. I've had enough of all this. This crossing is a record for us. We've been living on the edge, pushing all the limits of extreme sailing for weeks. And it's not over yet. I was going to call in at the island Tristan da Cunha, but after the unfriendly welcome I encountered at South Georgia Island, I don't want to risk getting into more hot water. Never mind, we'll keep going and head for the coast of South Africa.

Somehow, we manage to keep sailing in spite of all the depressions that come our way—which always blow harder at night, of course. That's just my luck. I've gotten used to it. I try to make light of it all. "Well, Momo," I joke, "our Internet might be offline, but at least we have the storms to keep us company, eh?"

We're at 39 degrees south now.

Since the accident, *Yvinec* has kept falling to pieces. The tiller extension is coming loose, but the conditions are too heavy for me to bring out my welding gear. I do my best to lash it together with straps, and it seems to be holding all right. This sailboat of mine is becoming a real pirate ship. It's a good thing I'm a natural optimist.

It's April 10, and it feels like we've been sailing forever. We should be able to see land by now. But we can't, because we've been slogging our way upwind for days and making slow progress. The swell has eased, but there are still some massive gales blowing through. The last one hit so hard, I fell and bashed my face on the card table. I was worried I'd lost a tooth. My provisions have gone bad. Even the butter is moldy. Every day, I have to throw some food overboard.

A stray line is tangled up in the propeller, and I have to dive down to untangle it. It's a good thing the seas are calmer and the temperatures have warmed up a bit. Barely an hour later, when I see fins cresting the surface beside the boat, I realize my decision to take a dip could have ended very badly. I'd forgotten this was great white shark territory. Just thinking about that gives me the shivers.

As Cape Town welcomes us with open arms, our white-knuckle journey is finally over. At last! A sense of joy fills me as the mountainous curves of the coast come into view. What a relief! But the closer we get to the harbor, the more the things I see, hear, and smell feel like an assault on my senses. The buildings, the concrete, the car horns, and the smells of the city are making me feel queasy. The return to civilization after four months of self-sufficiency at sea is too brutal. I wasn't expecting the change to hit me this hard. I have to look away and keep to myself for a while. Nevertheless, this stopover is the best thing we could have hoped for. The list of damage is never-ending. We'll have to rest here for a while to get *Yvinec* back on her feet again. As for Monique, she's not complaining about having the boat back on an even keel. She's such a stickler for cleanliness in her coop; she's happy that not everything is flying around in there anymore.

After I've filled out all the entry paperwork and compared a few boatyards, I roll up my sleeves and get to work. It ends up taking me two and a half months of hard work to make *Yvinec* good as new again. Welding, waterproofing, electrical work, and rust removal, repairing the cockpit, sails, genoa furler, rigging, and gooseneck—I do it all. I don't want to leave anything to chance for my journey home.

Before I set sail again, I decide to take a little time to explore the area. The view from Table Mountain is well worth the hike. I head down to the Cape of Good Hope too, curious to see this mythical place I've heard so much about. I'm surprised to learn that the true dividing line between the Atlantic and Indian oceans doesn't lie here, but rather at Cape Agulhas, some eighty miles farther east. As I keep exploring, I find my way to Boulders Beach, where a penguin colony has taken up residence. Watching the penguins go about their lives is like tuning in to a reality TV show. I sit here for a while and enjoy the view while I think about the next chapter of adventures waiting for me and Monique.

Monique, chicken of the sea, gazes upon her ocean domain

Photo by Likka Photographie

PART 6

~~~~~

The Long Journey Home

I T'S JUNE 27. I've been waiting for calmer seas for the last two weeks. But the call of the open ocean is too hard to resist, so we're setting sail. To make the most of favorable winds and currents, we're taking the scenic route. Rather than sailing all the way up the African coast, we're going to do one big zigzag—that's right, two transatlantic crossings.

As we head toward smoother latitudes, it's reassuring for Monique and me to know that our boat is built to last, especially as the conditions in the next few days really put her through her paces. Poor *Yvinec* is pitching and rolling in these heavy seas, catching a little air off the crest of every wave before all twelve tons slam back down with a splash. We're barely making any headway; three hundred nautical miles in four days is pitiful.

Water is seeping in through the sail locker adjacent to my berth, so my bunk is soaking wet. The sea has washed away my spinnaker pole, even though it was lashed down tightly on deck. And to top it all off, the safety line I leave trailing behind the boat has gotten caught in the propeller. This time, diving down to untangle it is out of the question. I'll have to wait a few days until the weather improves and we're out of shark-infested waters. The commercial shipping traffic isn't doing anything to ease my stress either, but that won't be a problem for too long.

After four days, the bad weather has given way to bright sunshine and favorable tailwinds. The conditions are perfect for me to fly my brand-new spinnaker.

Because I've lost my spinnaker pole, I have to cobble together a tack fitting on one of the forestays to hold the sail out. Because I'm essentially flying the sail out to one side as an asymmetrical spinnaker, I can't sail directly downwind. Still, we're zipping along on a broad reach. I'm thrilled to have a spinnaker with a sock cover at last. It makes launching and retrieving the sail an absolute breeze, and much quicker too. All I have to do is pull on a line and the sail billows out from the sock, and I do the same thing when I want to pull it in again. It's a total game changer. How did I ever live without this?

Yvinec is flying along now. Monique is in good spirits. She's happy she can spend all her time out on deck again. This fine weather is giving me the chance to air out my sheets, pillows, and mattress, which were starting to go moldy. The nights are dreamy. I've been sleeping like a baby as the gentle rolling of the sea beneath the hull and the whispering of the spinnaker lazily filling with wind lull me into slumber. These conditions are reminiscent of

my first transatlantic crossing—pure bliss. Life on board is pretty
sweet. Monique and I have been enjoying our alfresco lunches.
The tempestuous southern latitudes are now just a distant
memory—I've been promising myself that I'll go back there
someday with a boat that's better equipped to handle the monstrous breakers.

Now that the wind has dropped, I'm going to have to dive down
and free the propeller. Before I go into the water, I set out two
extra safety lines, just in case. We're swaying side to side in the
gentle residual swell, and I'm holding on to the rudder because
the boat is drifting a little. The line is tangled up like crazy down
there, so I have to cut it free. I'm not usually a worrier, but the
image of those sharks keeps swimming around my mind—I
could sure do without that. Still, I'm taking the time I need to
do the job properly, and to save enough strength to climb back
aboard without a ladder.

On July 10, we're flying the staysail and genoa wing-on-wing
as we cross the Greenwich Meridian, the official prime meridian
of longitude dividing the eastern and western hemispheres. I'm
glad I opted for the double-transatlantic route rather than one
long slog upwind. I have to admit, *Yvinec* really isn't designed to
sail close-hauled. I'd far rather enjoy sailing her on a broad reach,
even if it means taking weeks longer to get where we're going.

Land ho! It's Friday the thirteenth, and after sixteen days at sea,
I can see the coastline of the island of Saint Helena bobbing in
and out of view as we skim atop a smooth ocean swell, all sails
flying. Saint Helena was Napoleon's last place of exile. There's
something mystical about the atmosphere as we make our

approach. I like this place already. As we're sailing in, I call the harbormaster on the VHF radio. Here, I have to tie up to a buoy, and I'm not allowed to go ashore in the dinghy. It's too dangerous to approach the wharf in this swell. Instead, there's a shuttle boat coming over to pick me up. Monique knows the score, and makes herself scarce. I have to hurry to get my customs clearance out of the way. The office is closing soon for the weekend.

Once the formalities are taken care of, I figure I'd better withdraw some cash so I can treat myself to a meal at a local restaurant. But the bank is closed already, so I'll have to wait until Monday. I figure I might as well keep walking around anyway, now that I'm ashore. Farther up in the village, I come across a little bistro and the owner invites me in. I explain that I don't have any way to pay for a meal right now, but he agrees to give me credit until Monday. The people of Saint Helena are remarkably hospitable. The next day, I'm invited to watch the World Cup soccer final with a group of complete strangers. Who'd have thought that I'd get to see my native France win the world's biggest soccer event perched on a remote rock more than twelve hundred miles away from the nearest land?

I'm really enjoying myself. It hasn't taken long for me to get to know everyone here. Before I know it, I've been here two weeks. Between hikes in the lush mountains and living the good life in the village, the days have flown by. But the time has come to say goodbye to this very friendly island. Monique is playing the lookout as I hoist the spinnaker. She's keen to see what we're going to encounter next on our big adventure. A whale and her calf are there to escort us out into the big blue. Again, I think of Raino and his parting words to me: "Animals never appear by chance. Their presence is always a sign."

It's getting hotter and hotter as the days flow by to the gentle rhythm of our little domestic routine. Our second Atlantic crossing of the year is nearly over. Brazil isn't far away now, and I have my sights set on Fernando de Noronha. I've heard so much about this island paradise, and I can't wait to discover it for myself. But just a few days before we get there, I run into technical difficulties again. The wind has busted my shiny new spinnaker, and all the cloth is trailing in the water. I'm gutted. I don't understand. The wind was light, so the cloth must have been chafing badly against something for the sail to fail so catastrophically. And, because problems never come one at a time, the genoa furler is the next thing to give out. I repaired the drum back in Cape Town, but now the entire torque tube is broken. There's not much I can really do about that. At least I still have the staysail.

We make our grand entrance into Fernando de Noronha on August 13. No sooner have I cast anchor in thirty feet of water than a pod of lively dolphins start leaping all around the boat. I can't believe my eyes. The temptation is too hard to resist, so I dive right into the water and swim with them. Around twenty minutes later, they swim away, but I could have stayed there with them for hours.

The next day, I figure I'd better get the entry formalities out of the way before too long. As usual, I neglect to mention Monique. In any case, she'd rather stay on the boat. I've allowed myself three days to explore this unspoiled island oasis. It's rare to see water as clear as this. Fish are swimming around by the thousand to a stunning backdrop of rocky peaks and lush green mountains. Now I can understand why this is one of the most expensive places in the world for moorage. Here, the authorities are serious about protecting the environment. There's even a cap on the number of tourists allowed to visit.

I check the compass and steer us on a heading of 290 degrees. Next stop, French Guiana! The winds and currents are so amenable right now, it's like we're sailing on a magic carpet. The heat is scorching, and I'm walking around naked on deck. Monique wishes she could trade her feathers for something a little cooler. I've been hiding little treats for her to find all over the place to take her mind off the heat and help her brush up on her hunting skills. As we near the coast, the color of the water changes dramatically—first from clear blue to cloudy, then from cloudy to murky brown. *Yvinec* glides her way between the inshore Îles Rémire before turning into the mouth of the Mahury River. Sailing up the river, the first things I notice are the overgrown jungle on the shore and the heady sound of birdsong filling the air.

I cast anchor in front of the port of Dégrad des Cannes. We're in the current, and a tree trunk has just bashed into the side of the bow, so we won't be sticking around here for long. I've been looking forward to going ashore and stocking up on all sorts of French delicacies. Fruit, vegetables, grated cheese, cereal, yogurt, and gourmet canned food, just like at home—I'm licking my lips at the thought of it. The customs officials warn me to be on my guard for the next part of my journey. After Suriname, it's wise to avoid sailing too close to shore, especially around Venezuela, because there might be pirates sailing those waters. I wouldn't be the first sailor to have my boat hijacked. I'm not changing my course, in any case. We're already well on our way toward the Caribbean.

Six days later, we're passing by Trinidad, waving from a fair distance offshore. It's like we're passing a milestone. Trinidad was where *Yvinec* came out of the boatyard three years ago, ready at last to take on the ice up north. "Hey Momo, this looks familiar, doesn't it? We've come around full circle!" Well, almost. For me, the loop will only be complete when we return home to Brittany. Something inside me has shifted, and there's a twinge in my heart. I feel an overwhelming urge to be at home on my little island. I miss my father. And the closer I get to home, the more it sinks in that he won't be there to greet me. I'm trying not to think about it. I almost just want to get the trip over and done with. It's a good thing we're in the tropics; it's going to do me a world of good.

Here we are, in the Grenadines! The bay at Carriacou is chock-full of boats at anchor. There's a cyclone warning farther up the Caribbean chain and all the boaters have come here to take shelter. This archipelago is in the Intertropical Convergence Zone, so it's much less exposed to the risk of cyclones than the islands farther north. It's September 15, and it's the middle of the wrong season to be in the Caribbean.

I've been having a blast snorkeling, kitesurfing, and enjoying fresh coconuts as I hop my way around the Grenadines from one island to the other—Carriacou, Mopion, Petit Saint Vincent, Union Island, Bequia, just for starters. My skin has turned its usual bronze again, and Monique's feathers have never looked redder. Just the two of us have been hanging out in the hammock on deck, enjoying the flamboyant sunsets every evening. We've been spoiled. The frequent squalls are helping to replenish my reserves of fresh water too. Showers have become a daily occurrence again, so I'm making up for the last few years of neglecting my personal hygiene on board!

We have to keep heading north toward Martinique. I've made a plan to pull *Yvinec* out of the water there before our final Atlantic crossing. That'll be the third one this year, and the fourth since we set out on this globe-trotting adventure of ours.

It's October 8, and we've just sailed into the harbor at Le Marin, in the south of the island of Martinique. Waiting for us when we dock is my doctor friend Maxence, who saved my life two years ago when he diagnosed me with peritonitis over the phone. It's great to see him again, and we spend a few days enjoying the local surf spots before it's time for me to roll up my sleeves and start working on the boat. I've found a great marine supply store called Caraïbe Marine. The guys there, Philippe and Gaëtan, soon turn out to be the saviors of our adventure. They help me in every possible way, taking care of the work and even finding some new partners that are happy to contribute an endless list of vital equipment to our cause. Thanks to them, I now have a new furler, refrigerator, dinghy, spinnaker pole, and boom (that's right, I can say goodbye to having to weld the gooseneck back together at sea!). They've even changed all the standing rigging for me, every last shroud. Every night, Monique gets to chow down on pizza at Aurélie's—she's Gaëtan's wife, and she runs a pizza boat. I'm in seventh heaven here. I could never dream of such a warm welcome. Our new partners and friends are a real blessing. We've even overhauled the entire electrical system. The sails have been given the once-over by the team at Voiles Caraïbes; this is where I got my new sails three years ago. And honestly, their sails have really gone the distance. Now, our pit stop is over, and the time has come to put *Yvinec* back in the water and be on our way again. I want to call in at St. Barts and

Saint Martin. I'm keen to catch up with friends, and I'm curious to see what my old stomping ground looks like three years after I was last there.

We sail past the islands of Dominica, Guadeloupe, Montserrat, Saint Kitts, and many others. As we approach St. Barts, I pass to the windward side of the island so I can sail right into the bay at Saint-Jean beach, where I had my anchorage. So many memories come flooding back to me. Jean-Mi motors out in his dinghy to greet me. He and all my old friends have organized a beach party to celebrate our return. It feels funny to be back; so much has changed. Actually, I'm probably the one who's changed the most. Antonin, one of the kids I used to hang out with at the windsurfing center, is there, but all the others have gone away to school in Canada.

It's great to see everyone, but being back here is making me think about everything that's happened in the last few years. I've barely set foot on board *Yvinec* when I feel a knot in my stomach; this homecoming-of-sorts has been fun, but I really am ready to go home now. It's been a very intense year, to say the least. My limited living quarters here on board are starting to get me down. In my mind, I'm already back home in the other Yvinec—my little island—hauling up my lobster traps. But I know the final Atlantic crossing we're about to embark on might not be an easy one.

I'm going to call in quickly at Saint Martin on the way. I can't leave without saying goodbye to Johann. He's been a huge support to me all throughout this adventure. He's waiting for me in the marina at Anse Marcel when I sail in. A year ago, Hurricane Irma barreled through here, causing carnage in the marina, which is usually very well protected. It's freaky to see the aftermath of it all, even now. There are still sunken boats out there in the bay, and *Gadjo*, my friends Christian and Claudine's boat, is one of them. I know they're safe, but it still pains me to know their whole life was turned upside down in a single night. They've had to go back to France, and I hope I'll see them again.

It's about time we set sail. Right as we're heading out, the Route du Rhum transatlantic race is starting on the other side of the Atlantic. Once again, Monique and I are doing the opposite of everyone else. But that doesn't matter, because we'll have a victory of our own to celebrate.

We have to head due north for a while to catch the west winds that I'm hoping will carry us across to Brittany. We want to steer clear of the Azores High so we don't get stuck in dead calm waters. It seems to take us forever to work our way up the coast of North America, albeit far offshore. We're sailing close-hauled, into the wind, and only averaging about four knots of boat speed. After two weeks of exhausting sailing, we finally get to a point where we can steer onto a more easterly course. I thought this would give us a bit of a break, but now the automatic pilot has decided to let me down. A hose has burst between the pilot motor and cylinder, so it's time for me to roll up my sleeves and fix it. With time and experience, I've gotten better and faster at diagnosing issues on the boat. It's amazing how quickly you can figure out how to do something when it's your only option.

And because these things never happen one at a time, now the genoa halyard shackle has broken. It's going to be a tricky thing to fix. This time, it won't be as simple as climbing the mast and yanking a stuck sail free, then climbing back down again. I have to steady myself at the head of the mast with very little in the way of safety gear. I've rigged up the bosun's chair and wrapped a safety line around my shoulder. Once I've shimmied my way up there, I use one hand to attach the safety line and hang on for dear life with the other. The sea might be calm, but up here, the slightest movement of the boat down below makes me sway perilously—this is turning out to be more of a daredevil undertaking than I thought. I'm only using one hand to do the job because I don't want to let go of the mast with the other. Once I've eventually managed to replace the shackle, I don't waste any time getting back down on deck.

It's November 25, 2017—two years to the day since I began my hibernation in Greenland—and there's been a change of plan. I hadn't anticipated making a pit stop in the Azores, but it looks like I don't have the choice. A gale has blown through and broken off all the blades of my wind generator, and the weather forecast is calling for a massive storm forty-eight hours from now. That means we have to head for the nearest port in the northwest of the archipelago on Flores Island. It's after dark when I get there. I'm feeling pretty stressed. This is an unfamiliar place and the wind is blowing a solid thirty knots. There's a swell running, and a squall is passing overhead. As I approach the end of the jetty I can hear someone shouting. A man on the shore is gesticulating and warning me to steer a tight course into the harbor. The channel is just a few feet wide now because part of the breakwater on the other side collapsed a few days ago. Phew! It's a good thing he was there just at the right time. We make it into the marina safely and I moor *Yvinec* in the first empty slip I can find.

The next morning, the harbor pilot is helping all the fisher-men lift their boats out of the water. They warn me it isn't very sheltered here at all and tell me I should have kept on going to the marina in Horta, on nearby Faial Island, to find safety. There's not enough time, though. They're insisting I can't stay moored up at the dock, so they decide to help me. Now *Yvinec* is trussed up in a spider's web of mooring lines in the middle of the marina basin. We've weighted the hawsers down with "pigs"—cast-iron weights—to act as ballast and soften the pulling of the lines as the boat is buffeted around. I wasn't familiar with this technique.

The storm is here now, and I'm hunkered down on *Yvinec*, steeling myself for a sleepless night on board.

Several times, the seamen who've stayed on the wharf to watch over their boats in cradles put their lives on the line to throw me more hawsers between two gusts, because they keep breaking, one after the other. Every time it happens, I have to compensate with the engine to ease the tension on the lines and move a little closer to catch the hawser. Sometimes, the water level in the basin might go up and down by as much as twelve feet in a matter of seconds. The current is whirling beneath the hull, and the wind is whipping the gravel from the wharf into my face. For twenty-four hours, setting foot on land isn't even an option. Monique is tucked up warm and cozy in the cabin. If she dared to poke her beak outside, this wind would carry her all the way to Brittany.

When all is calm again, I don't know how to thank my guard-ian angels on the shore. At the peak of the storm, the wind was howling over 140 miles per hour, and the waves outside the breakwater were close to sixty-five feet. After two days holed up here, we have to get going. We've come this far, and winter is setting in, so we're not giving up now. From here we'll be on the home stretch.

There are only 1,300 nautical miles left to go now. With a generous tailwind pushing us along, we're making good progress. I can't wait to get this last stretch over with. I'm not letting my guard down for a second as we approach the Bay of Biscay. This body of water can be as cruel as the Southern Ocean. I've just found out that a depression is coming this way and might give us trouble as we're nearing the coast of Brittany. According to my calculations, we should be able to make it into sheltered waters in time. If worst comes to worst, we can always beat a hasty retreat to the south and take shelter in Brest. I've come so far, and I'm so looking forward to seeing my home coastline again that I'm sure nothing can happen to me now. But still, there's a little voice reminding me not to take anything for granted, and not to do anything stupid.

The depression is deepening, and it's right on our heels. It's after dark, and we're not far from the island of Ushant, just off the tip of the Brittany peninsula. The continental shelf rises sharply here, so a storm can whip the sea into a frenzy in no time at all. This is Europe's answer to Cape Horn. It's a dangerous area to be in, so we have to steer well clear. It's going to be a rough night. *Yvinec* puts her big-wave-surfer's hat on again and tips over onto her side twice. My solar panel has been swept away, and inside the cabin, the radar screen is broken.

We're getting really close to the tip of the peninsula now. Once we've rounded the point, I figure I'll head for the nearest harbor in Aber Wrac'h. But as we make our way closer, all I can see is the spray from the breakers. It isn't safe to go ashore in these conditions, so we'll just have to hold tight until daybreak. First thing in the morning, I muster up the courage to charge my way in through the breakers to the marina entrance. All around, there are rocks poking their heads above the surface. I don't know how, but we end up making it through this rocky mine-field in one piece.

At last, we're safely ashore in France! I'm happy to have a moment to catch my breath and tidy up on board. Only eighty nautical miles left to go along the coast to Paimpol, then we'll be home. To make sure we're sailing with the current, I set off again at low tide, so the inflow will carry us east.

On the morning of December 15, as I guide *Yvinec* into the nar-row channel between the little islands of Bréhat and Béniguet on the approach to Paimpol, I see a boat I crossed paths with three years ago in the Caribbean, the *Boulmic*. The skipper has come out to keep me company for the home stretch. Other friends in their boats soon gather around to escort us ashore.

Now the bay of Paimpol is opening up before us, and we're making our final approach under sail. *Yvinec* is gliding through the water with speed and grace. Monique is standing tall with the wind in her feathers, and I'm totally pumped. I'm so proud of my co-skipper—my little hen and her golden eggs.

My heart skips a beat when I see the crowd gathered at the end of the jetty to welcome us home to the sound of traditional Breton bagpipers. I feel overcome with emotion as a wave of pride and accomplishment washes over me. My head is spin-ning. I can't believe what we've achieved. Everything is flashing before my eyes. We could have died out there, what, seven times at least? But we pulled through, and we made it home. "We've done it, Momo! This is it; we're home at last!" I cry.

On the wharf, all my family are here, eager to give us a hug and welcome us home. It's time to lower the sails. Our journey is complete.

All that's missing is you, Dad.

Guirec and Monique, home at last

Photo by Likka Photographie

Acknowledgments

~~~~~~~~~~

I WANT TO GIVE a huge thank-you to Lauren and Alice for helping me make this book happen. Lauren, I'm immensely grateful for your commitment, your patience, and your support. I don't know what I would have done without you these last few years.

I would like to thank the amazing people I have met through my northern voyage: Uno, Adam, Lukaka, Jonas, and everyone in Saqqaq village and Greenland; Raino and Bosco in Alaska; Claude, Emmanuel, Sharon, Ted, and Damien in Canada; and so many more.

I was alone at sea, but I certainly wasn't alone on land. This adventure was made possible in large part because of the support of people and businesses around the world and from all walks of life. We are all united by a shared passion for adventure and for this beautiful planet of ours. To everyone who donated to our cause through Ulule and Patreon, our hundreds of anonymous helpers and tens of thousands of followers on social media, and to all the new friends we met along the way, thank you for your support, for lending a helping hand, and for your words and messages of encouragement that made us smile when we needed it the most.

Above all else, never forget that if *you* want to do something, you can. All you have to do is set your mind to it—just look at Monique! Now it's your turn to get out there and do whatever floats your boat.

Life is there for the living!

GUIREC

Glossary

AIS TRACKING SYSTEM—safety system using a transceiver to broadcast a vessel's position and track it on a screen in a radar-like display format

ALTERNATOR—device used to charge a vessel's batteries and power its electrical system when the engine is running

ANEMOMETER—device used to measure current wind strength

ANGLE GRINDER—handheld power tool used for grinding and polishing

ANTIFOULING—protective treatment applied to a boat's hull to prevent barnacles and other marine growth from building up below the waterline; helps to reduce corrosion and drag

AUTOMATIC PILOT SYSTEM—electronic system enabling a vessel to remain on a preset course with no one at the helm

BILGE PUMP—pump used to remove excess water buildup from beneath the cabin floor

BOOM—the pole that holds the bottom of the mainsail, attaching to the mast

BOSUN'S CHAIR—a harness-like seat suspended from a rope, used to climb a sailboat's mast in order to carry out work in comfort and safety

BOW—nose (front) of the boat

BREAKERS—waves that are breaking, more powerful than rolling swells and more dangerous for a boat to navigate

CLOSE-HAULED—sailing upwind as close to the wind as possible; no sailboat can point closer than forty-five degrees toward the wind, and *Yvinec* can only point as high as seventy degrees

DEPRESSION—area of low atmospheric pressure, typically bringing strong winds and unsettled weather

DEPTH-SOUNDER—device used to measure water depth beneath the hull of a vessel

DINGHY—small boat carried or towed by a larger vessel to serve as a lifeboat or to travel ashore when moored in open water

DODGER—a canopy covering the cockpit of a sailboat to keep the cabin sheltered from rain, spray, and wind

DRAFT—the vertical distance between the waterline and the bottom of a boat's hull; this determines the minimum depth of water the boat can safely navigate

DRY SUIT—waterproof suit designed to be worn over clothing or thermal underwear for comfort and safety when immersed in cold water

FIXED KEEL—a permanently fitted keel which cannot be moved or repositioned; typically found on larger boats

FLOAT SWITCH—switch that automatically activates a bilge pump to remove any excess water entering a vessel's hull

FORESTAY—a wire attached to a sailboat's mast and the bow to prevent the mast from falling backward, part of a sailboat's standing rigging; used to rig a jib or genoa sail in front of the mainsail

FURIOUS FIFTIES—name used to refer to latitudes below fifty degrees south in the Southern Ocean, which are notorious for their strong westerly winds

FURLER LINE—rope attached to a jib or genoa, used to roll up a sail around the forestay when not needed, and unroll it when needed

GENOA—a large sail that extends past the mast when rigged, overlapping the mainsail and helping to increase boat speed

GENOA FURLER—device used to roll up a genoa around the forestay when not needed, and unroll it when needed

GROWLERS—small chunks of broken-off icebergs

GUNWALE—the upper edge of the side of a boat

HALYARD—rope used to hoist a sail

HALYARD SHACKLE—shackle used to connect a halyard to the sail, allowing it to be hoisted

HAWSER—a heavy rope or cable for mooring a sailboat

HEELING—the action of a sailboat tipping over to its side from the force of the wind on its sails; heeling is more pronounced when sailing upwind

HELM—the wheel that steers a sailboat; to be at the helm is to be (theoretically!) in control of the sailboat

IRIDIUM SATELLITE PHONE—type of satellite-based phone used to ensure communication at sea, regardless of global position

JIB—triangular foresail rigged ahead of the mast; functions with the mainsail to provide propulsion and improve performance and stability

JIBE—to turn the boat from one direction to the other, away from the wind; opposite of "tack"

JIGSAW TOOL—handheld saw using a reciprocating blade

KEEL—flat blade attached to the bottom of a sailboat's hull that extends down into the water to increase stability and prevent the vessel from being blown sideways by the wind; can be either fixed in place (fixed keel) or movable (swing keel)

KNOT—measure of wind and boat speed; 1 knot = approximately 1.15 mph or 1.85 km/h

LUFF—the forward (leading) edge of a sail, attached to the mast

LUFF WIRE—a wire sewn into the leading edge of a sail to allow it to be inserted into the mast and hoisted and lowered

MAINSAIL—sail rigged on the main mast of a sailboat

MONOHULL SAILBOAT—a type of sailboat having only one hull, as opposed to multihulled boats such as catamarans and trimarans, which respectively have two or three individual hulls connected to one another

PIG—a cast-iron weight attached to a mooring line to help stabilize a sailboat at anchor in strong winds and turbulent water

POLE OUT—a technique using a pole to fly a jib or genoa sail out to the opposite side of the mainsail when sailing downwind, in order to maximize the sail area exposed to the wind

REEF THE SAILS—technique used to reduce sail area in stronger winds in order to maintain control and stability

ROARING FORTIES—name used to refer to latitudes below forty degrees south in the Southern Ocean, notorious for their strong westerly winds

ROLLY ANCHORAGE—term used to describe the location of a sailboat at anchor where the sea is less calm than desirable

RUDDER—underwater blade at the stern of a sailboat, connected to the helm and used to steer the vessel

SCREAMING SIXTIES—name used to refer to latitudes below sixty degrees south in the Southern Ocean, notorious for their strong westerly winds

SELF-STEERING SYSTEM—mechanical system used to keep a sailboat sailing on the same course in relation to the wind and enable a sailor to step away from the helm; unlike an electronic automatic pilot system, does not require electrical power to function

SHOAL—sandbar in an area of shallow water

SLIP—a space in a marina for a boat to tie up at the dock

SPINNAKER—a light, billowy sail flown from the front of the boat to maximize boat speed when sailing downwind

STAYSAIL—smaller foresail used in stronger winds

STERN—tail (back) of the boat

SWELL—series of rolling (and not breaking) waves typically found on the open sea

SWING KEEL—a keel that can be lifted to enable access to shallower waters; typically found on smaller boats

TACK—to turn the boat from one direction to the other, up toward the wind; opposite of "jibe"

TILLER—lever used to steer a sailboat; attached to the rudder

TOUK—an implement with a large metal blade and a long wooden handle, used by the Inuit in Greenland to test the strength of the ice and make holes for ice fishing

TRADE WINDS—the east-to-west prevailing winds that flow in the earth's equatorial regions, between thirty degrees north and thirty degrees south

TRIM THE SAILS—to adjust the angle of the sails in relation to the wind in order to ensure maximum boat speed and efficiency

VHF RADIO—worldwide system of two-way radio transceivers used for vessel-to-vessel and emergency communication

WING-ON-WING SAILING—technique for sailing downwind with the wind directly behind the boat, using a pole to fly the jib or genoa on the opposite side of the boat to the mainsail in order to increase boat speed by maximizing sail area exposed to the wind

Partners